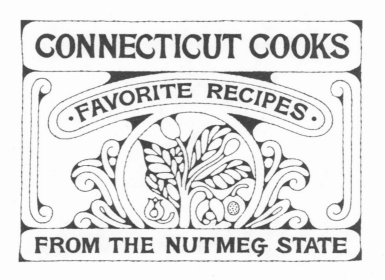

CONNECTICUT COOKS
·FAVORITE RECIPES·
FROM THE NUTMEG STATE

Designed & Illustrated by
NAIAD EINSEL

For the Benefit of
THE AMERICAN CANCER SOCIETY
CONNECTICUT DIVISION, INC.

For your convenience
CONNECTICUT COOKS
may be purchased
at all unit offices of the
American Cancer Society
in Connecticut.
Copies may also be obtained
by using the order forms
in the back of the book.

Copyright © 1982 American Cancer Society, Connecticut Division, Inc.
Copyright © 1982 Naiad Einsel, Illustration

ISBN: 0-9608732-0-1
LIBRARY OF CONGRESS CATALOG CARD NUMBER: 82-72387

Printed in the United States of America by
R. R. DONNELLEY & SONS COMPANY

First Printing September 1982   20,000 copies

Forward

Variety is one of Connecticut's most valuable spices. Throughout its history, the Nutmeg State has enjoyed a rich and diversified cultural heritage. Today, more than sixty separate ethnic groups provide our state with a broad and interesting personality. CONNECTICUT COOKS reflects that personality. Inside you will find a medley of recipes from Eierkuchen, traditional German pancakes, to a distinctive Seafood Chardonnay from one of Connecticut's five vineyards.

The recipes collected in CONNECTICUT COOKS have been selected from the hundreds submitted by friends of the American Cancer Society, including many of our state's most noted celebrities. The recipes were selected by a panel of professional Home Economists, and tested enthusiastically by friends and families of our volunteers.

The proceeds from the sale of the cookbook will be used by the American Cancer Society for research, education, service and rehabilitation.

We are proud to present this book and are assured that all will find the recipes in CONNECTICUT COOKS to be intriguing as well as delicious.

Cookbook Committee

Chairman: *Norma E. Volk*
Co-Chairman: *Sona A. Current*

Danbury Unit: *Mary Setaro, Lucy Lavelle*

Eastern Fairfield County Unit (Bridgeport)
Callista Healey, Joan E. Chiota, Ede D. Baldridge

Greater Hartford Unit: *Brenda Colgate, Laura R. Soll*

Manchester Unit: *Ginny Wickersham, Elsa Dobkin*

Middlesex/Meriden/Wallingford Unit
Carmel Correll, Anita Carofino

New Britain Unit
Debbie Chellstorp, Linda Krasner, Irene MacArthur

New London Unit: *Jeanne Martin, Eileen Marshall*

Northwestern Unit (Torrington)
Olga M. Mason, Patricia Fields

Norwich/Quinebaug Unit
Gen Bergandahl, Tete Masterson

South Central Unit (Woodbridge)
Nancy Cassela, Beverley Clarke

Southern Fairfield Unit (Darien)
Ann B. Lillis, Rene Purcell, Susan Cameron

Greater Waterbury Unit: *Lillian Lenkowski*

Windham Unit (Willimantic)
Mari-Carole Shooks, Jean Sawicki

Home Economists
Sue Haman, Rita Kraushaar, Ruth Russell

Table of Contents

1 Appetizers & Beverages

35 Salads & Dressings

63 Breads

83 Soups

97 Pasta, Cheese & Eggs

125 Meats

153 Poultry

177 Seafood

197 Sauces, Preserves, & Relishes

215 Vegetables

241 Desserts

293 Contributors

301 Index

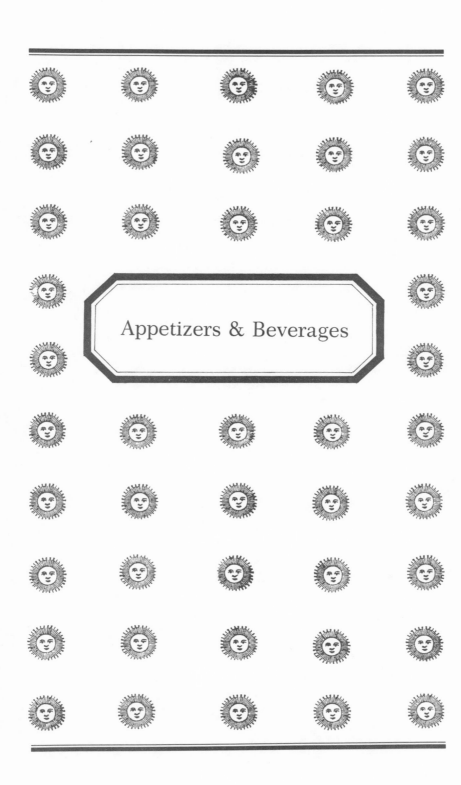

Appetizers & Beverages

Hot Artichoke Dip

1 (14 ounce) can artichoke
   hearts
1 cup mayonnaise
½ cup Parmesan cheese
¼ teaspoon seasoning salt

Garlic powder to taste
½ can chopped jalapeno peppers
   (black olives or green chilies
   may be substituted)

Drain and quarter artichoke hearts. Mix artichoke and remaining
ingredients together in small casserole. Sprinkle Parmesan cheese
on top. Bake at 350° for 20 minutes.

Spinach Dip

Makes 3 Cups

1 (10 ounce) package frozen
   chopped spinach
1 cup mayonnaise
1 cup sour cream

1 medium onion, chopped
1 (8 ounce) can water
   chestnuts, chopped
1 package vegetable soup mix

Thaw spinach and drain well until barely moist. Combine with
mayonnaise, sour cream, chestnuts and vegetable soup mix. Stir
well. Cover and chill several hours. Serve with crackers or raw
vegetables.

Artichoke Pie

1 (9 ounce) package frozen
   artichoke hearts, defrosted
4 eggs, well beaten
½ cup diced pepperoni
1 scant teaspoon salt

1 cup diced Mozzarella cheese
½ teaspoon pepper
¼ cup grated Romano cheese
1 unbaked frozen pie crust,
   9-inch

Pat artichokes dry and cut in half. Blend artichokes with eggs,
pepperoni, cheeses, salt and pepper. Pour into pie crust. Bake at
350° for 45 minutes or until a toothpick inserted in center comes
out clean. Serve warm or cold.

Clam Bake Dip

2 (7 ounce) cans minced clams
  with juice
1 teaspoon lemon juice
1 medium onion, chopped
1 garlic clove, minced
½ green pepper, chopped
1 teaspoon chopped parsley
½ cup butter or margarine

1 teaspoon oregano
1 dash tabasco
1 dash red pepper
½ cup Italian bread crumbs
Velveeta cheese
Parmesan cheese
Paprika

In saucepan simmer clams with juice and lemon juice. In separate pan simmer the next 8 ingredients until soft. Add bread crumbs. Place in 9×10 baking dish. Top with thin slices of Velveeta cheese. Sprinkle top with Parmesan cheese and paprika. Bake at 350° for 20 minutes or until cheese is melted and bubbly. Recipe can be frozen. Thaw and bake when needed.

Holiday Appetizer Pie

Makes 2 Cups

1 (8 ounce) package cream
  cheese, softened
2 tablespoons milk
1 (2½ ounce) jar chipped beef,
  finely snipped

2 tablespoons instant minced
  onion
2 tablespoons finely chopped
  green pepper
½ cup sour cream
¼ cup coarsely chopped walnuts

Blend cream cheese and milk. Stir in beef, onion, and green pepper. Mix well. Stir in sour cream. Spoon into baking dish. Sprinkle walnuts over top. Bake at 350° for 15 minutes. Serve with your favorite crackers. May be prepared a day or so in advance. Bake before serving. Freezes well.

Hot Shrimp Dip

1 (8 ounce) can mushrooms,
    sliced and drained
2 tablespoons butter
1½ cups cream cheese, softened
¼ cup sour cream
¼ teaspoon salt

¼ teaspoon garlic salt
½ teaspoon soy sauce
1 (5 ounce) can shrimp or
    crabmeat
2 tablespoons Italian salad
    dressing

Mix all ingredients together and heat until hot.

Governor and Mrs. William A. O'Neill

Inez Hodges Shrimp Dip

Makes 5 Cups

3 cups shrimp, boiled and peeled
1 cup mayonnaise
½ cup evaporated milk
1½ cups ketchup
1 tablespoon yellow mustard

1 large onion
2 garlic cloves
1½ teaspoons tabasco
1½ teaspoons Worcestershire
    sauce

Put all ingredients in food processor or blender and puree. Serve cold with corn chips or raw vegetables.

Havoc Herb Dip

Makes 2 Cups
Garden fresh herbs makes this a special summer treat

½ cup plain yogurt
1 cup sour cream
½ cup mayonnaise

2 tablespoons dried tarragon,
    crushed
1 teaspoon marjoram
Pinch of sage

Combine ingredients. Chill well. Serve with tostadas or crudites.

June Havoc
Actress

Artichoke Appetizer

Makes 18 Squares

2 (6 ounce) jars marinated
artichokes
1 small onion, finely chopped
1 garlic clove, minced
4 eggs
¼ teaspoon salt
⅛ teaspoon tabasco
⅛ teaspoon pepper
⅛ teaspoon oregano

2 tablespoons minced parsley
2 cups grated Cheddar cheese
¼ cup Italian style bread
crumbs
1 teaspoon lemon juice
Fresh minced parsley, add some
to mixture and reserve some
for garnish

Drain artichokes and save marinade. Saute onion and garlic in part
of the marinade. Saute for about 5 minutes. Beat eggs and add all
other ingredients. Bake at 325° for 30 minutes in 7×11 baking dish.
Cut into one inch squares for an appetizer and serve hot. May be
cooked in smaller container yielding thicker slices and can serve as
vegetable or side dish.

Cheese Filled Pumpernickle

Serves 15 to 20
A conversation piece

1 round pumpernickle
1½ pounds grated Cheddar
cheese
¼ pound bleu cheese or
Roquefort
1 teaspoon dry mustard

1 garlic clove, minced
2 teaspoons butter, softened
1 teaspoon Worcestershire sauce
⅛ teaspoon tabasco
12 ounces stale beer

Hollow out pumpernickle. Mix rest of ingredients together and stuff
pumpernickle. Serve on tray surrounded with assorted crackers and
small pieces of pumpernickle cut from hollowed out loaf. Cheese
can be made ahead. Store in refrigerator. Bring to room temperature
before serving.

Benne's Seed Wafers

Makes 4 Dozen

1 cup sesame seeds
2 cups flour
Salt and cayenne to taste

¾ cup butter or margarine
¼ cup water
Coarse salt

Toast seeds in 300° oven until brown. Combine flour and seasonings. Cut in butter as if for pastry. Add water. Knead in seeds. Roll out dough and cut into wafer shapes. Place wafers on cookie sheet and bake at 325° for 15-20 minutes. As soon as the wafers are removed from the oven, sprinkle them with coarse (Kosher) salt, lightly.

Black Olive Canapes

Makes 48 Canapes

1½ cans black pitted olives
½ cup mayonnaise
2 tablespoons minced onion

¼ teaspoon curry powder
1 cup grated sharp cheese
6 whole English muffins

Mince black olives. Mix with mayonnaise, onion, curry and cheese. Quarter and split the muffins. Spread on the mixture. Broil 3-4 minutes until bubbly. Serve hot.

Marinated Broccoli

Serves 8
Very different

3 bunches broccoli, flowerets
1 cup cider vinegar
1 tablespoon sugar
1 tablespoon dill weed

1 teaspoon salt
1 teaspoon ground peppercorns
1 teaspoon garlic salt
1½ cup vegetable oil

Blanch broccoli. Blend all remaining ingredients together. Marinate broccoli overnight. Drain and serve.

Derevi Sarma

Makes 30 to 40
(Grape Leaves Stuffed With Rice)

1 cup olive oil
3 large onions, finely chopped
1 cup long-grain rice
1 cup chopped dill
½ cup chopped Italian parsley
   (save stalks)
1 bunch scallions, chopped

3 tablespoons pine nuts
   (optional)
Juice of 2 large lemons
2½ cups cold water
Salt and pepper, to taste
1 jar grape leaves

Heat ½ cup olive oil in skillet and cook onions until transparent. Add rice and cook ten minutes, stirring occasionally. Add dill, parsley, scallions, pine nuts, juice of one lemon, ½ cup water, salt and pepper. Cook ten minutes until liquid is absorbed. Cool. Rinse and drain grape leaves in hot water. Place leaves, shiny side down, on flat surface and place one teaspoon of rice filling near stem end (cut off any extra stem), fold over sides and roll lightly like a cigarette. Place parsley stalks or a few small leaves in the bottom of pan to prevent grape leaves from burning and arrange the rolled leaves side by side in the pan and in two or three layers according to the size of the pan. Pour remaining oil, lemon juice, and one cup of water over leaves. Bring to high heat for five minutes. Add remaining cup of water, reduce heat and simmer about 1 hour. (Place a plate over the leaves to keep them in place and cover pan). Cool in the pan and chill. Serve cold. Sprinkle with olive oil to make them shine and garnish with lemon wedges.

Kielbasa Treats

Serves 8 to 10

1 medium sized ring kielbasa
1 (8 ounce) package cream
   cheese, softened
2-3 tablespoons red horseradish

White pepper to taste
Dry white wine
Party rye

With a fork, mix cream cheese, horseradish and white pepper. Add a little white wine to obtain creamy consistency. Spread on party rye. Diagonally slice kielbasa and place one piece on each slice of party rye.

Swedish Meatballs

Makes 300

1½ pounds lean ground beef
1 pound ground veal
½ pound ground pork
3 cups soft, unflavored bread
  crumbs
2 cups light cream
1 cup finely chopped onion
  sauteed in margarine

2 eggs
½ cup chopped parsley
3 teaspoons salt
½ teaspoon ginger
Dash pepper
Dash nutmeg

Soak bread crumbs in cream for 5 minutes. Mix in onions, eggs, parsley, ginger, pepper and nutmeg. Form 1-inch diameter balls. Saute in margarine and put aside.

Sauce:
3 tablespoons flour
3 tablespoons margarine

3 cans condensed beef broth
1½ teaspoons instant coffee

Melt margarine; add flour. Stir in broth and coffee. Water may be added to make sauce the desired consistency. Heat and return the meatballs. Simmer 45 minutes. (The coffee in this recipe is the real Swedish way).

Cheese Onion Bread

Makes 48

2 (10 ounce) packages chopped
  frozen onions, defrosted
  and drain well
2 eggs, slightly beaten
1 cup milk

3 cups prepared biscuit mix
2 cups grated Cheddar cheese
Poppy seeds
4 tablespoons melted butter

Mix eggs with milk. Add onions and 1 cup of the grated cheese and biscuit mix. Spread on well greased 10×15 cookie sheet. Sprinkle top with remaining cheese, poppy seeds and melted butter. Bake at 400° for 35-40 minutes. Cut in small squares and serve. May be frozen.

Mushroom Hors D'Oeuvres

Serves 12

24 slices very thin white bread
4 tablespoons butter
3 tablespoons finely chopped
onion
½ pound fresh mushrooms,
finely chopped
2 tablespoons flour

1 cup heavy cream
½ teaspoon salt
⅛ teaspoon cayenne pepper
1 tablespoon chopped parsley
1 tablespoon minced chives
½ teaspoon lemon juice
2 tablespoons grated cheese

To prepare cups: coat muffin tins with butter. Cut slices of bread with a 3-inch cookie cutter. Press slices of bread into muffin tins. Bake cups at 400° for 10 minutes or until light brown. At this point can be frozen in a plastic bag.

To prepare filling: melt butter in heavy skillet and add onion, stirring constantly until transparent. Stir in mushrooms and cook over low heat until all the moisture disappears. Remove pan from heat. Sprinkle flour over onion and mushrooms. Add cream and bring to a boil. Reduce heat and cool a few minutes. Add seasonings and lemon juice. Filling may be frozen. Fill cups with filling and place on cookie sheet. Sprinkle grated cheese on top. Bake at 350° for 10 minutes.

Marie's Bleu Pecan Delights

Serves 6
Superb with sherry—monumental with martinis

5 ounces bleu cheese
2 tablespoons butter

2 ounces cream cheese
48-60 pecan halves

Have all ingredients at room temperature. With the cutting blade in a food processor or in a mixing bowl with a fork, combine the two cheeses and butter until well mixed. Refrigerate until firm. Put 1 teaspoon of mix between 2 pecan halves. Repeat process with all the pecan halves. Refrigerate until ready to serve.

Sesame Chicken With Honey Dip

Makes 2 Cups

½ cup mayonnaise
1 teaspoon dry mustard
1 teaspoon instant minced onion
½ cup fine dry bread crumbs

¼ cup sesame seeds
2 cups cubed cooked chicken or
    turkey

Honey Dip:
1 cup mayonnaise

2 tablespoons honey

Mix first three ingredients together and set aside. Mix bread crumbs
and sesame seeds. Coat chicken with mayonnaise mixture, then
bread crumb mixture. Place on baking sheet. Bake at 425° for 12
minutes or until lightly browned. Serve hot with honey dip. Chicken
may be cooked the day before. Can be rolled in the mixtures in the
morning and placed on baking sheet and stored in refrigerator.

Eggplant Caviar

1 small eggplant
1 medium onion, coarsely
    chopped
⅓ cup chopped green pepper
½ cup chopped mushrooms
2 garlic cloves, crushed
¼ cup salad oil
1 teaspoon salt

½ teaspoon pepper
½ teaspoon oregano
1½ teaspoons sugar
1 cup tomato sauce
1 tablespoon wine vinegar
½ cup chopped olives
3 tablespoons pignolia nuts
2 tablespoons capers

Finely chop unpeeled eggplant. Combine eggplant and next 5
ingredients in large skillet. Cover and simmer 10 minutes. Add
remaining ingredients. Stir and simmer, covered, for 25 minutes
until eggplant is cooked but not mushy. Chill overnight or freeze.
Serve with crackers.

Guacamole Specialty

Makes 20 Appetizer Servings
Gets rave reviews

2 medium ripe avocados
2 tablespoons lemon juice
½ teaspoon salt
¼ teaspoon pepper
1 cup sour cream
½ cup mayonnaise or salad
  dressing
1 package taco seasoning mix
2 (10½ ounce) cans plain or
  jalapeno-flavored bean dip

1 large bunch green onions with
  tops, chopped (1 cup)
3 medium-sized tomatoes, cored
  and coarsely chopped (2 cups)
2 (3½ ounce) cans pitted ripe
  olives, drained, coarsely
  chopped
½ cup sharp Cheddar cheese,
  shredded
Large round tortilla chips

Peel, pit and mash avocados in medium sized bowl with lemon
juice, salt and pepper. Set aside. Combine sour cream, mayonnaise
and taco seasoning mix in bowl. To assemble, spread bean dip on
large shallow serving platter. Top with seasoned avocado mixture.
Layer with sour cream-taco mixture. Sprinkle with chopped onions,
tomatoes and olives. Cover with shredded cheese. Serve chilled or at
room temperature with round tortilla chips.

Homos Bi Tahini

Makes 2 Cups

1 (20 ounce) can chick peas
½ teaspoon salt
Juice of 3 lemons
6 tablespoons Tahini paste
1 garlic clove, minced

⅓ to ½ cup water
Olive oil
Parsley
Ground red pepper

Rinse and drain chick peas. Place in blender with salt, lemon juice,
Tahini paste, garlic and water. Puree 1 to 2 minutes until smooth.
Garnish with olive oil, parsley and red pepper. Serve with Pita bread
cut in 2-inch pieces.

Marinated Chicken Wings

Serves 10 to 12
Everybody's favorite

1 cup soy sauce
1 cup brown sugar
½ cup butter

1 teaspoon dry mustard
¾ cup Sauterne wine
3 pounds chicken wings

Combine soy sauce, sugar, butter, mustard and Sauterne in saucepan. Stir until melted. Spread wings in baking pan. Pour hot mixture over wings. Marinate for one hour in refrigerator. Bake at 350° for 1 hour, turning once after 30 minutes.

Foo Yung Fritters

Makes 36

6 eggs
1 cup flour
1½ teaspoon baking powder
1 tablespoon soy sauce
1 (8 ounce) can mushrooms,
   drained

½ teaspoon Worcestershire
   sauce
1 pound can bean sprouts,
   drained
1 envelope onion soup mix
Oil for deep fat frying
Sweet and sour sauce

Beat eggs. Sift together flour and baking powder. Add to eggs. Beat until smooth. With scissors, snip bean sprouts into short lengths. Finely chop mushrooms. Add remaining ingredients and fold into batter. Blend well. In deep fryer or wok, heat oil. Drop mixture by teaspoonful into hot oil. Fry until golden brown and puffy. Drain. Serve with sweet and sour sauce. Can be frozen and reheated at 350° for 10 minutes.

Louraine's Baked Stuffed Mushrooms

Smoked cheese lends exceptional flavor

2 pounds fresh mushrooms
2-3 tablespoons oil
½ cup grated salami
½ to ¾ cup grated smoked
  cheese

1 small onion, chopped
Bread crumbs
Dash of garlic powder, optional

Remove stems from mushrooms and reserve. Slowly cook
mushrooms in oil until tender. Chop stems and onion and cook in
oil until soft. Drain. Mix salami, cheese, mushrooms and onion with
bread crumbs until mixture sticks together. Stuff mushroom caps.
Place on cookie sheet with a drop of oil on each mushroom and
bake at 425° for 10 minutes.

Cocktail Meatballs

Makes 60 to 70

4 slices white bread
¾ cup milk
1 onion, minced
2 teaspoons salt
¼ teaspoon pepper
1 pound ground beef

1 pound ground veal
½ pound ground pork
⅛ teaspoon nutmeg
⅛ teaspoon allspice
1 garlic clove, minced
2 eggs

Soak bread in milk. Add remaining ingredients. Let stand 15
minutes. Form into small balls the size of walnuts. Brown on all
sides. Simmer in sauce for 1 hour.

Sauce:
2 tablespoons brown sugar
½ cup water
2 teaspoons mustard
2 tablespoons Worcestershire
  sauce

1 cut ketchup
⅓ cup vinegar
2 tablespoons butter
⅓ cup minced onion

Simmer sauce for ½ hour. Add meatballs.

Mushroom Strudel

Serves 12
Elegant

1 pound fresh mushrooms,
  thinly sliced
1 small onion, chopped
2 tablespoons butter or
  margarine
¾ teaspoon salt
⅛ teaspoon pepper
1 tablespoon sherry

4 ounces cream cheese
1 teaspoon fresh dill or ½
  teaspoon dill weed
1 tablespoon dry bread crumbs
6 frozen fillo strudel leaves,
  thawed
Melted butter
1 tablespoon dry bread crumbs

Saute mushrooms and onion in 2 tablespoons butter in large skillet until mushrooms are tender, about 3 minutes. Stir in salt, pepper, sherry, cream cheese and dill. Stir until smooth. Remove from heat. Stir in bread crumbs. Cool to room temperature. Heat oven to 375°. Layer 3 fillo leaves on damp kitchen towel, brushing each with melted butter. Spoon half the mushroom mixture on short end of fillo in 2-3-inch wide strips, turning long sides of fillo about one inch to keep filling in place. Lift towel, using it to roll fillo like a jelly roll starting from narrow end closest to filling. Place roll, seam side down on lightly buttered jelly roll pan. Brush top and sides of dough with melted butter. Sprinkle with bread crumbs. Repeat procedure with remaining ingredients. Bake strudels until brown and crisp, 30-35 minutes. Let cool slightly. Cut each strudel into six pieces.

Washington, Connecticut was the first town in the United States to be named for George Washington.

Brandied Meatballs

Makes 36 Meatballs

1 pound ground beef	1 teaspoon minced onion
½ cup fine bread crumbs	1 egg
1 teaspoon salt	Dash of paprika
½ teaspoon pepper	

In 2-quart mixing bowl combine beef, bread crumbs, salt, pepper, onion and egg. With wet hands, shape into 36 tiny balls. Place on greased cookie sheet. Bake at 400° for 10 minutes (5 minutes on each side). Sprinkle with paprika. Serve hot or cold with cherry brandied sauce.

Cherry Brandied Sauce:

¾ cup red currant jelly	1 tablespoon corn starch
2 tablespoons vinegar	½ cup wild cherry brandy
¼ teaspoon tabasco	

In a one-quart saucepan combine jelly, vinegar, tabasco and cornstarch. Use whisk for blending. Cook over low heat, stirring constantly until thickened. Add brandy. Serve hot as a sauce for meatballs or pour over meatballs in chafing dish.

A Special Note About Pâtés

Be as accurate as possible about measuring liquids when making a pâté. It is better to have less liquid than more.

The best ratio for meat to fat is one part fat to three parts meat.

Blenders and food processors will give you the finest of pâtés, while using the old-fashioned chef's knife will give you a rougher pâté called a country pâté or woodsmen's pâté.

All pâtés improve with aging. About one week in the refrigerator is all it takes for the flavors to marry.

The density can be controlled by weighting the pâté while it is chilling. A piece of wood cut to the inside measurements of the mold wrapped in foil and weighed down with an iron or a book will do the job.

Pâté Champagne

Serves 6
A favorite of young and old alike

½ pound pork
½ pound veal
½ pound ham
4 slices bacon
1 garlic clove, minced
½ cup champagne

1 whole egg
Salt and white pepper, to taste
⅛ teaspoon basil
⅛ teaspoon oregano
1 tablespoon chopped parsley

Finely grind together pork, veal, ham and bacon. Add remaining ingredients and whisk into a smooth paste. Put mixture in a 6-inch loaf pan, packed down tightly. Bake at 325° for 1 hour. To test for doneness place a skewer in center. It should be warm to the touch. Special Note: Because of the food animals eat, pork, veal and ham may vary in water content. Unless you know your butcher, it is best to add the champagne last.

Chicken Liver Pâté

1 large Bermuda onion, finely
  chopped
1 cup butter
1 pound fresh chicken livers

¼ cup brandy
Salt and pepper to taste
Few drops lemon juice

Saute onion lightly in 4 tablespoons butter. Add 4 tablespoons butter and saute chicken livers until browned on the outside. Put brandy in ladle and flame. Pour over livers in pan. Put mixture in blender and beat 2-3 minutes. Cream remaining butter and add to mixture. Add salt, pepper and lemon juice. Beat until mixture is smooth. Place mixture in crock and refrigerate. Melt a little butter and pour over chicken livers to seal the exposed top. Refrigerate again until ready to serve. Delicious served on party rye with egg yolk sprinkled on top.

Lentil Pâté

Serves 4
Vegetarian's Delight

1 garlic clove, crushed
1 medium onion, chopped
1 teaspoon oil
1 cup cooked lentils, pureed in blender
2 slices whole wheat bread, soaked in water to soften

2 tablespoons miso (fermented soy bean paste)
4 tablespoons tahini (sesame seed butter)
1 tablespoon chopped parsley
Pinch nutmeg

Saute garlic and onion until soft. Add lentils, bread, miso, tahini, parsley and nutmeg. Mix and cook 10 minutes, stirring constantly. Chill pâté. Serve cold. Can be used as a spread for bread and crackers or stuffed in a tomato or avocado for main dish.

Chutney-Cheese Pâté

Makes 1 Cup

1 (3 ounce) package cream cheese, softened
½ cut shredded sharp cheese
2 teaspoons dry sherry
¼ teaspoon curry powder

⅛ teaspoon salt
¼ cup finely chopped mango chutney
Green onions with tops, finely sliced

Beat together first 5 ingredients. Spread on serving platter in ½-inch thick layer. Chill until firm. Before serving, spread with chutney and sprinkle with green onions. Serve with wheat thins or sesame wafers.

Sausage Quiches

Makes 48 Small Quiches

1 (8 ounce) package refrigerated
  crescent rolls
½ pound hot sausage, crumbled
2 tablespoons dried onion flakes
4 eggs, lightly beaten
1 pint cottage cheese, small curd

2 tablespoons minced chives
2 cups grated Swiss or Cheddar
  cheese
⅓ cup grated Parmesan cheese
Paprika

Generously grease 4 miniature muffin tins. Separate dough pieces
and cut up to fit into tins about ⅔ way up the sides. Brown sausage
lightly with onion. Drain well. Add chives. Spoon equally over
dough. Mix eggs and cheeses. Fill tins with mixture. Sprinkle top
with paprika. May be frozen at this point, tightly covered. Bring to
room temperature. Bake at 375° for 20 minutes.

Skewered Swordfish and Cantaloupe

Serves 4
Interesting combination

1 pound swordfish
¾ cup lime or lemon juice
¼ teaspoon salt

1 large cantaloupe
Lime wedges

Cut swordfish into ¾-inch cubes. Place in a large bowl and cover
with a marinade of lime or lemon juice and salt. Cover bowl and
chill 1 hour. Remove rind and seeds from cantaloupe and cut in ½
inch cubes. Alternate cubes of swordfish and cantaloupe on long
thin skewers. Cook over hot coals or under preheated broiler until
swordfish is done, 10-15 minutes, turning to cook on all sides. Serve
with lime wedges. Swordfish and cantaloupe have firm textures and
mild, sweet flavors which the citrus marinade enhances.

Pepperoni Bread

Makes 1 Loaf

1 loaf frozen bread dough
1 package pepperoni, sliced
2 green peppers, cut in strips

½ pound Provolone cheese
Grated Parmesan cheese
Garlic salt

Thaw bread dough. Fry peppers in oil and cool. Roll dough to measure 12×24 inches. Put on cookie sheet. Arrange down center (lengthwise) of dough the sliced pepperoni, overlapping slices of Provolone then green peppers. Sprinkle with Parmesan cheese and garlic salt. Fold up long sides to center. Seal well. Bake at 350° until golden brown, about 25 minutes. Slice and serve.

P. T. Barnum, the great circus impresario, was mayor of Bridgeport for many years. His mansion is now a unique museum of circus memorabilia.

Pineapple Cheese Ball

Makes a thoughtful gift

2 (8 ounce) packages cream cheese, softened
1 (8 ounce) can crushed pineapple, drained
2 cups chopped pecans

¼ cup finely chopped green pepper
2 tablespoons finely chopped onion
1 tablespoon seasoned salt

Mix together by hand cream cheese and pineapple. Add 1 cup of the nuts, green pepper, onion and salt. Chill well. Form into one large or 2 medium balls and roll in remaining nuts. Garnish with pineapple slice and cherry and/or parsley. Surround with crackers. May be made ahead of time.

Potted Cheese

Makes 2 Cups
Keeps well-handy for spur of the moment guests

1 pound grated Cheddar cheese
3 tablespoons chopped scallions
3 tablespoons chopped parsley
1 teaspoon Dijon mustard
Salt to taste

2 tablespoons butter, softened
2 tablespoons dry sherry
Dash of tabasco and
    Worcestershire sauce to taste

Mix in food processor until creamy. Pack in jar or crock and
refrigerate. Serve at room temperature with crusty bread or
crackers.

Spinach Roll-ups

1 loaf soft white sandwich bread
1 (10 ounce) package chopped
    spinach
2 ounces Swiss Gruyere cheese,
    melted

1 (3 ounce) package cream
    cheese, softened
Dash oregano
Salt and pepper
Butter or margarine, melted

Remove crust from bread slices and roll thin with rolling pin. Cook
spinach and drain well. Combine in bowl with remaining
ingredients. Everything should blend and look like creamed
spinach. Spread one teaspoon of spinach mixture on each slice of
bread and roll up jelly-roll fashion. Cut in thirds. Brush with melted
butter or margarine. May be frozen until ready for use. Bake frozen
roll-ups at 400° for 25 minutes, or until brown.

State Senator Richard F. Schneller

Spanish Woodcock

Serves 4 to 6

2 medium onions, diced
1 (28 ounce) can tomatoes
Salt and pepper to taste

1 pound Cheddar cheese, diced
2-3 eggs, slightly beaten

Saute onion in large frying pan. Add tomatoes, salt and pepper.
When hot, add diced cheese, stirring constantly until cheese melts
and blends. Add eggs and blend well. Simmer until thickened, do
not let boil. Serve on saltines or crackers. (Any type cheese may be
used depending on how mild or sharp a flavor you desire).

Spinach Balls

Makes Approximately 60
Very popular

2 (10 ounce) packages frozen
  chopped spinach
1 cup coarsely ground Parmesan
  cheese
1½ cups herb stuffing

¾ cup melted butter or
  margarine
3 eggs, beaten
Salt and pepper, to taste
¼ teaspoon thyme (optional)

Cook and drain spinach well. Mix with all remaining ingredients.
Chill 2 hours or more. Form into bite sized balls. Bake at 350° for
15 minutes. Serve hot or cold.

Glazed Spicy Wieners

Makes 48

3 (5½ ounce) packages small
  frankfurters
1 cup jellied cranberry sauce

3 tablespoons prepared mustard
1 tablespoon lemon juice
½ teaspoon salt

In saucepan, cook all the ingredients except frankfurters. Stir sauce
until smooth. Make thin slashes in frankfurters and place in sauce
and heat through. Serve hot with cocktail picks.

Zucchini Hors D'Oeuvres

Makes 40 Pieces

1 cup Parmesan cheese
3 cups cubed zucchini
½ cup chopped onion
3 garlic cloves, mashed

2 tablespoons chopped parsley
4 eggs, slightly beaten
½ cup oil

Mix all ingredients together and bake in a 9×13 greased baking dish at 350° for 25-30 minutes or until top is nicely browned. Cut into bite sized pieces when cool.

American Cookery, by Amelia Simmons, a phamplet of 48 pages, was published in Hartford in 1796. It is credited as the first American Cookbook.

Elegant Caviar

Serves 8 to 10

4 eggs, hard-cooked
2 medium onions
Mayonnaise
½ pint sour cream
1 (8 ounce) package cream
   cheese, softened

1 envelope green onion dip
1 (3 ounce) jar caviar (black or
   red)
¾ cup chopped parsley

Chop eggs and onions lightly in food processor mixing with a little mayonnaise to hold together and layer in a pie plate. Mix cream cheese and dip and spread on top of egg mixture. Top with caviar, all black or combination of red and black. Decorate edge with parsley. Refrigerate at least 4 hours or day ahead. Serve with crackers.

Ceviche (Pickled Raw Fish)

Serves 8

2 pounds raw firm white fish
  (cod or haddock filet) cubed

1 cup lemon juice

Marinate fish 4-6 hours in lemon juice in refrigerator. Make a sauce of the following ingredients:

2 cups chopped onion
½ cup tomato puree
½ cup tomato juice
1 tablespoon salt
2 tablespoons Worcestershire
  sauce

1 teaspoon tabasco
2 small green chilies, chopped
3 firm tomatoes, chopped
Chopped parsley

Pour off half the lemon juice, add sauce and let stand overnight. If too dry, add a little more of the marinade. Serve with crackers or as first course on lettuce leaves.

Clam Rolls

Makes 36 to 48 Rolls

2 tablespoons onion, minced
1 tablespoon butter
1½ tablespoon flour
1 (7 ounce) can minced clams
¼ teaspoon Worcestershire
  sauce

Dash of garlic powder
12 slices white bread, crusts
  removed
Butter, softened

In medium saucepan saute onion in butter. Cook 3 minutes. Remove from heat and add flour. Gradually add liquid from clams. Add Worcestershire sauce, garlic and clams. Boil 1 minute and remove from heat and cool. Roll the slices of bread thin with a rolling pin. Spread with softened butter and the cooled clam mixture. Roll as for jelly roll and slice to desired size. Place on greased cookie sheet and brush with melted butter. Bake at 425° for 8-10 minutes. Serve hot. May be prepared ahead and frozen until ready to use. Freeze rolls whole and slice just before baking.

Stuffed Clams

Serves 8

2 dozen cherrystone clams or
   2 (7 ounce) cans chopped
   clams
2 slices white bread
1 medium onion, finely chopped
2-3 medium celery stalks,
   chopped

¼ cup butter or margarine
12-15 Ritz crackers, crushed
1 (7 ounce) can small shrimp, or
   8 fresh small shrimp, chopped
Freshly ground pepper to taste
White wine or sherry

Wash clams thoroughly before steaming open. Reserve 1-2 cups of broth. Soak bread in broth. If canned clams are used, soak in canned broth. Saute onions and celery in butter. Crush crackers to semi-fine texture. Add soaked, squeezed bread, crackers, clams, shrimp, celery, onions and pepper. Moisten with clam broth and wine or sherry. Fill clean clam shells with mixture. Brush with melted butter and wine. Bake at 400° for 30 minutes brushing occasionally with butter/wine mixture.

Crabbies or Shrimpies

Makes 72 Bite-Sized Triangles

½ cup butter, softened
1 jar Old English cheese
1½ teaspoons mayonnaise
1½ teaspoons garlic salt

½ teaspoon seasoned salt
1 (7 ounce) can crabmeat or
   shrimp
6 English Muffins

Place first 5 ingredients in blender or processor. Add fish and mix slightly. Spread mixture on split muffins. Place on cookie sheet and freeze. When frozen, cut each split muffin into 6 wedges. Bag and freeze until needed. When ready to serve, take amount needed and spread mixture side up on a cookie sheet. Broil until slightly browned and bubbly. Serve immediately. These can also be made and cooked without freezing.

Crab-Swiss Bites

Makes 36

1 (7 ounce) can crab meat
1 tablespoon chopped green
  onion
4 ounces Swiss cheese,
  shredded
½ cup salad dressing

1 teaspoon lemon juice
¼ teaspoon curry powder
1 package flaky rolls (12 rolls)
1 (5 ounce) can water
  chestnuts, drained and sliced

Combine crab meat, onion, cheese, salad dressing, lemon juice and curry powder; mix well. Separate rolls into 3 layers. Place on ungreased baking sheet. Spoon on mixture. Top with chestnut slices. Bake at 400° for 10-12 minutes.

Salmon Ball

Serves 10

1 (1 pound) can salmon
1 tablespoon lemon juice
1 teaspoon horseradish
¼ teaspoon liquid smoke
1 (8 ounce) package cream
  cheese, softened

2 teaspoons grated onion
¼ teaspoon salt
½ cup chopped nuts
Fresh parsley

Drain and flake salmon. Remove skin and bones. Combine all ingredients except nuts and parsley. Mix thoroughly. Chill several hours. Shape into a ball and roll in nuts and parsley. Serve with crackers or party bread.

Water Chestnuts and Bacon

Makes 40

2 (6 ounce) cans whole water
    chestnuts, drained
½ (12 ounce) bottle seafood
    cocktail sauce

1 pound bacon
¼ cup brown sugar
Wooden toothpicks

Marinate chestnuts in cocktail sauce for 1 hour. Slice bacon in half
for strips. Wrap each marinated chestnut in strip of bacon and
pierce it closed with a toothpick. Place in a shallow baking dish.
Sprinkle with brown sugar and top with remaining bits of seafood
sauce. Bake at 350° for 20 minutes. Then remove each chestnut to
a clean baking dish. Reheat for about 15 minutes at 325° before
serving.

Salmon Stuffed Eggs

Serves 8
Easy Appetizer

4 hard-cooked eggs
1 (3 ounce) can smoked salmon
¼ cup sour cream

1½ tablespoons lemon juice
Salt and pepper to taste

Halve the eggs lengthwise. Remove yolks and arrange the whites on
a plate lined with paper towels. In a food processor fitted with steel
blade or in blender, blend yolks with salmon, sour cream, lemon
juice, salt and pepper. Transfer mixture to bowl and chill, covered
for 30 minutes. Transfer the mixture to a pastry bag fitted with
small ribbon tip and pipe it decoratively into the whites.

Banana Delight

Serves 2

4 ice cubes, chopped
Juice of 1 lime
2 teaspoons confectioners' sugar

6 tablespoons white rum or
  5 tablespoons pineapple juice
1 ripe medium banana, cut into
  chunks

In blender combine half the ice, lime juice, sugar, rum or pineapple juice and banana. Blend at high speed 1 minute or until smooth. Add remaining ice; blend 1 minute more. Pretty served in stem glasses.

Frosty Beverage

Serves 4 to 6
Refreshing on hot summer days

Juice and rind of one lemon
8 ounces heavy cream

¾ cup sugar
7-Up, Sprite or Fresca, chilled

Grate lemon rind and squeeze out all the juice. Add all ingredients except 7-Up; stirring until sugar is dissolved. Freeze until solid (6-8 hours). Fill a tall glass ⅓ to ½ full with frozen cream mixture; add 7-Up. Stir slightly to dissolve cream. Drink will be frothy. Enjoy.

Nectarine Float

Serves 4

3 cups peeled sliced nectarines
  or peaches
1 (11 ounce) can apricot nectar
2 cups milk

2 teaspoons lemon juice
1 pint vanilla ice cream
Mint sprigs (optional)

Whirl nectarines, nectar, milk and lemon juice in blender until well blended. Pour into 4 chilled tall glasses and top with scoop of ice cream. Garnish with mint.

Frosty Yogurt Delight

Serves 2 to 3
"High energy drink"

¼ cup milk, whole or skim
¼ cup powdered milk
1 cup fruit juice, fresh or
   bottled: concord grape,

boysenberry, raspberry,
   cherry, prune, pear, etc.
2-3 teaspoons honey
1 cup crushed ice
1 cup plain yogurt

Blend milk, fruit juice, honey and ice. Pour into bowl. Add yogurt;
stir gently. Garnish with fruit and sprigs of mint.

Tomato Bouillon

Serves 18 to 20

1 (46 ounce) can tomato juice
1 (46 ounce) can water
7 beef bouillon cubes

⅔ cup sugar
1 small stick cinnamon, ½ inch
1 teaspoon whole cloves

Spices may be put into a small cloth bag for easy removal. Mix
ingredients in large saucepan. Bring to boiling point. Remove from
heat and allow to steep for 20 minutes or longer. Remove spices.
Serve hot or cold.

Mulled Cider

Serves 24 to 30
A New England autumn favorite

1 gallon cider
1 quart tea
1 cup sugar

4 sticks cinnamon
1 teaspoon whole cloves

Simmer all ingredients for 20 minutes. Refrigerate 24 hours. Serve
hot or cold.

Spicy Instant Tea

Makes 6 Cups

2 cups powdered orange juice
½ cup instant tea
2 (6 ounce) packages lemonade
2 cups sugar

2 teaspoons cinnamon
1 teaspoon cloves
1 teaspoon allspice

Mix and "age" about 4 days. Serve 2 teaspoons per cup of boiling water. Ice to serve cold.

Spiced Ice Coffee

Serves 4

1 cinnamon stick
4 whole cloves
6 tablespoons sugar

4 cups hot strong coffee
Ice
Cream (optional)

Add cinnamon, cloves and sugar to coffee; chill. Remove spices and pour coffee into 4 ice-filled tall glasses. Serve with cream.

Teetotaler's Revenge

Serves 8
A rum and tea warmer

2 cups dark rum
⅔ cup sugar
1 cup orange juice

¼ cup lemon juice
¼ cup arrack
4 cups hot strong tea

In a saucepan combine rum and sugar and bring to a boil over low heat, stirring. Increase the heat to medium-high and reduce the liquid by one third. Stir in orange and lemon juices, arrack and tea. Serve in mugs. Garnish with a thin slice of lemon or orange.

Cherry (or Fruit) Wine

Makes 3 Gallons

4 quarts cherries or fruit
7½ pounds sugar
2 gallons water

1 package dry yeast
3 lemons
3 pounds raisins

Chop fruit in blender. Put in 5 gallon container. Add sugar and water. Stir well. Add yeast and stir again. Add lemons and let stand for one week. Stir daily. After one week, add raisins and let stand three more weeks. Be sure to stir each day. After four weeks strain through cheese cloth and let it stand until it settles, about 3 days, then siphon it off from the top. It will be clear and taste sooo good.

Brandied Pear Punch

Serves 20 to 25
A toast to the garden club

2 cups water
1 cup sugar
24 whole cloves
12 strips lemon peel
2 cinnamon sticks, broken into
  pieces
1 fifth brandy
1 (23 ounce) bottle sparkling
  water

2 cups orange juice
2 cups liquid from drained
  canned pears
1 cup fresh lemon juice
Block of ice
Pear halves and/or frozen
  quartered pears (garnish)

Combine first 5 ingredients in medium saucepan. Bring to a boil, stirring constantly until sugar is dissolved. Remove from heat and let stand until cool. Strain into large bowl. Add next 5 ingredients and blend well. Pour over block of ice in punch bowl. Float pear halves for garnish. Serve in old-fashioned glasses, adding pieces of frozen pear to each serving.

Champagne-Orange Punch

Serves 30

2 (6 ounce) cans frozen orange
   juice
1 (6 ounce) can frozen
   lemonade

1½ quarts club soda, or water
½ to 1 bottle champagne
½ pint orange or lemon sherbet
   (optional)

Thaw orange juice and lemonade. Add remaining ingredients and
top with sherbet. Voila!! (Rum or vodka may be substituted for
champagne).

Fish House Punch

Serves 20 to 25
A Connecticut favorite since the early 1800's

2 quarts water
1 cup superfine sugar
2 cups fresh lemon juice
1 fifth light rum

1 fifth dark rum
1 fifth Cognac or brandy
½ cup peach brandy

Combine all ingredients in large bowl. Allow to "mellow" several
hours. Serve from punch bowl containing ice mold or over ice in
individual glasses.

Gae's Party Punch

Serves 8

1 cup cranberry juice
1 cup apricot nectar
1 quart chilled ginger ale

1 pint raspberry sherbet
Mint sprigs

Combine cranberry juice and apricot nectar. Add ginger ale. Pour
over block of ice. Slide in sherbet. Fresh mint can be floated on top.

Christmas Punch

Makes 24 punch cups

8 cups cranberry-juice cocktail
1 (6 ounce) can frozen orange
   juice, thawed
1 (6 ounce) can frozen
   pineapple juice, thawed

1 (6 ounce) can frozen lemon
   juice, thawed
2 cups brandy
2 bottles chilled champagne
Lemon and lime slices for
   garnish

Mix juices and brandy in a large punch bowl over a block of ice.
Just before serving add chilled champagne. Garnish with slices of
lemon and lime. For teetotalers, substitute 2 quarts of gingerale for
champagne and 2 cups grape juice for brandy.

*Noah Webster, whose dictionary formalized American English, was born in a West
Hartford farmhouse which is now open to the public.*

Venezuelan Rum Punch

Makes 20 to 25
And don't forget the orchid!

1 bottle light rum
1 bottle Cinzano red
4 (12 ounce) cans pineapple
   juice

½ cup fresh lemon juice
3 (10 ounce) bottles club soda
½ cup grenadine syrup
10 drops Angostura bitters

Mix all ingredients. Fill tall glasses with crushed ice or ice cubes
and decorate with mint, pineapple and cherry.

James L. Buckley
U.S. State Department Counselor

Authentic Spanish Sangria

Makes 18 to 20 Punch Cups
An old Spanish recipe

2 bottles red Spanish Rioja wine	½ lemon
½ pear	Sugar
½ peach	1 (12 ounce) bottle club soda
½ orange	4 ounces cointreau (optional)

Slice fruit; combine with wine. Add sugar to taste. Marinate in refrigerator for 1 hour. When serving add ice and chilled club soda. For additional zest, add cointreau. Ole!

John Fitch launched the world's first practical steamboat on the Connecticut River near his South Windsor home.

Holiday Eggnog

Serves 10 to 12

12 eggs	2 quarts heavy cream
1 pound confectioners' sugar	1 cup peach brandy (optional)
5 cups brandy or dark rum	

Separate eggs; reserve whites. Beat egg yolks until light in color. While still beating, gradually add sugar. Continue beating and slowly pour in 2 cups brandy. Let mixture stand, covered, for 2-3 hours to allow eggs to cook in the brandy. Add remaining brandy and cream, beating constantly. Refrigerate, covered, for at least 4 hours. Beat egg whites until stiff but not dry; fold lightly into mixture. Sprinkle nutmeg on top if desired.

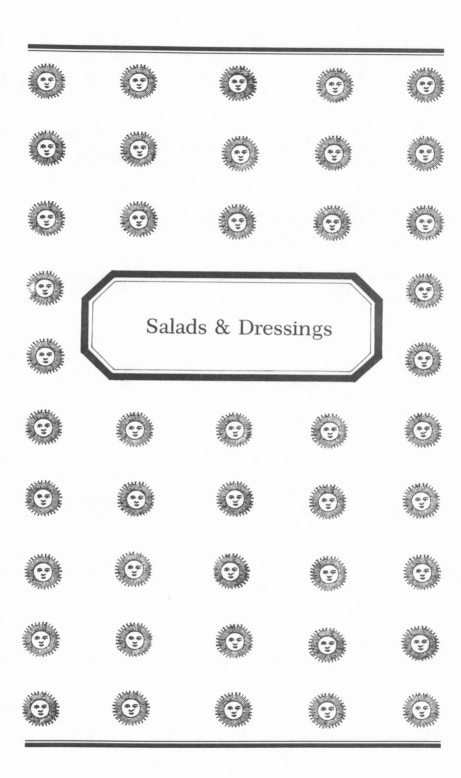

Salads & Dressings

Asparagus and Gruyere Vinaigrette

Serves 8

½ pound Gruyere cheese
2 (10 ounce) packages frozen
   asparagus, thawed
¼ cup red wine vinegar
¼ cup olive oil
2 tablespoons snipped chives
1 teaspoon salt

⅛ to ¼ teaspoon crushed red
   pepper
3 garlic cloves, crushed
1 tablespoon sugar
¼ teaspoon celery seed
¼ teaspoon dry mustard
Small amount chopped onion
   and pimiento for garnish

Cut cheese into ½×3-inch sticks. Arrange with asparagus in
shallow glass dish. In small bowl, combine remaining ingredients
except garnish; pour over cheese and asparagus. Sprinkle garnish
on top. Allow to marinate overnight.

Cabbage Salad

Serves 8 to 10
Colorful as a rainbow

1 small head cabbage
2 medium carrots, shredded
1 (8 ounce) can pineapple
   tidbits, reserve juice

2 red delicious apples, chopped
   with skin
Raisins or dates, chopped if
   desired
Nuts

Chop cabbage as for cole slaw. Add carrots. Drain pineapple,
reserving 3 tablespoons of the juice. Add apple to pineapple and
juice. Mix all ingredients together.

Dressing:
½ cup mayonnaise
½ cup sour cream
1 tablespoon vinegar or lemon
   juice

1 tablespoon honey
½ to 1 teaspoon salt
½ teaspoon celery seed
1 teaspoon dill seed

Mix all ingredients well. Pour over salad and toss.

Marinated Carrot Salad

Serves 8 to 10

5 cups cooked and sliced carrots
  (2 bunches)
1 medium onion, chopped
1 green pepper, chopped
1 (8 ounce) can tomato sauce or
  1 can tomato soup
½ cup cooking oil

¾ cup vinegar
1 cup sugar
1 teaspoon salt
1 teaspoon dry mustard
1 teaspoon pepper
1 teaspoon Worcestershire sauce

Mix sauce. Add carrots. Marinate in refrigerator at least 12 hours.

Cauliflower in Sour Cream Sauce

Serves 6
Refreshing, different summer salad

1 cauliflower
1 cup mayonnaise
1 cup sour cream
1 teaspoon Worcestershire sauce

½ teaspoon salt
Pepper to taste
½ cup grated Cheddar cheese
½ cup chopped scallions

Trim and separate cauliflower into flowerets. Cook in salted boiling water for 5 minutes or until tender, yet crisp. Drain and cool. In small bowl combine mayonnaise, sour cream, Worcestershire sauce, salt and pepper. In large bowl combine cauliflower with cheese and scallions. Toss mixture with the sauce.

Celery Italienne

Serves 6 to 8
Add spice to a buffet

2 large bunches celery
1 pound mushrooms, sliced
1 onion, sliced
1 garlic clove
½ cup chili sauce
⅓ cup salad oil

¼ cup red wine vinegar
½ teaspoon salt
½ teaspoon oregano
¼ teaspoon fennel
⅛ teaspoon dry mustard

Early in day or day before, cut up celery. Steam slightly to soften.
Combine remaining ingredients in saucepan and simmer 5 minutes.
Pour over celery. Refrigerate until ready to serve. Can also be made
with zucchini.

Green Bean Vinaigrette

Serves 8

6 green onions including tops,
   chopped
1 garlic clove
⅓ cup salad oil
3 tablespoons lemon juice
1 teaspoon salt
1 teaspoon sugar

1 teaspoon dry mustard
¼ teaspoon basil
¼ teaspoon oregano
¼ teaspoon marjoram
¼ teaspoon pepper
2 pounds fresh green beans

Mix dressing ingredients. Cook beans until tender, but crisp. To
serve hot, drain beans and turn into serving dish. Pour dressing
over beans. To serve cold, drain beans, run under cold water. Pour
on dressing. Cover and chill, stirring several times, 2 hours or
overnight. Garnish with cherry tomatoes and red onion rings.

Hungarian Cucumber Salad

Serves 4

2 cucumbers
¼ cup mayonnaise
¼ cup sour cream
1 teaspoon chopped dill
Juice of 1 lemon
½ teaspoon salt

Pepper to taste
½ medium onion, thinly sliced
1 tablespoon chopped chives
¼ cup green pepper, sliced
    julienne
¼ cup pimiento, sliced julienne

Peel and slice cucumbers. Mix all ingredients. Chill and serve.

Peas Pizzicato

Serves 8
Great for a hot day

2 (10 ounce) packages frozen
    tiny peas
1 cup sour cream
2 green onions, finely
    chopped

6 slices bacon, cooked
    and chopped
½ teaspoon salt
½ teaspoon finely ground
    pepper

Completely thaw peas and toss with remaining ingredients. Chill
until serving time.

Seven Layer Salad

Serves 6
Must be made ahead of time

1 small head lettuce, torn into
    bite sized pieces
½ pound bacon, cooked and
    crumbled
1 small Bermuda onion, thinly
    sliced

1 (10 ounce) package frozen
    peas, thawed, uncooked
2 hard cooked eggs, chopped
1 cup mayonnaise
1 cup yogurt
1 cup Cheddar cheese, shredded

In medium salad bowl layer half the lettuce, bacon, remaining
lettuce, onion, peas and eggs. Mix mayonnaise and yogurt and pour
over top, spreading evenly to edges. Sprinkle with Cheddar cheese.
Refrigerate 12 hours. To serve, dig deep. Do not toss.

Pickled Garden Salad

Serves 6
Refrigerate at least 24 hours

¼ small cauliflower, cut into flowerets
2 carrots, pared, sliced julienne
2 stalks celery, cut in 1-inch pieces
1 green pepper, cut in 2-inch slices
¾ cup wine vinegar
½ cup oil
1 tablespoon sugar
1 teaspoon salt
1 teaspoon oregano
¼ teaspoon pepper
¼ teaspoon garlic powder
Pinch of hot pepper

In large skillet, combine all ingredients with ¼ cup water. Bring to boiling, stirring occasionally. Reduce heat. Cover. Simmer 5 minutes. Let cool. Remove from pan. Refrigerate at least 24 hours. Store in covered jars. Fresh broccoli may also be added, if desired.

Perfect Potato Salad

Serves 6 to 8

2½ cups sliced cooked potatoes
1 teaspoon sugar
1 teaspoon vinegar
1 tablespoon chopped parsley
½ cup sliced celery
½ cup chopped onion
1¼ teaspoons salt
1 teaspoon celery seed
¾ cup mayonnaise
2 hard-cooked eggs, sliced

Sprinkle potatoes with sugar and vinegar. Add parsley, celery, onion, seasoning and mayonnaise. Toss to blend. Carefully fold in eggs. Refrigerate, covered, until well chilled (several hours). Serve in lettuce-lined bowl and garnish with parsley, sliced radishes, cucumber, and extra egg slices. For hot potato salad omit sugar, vinegar, salt and mayonnaise and use Pennsylvania Dutch Salad Dressing.

Lake House Spinach Pasta Salad

Serves 10 to 12
Cook noodles night before

8 ounces cooked spinach
  noodles
4 ounces Genoa salami
1 medium green pepper
1 medium onion
1 small bunch celery
16-20 canned artichoke hearts

1 large tomato
¼ cup mayonnaise
¼ cup sour cream
2 tablespoons tarragon vinegar
1 teaspoon chopped basil
Salt and pepper to taste

Cook noodles according to package directions. Drain, rinse and chill until ready to use. Slice salami into julienne strips (cold cooked ham or veal may also be used). Dice pepper, onion and celery. Drain and halve the artichokes, cut tomato into wedges. Toss meat and vegetables with noodles. Chill. Combine mayonnaise, sour cream, vinegar, tarragon and basil. Add salt and pepper. Dress the salad and toss before serving.

Variegated Salad

Serves 8
Tailgate Party Special

2 pounds zucchini, halved
  lengthwise and thinly sliced
2 teaspoons salt
¼ cup lemon juice
1 teaspoon salt
Pepper

⅔ cup oil
2 cups hot cooked rice
½ cup thinly sliced scallions
½ cup thinly sliced black olives
½ cup thinly sliced radishes

Place zucchini in large colander. Toss in salt. Let drain for 30 minutes. Press out moisture and pat dry with paper towels. In large glass salad bowl combine lemon juice, salt and pepper. Add oil in stream, beating with wire whisk until well mixed. Add rice and zucchini and toss. Add remaining vegetables. Toss all together. Season with salt and pepper. Chill for at least 2 hours. Serve from bowl or platter lined with lettuce.

Vegetables A La Greque

Serves 12
For a cold buffet

2 green zucchini, sliced
2 yellow zucchini, sliced
2 summer squash, sliced
½ pound green beans, chopped
1 small cauliflower in flowerets
4 carrots, peeled and cut up

12-15 small white onions, peeled
2 red peppers, cut in ½ × 1-inch pieces
2 green peppers, cut in ½ × 1-inch pieces
1 large cucumber

Marinade:
4 cups chicken broth
1¼ cup dry white wine
1½ cups olive oil
1 tablespoon bruised coriander seeds
1 tablespoon bruised peppercorns

4 garlic cloves
3-4 teaspoons salt
1 teaspoon thyme
2 small bay leaves
¾ cup lemon juice
Chopped parsley

Combine ingredients for marinade in large pot. Bring to a boil and taste for seasoning. Add salt and lemon juice. Cook vegetables in marinade according to each one's cooking time. Start with onions and carrots. Cook to al dente stage. Remove with slotted spoon. Cook squash, remove. Repeat process for all vegetables, cooking only until crisply tender. When all are done, place in large bowl, pour marinade over all; refrigerate overnight. Serve on large platter sprinkled with parsley.

Mandarin Salad

Serves 6 to 8
For best results, make day ahead

2 (11 ounce) cans mandarin oranges, drained
1 (1 pound) can pineapple tidbits or chunks, drained

1 cup miniature marshmallows
1 cup shredded coconut
½ cup chopped pecans
1 pint sour cream

Mix all together. Chill.

Spinach Salad

Serves 8

Salad:
1 pound spinach, washed and
  torn
1 (14 ounce) can bean sprouts,
  drained

1 (8 ounce) can waterchestnuts,
  sliced and drained
2 hard cooked eggs, sliced or
  grated
6 slices crisp bacon, crumbled

Place salad ingredients in layers in large glass or lucite bowl. Do not toss. Pour dressing over salad just before serving.

Dressing:
1 cup salad oil
½ cup sugar, or less
¼ cup vinegar
½ cup ketchup

¼ teaspoon salt
1 grated onion
2 teaspoons Worcestershire
  sauce

Put all ingredients in blender and blend well. Keep refrigerated.

Regal Chicken Salad

Serves 12

4 cups cooked and diced
  chicken
1 (1 pound 4½ ounce) can
  pineapple chunks, drained,
  reserve juice
2 cups seedless green grapes
1 cup chopped celery
⅔ cup dry roasted, coarsely
  chopped salted peanuts

Salt to taste
1 cup mayonnaise
2 tablespoons lemon juice
2 tablespoons juice drained from
  pineapple
1 (7 ounce) package small ring
  or twist noodles, cooked and
  drained

Combine chicken, pineapple, grapes, celery and peanuts. Combine mayonnaise, lemon juice and pineapple juice. Fold into first mixture. Add cooked noodles.

Carrot Gelatin Salad

Serves 9
Crunchy texture makes this special

1 (3 ounce) package
   lemon-flavored gelatin
1 cup warm water
1 cup canned pineapple juice
1 tablespoon vinegar

½ teaspoon salt
1 cup canned diced pineapple
1 cup grated raw carrots
½ cup diced celery
⅓ cup chopped pecans

Dissolve gelatin in warm water. Add pineapple juice, vinegar and salt. Chill. When slightly thickened, add pineapple, carrots, celery and pecans. Chill until set.

Old Saybrook's David Bushnell launched the world's first submarine in 1775.

Cucumber Salad Mold

Serves 6

1 (3 ounce) package
   lime-flavored gelatin
¾ cup hot water
1 cup small curd cottage cheese
1 cup mayonnaise (or ½ cup
   mayonnaise and ½ cup sour
   cream)

1 tablespoons horseradish (or
   tablespoons grated onion)
1 large, unpeeled cucumber,
   seeded and grated

Mix gelatin with hot water and let cool. Fold in remaining ingredients and pour into greased 6-cup mold and refrigerate until firm.

Lemon-Cheese Ring

Serves 4 to 6
Refreshing on a hot day

1 (3 ounce) package
   lemon-flavored gelatin
1 cup hot water
½ cup mayonnaise
1 cup chopped celery

1 cup grated carrot
1 cup large curd cottage cheese
½ cup diced green pepper
   (optional)

Dissolve gelatin in hot water. Chill until partially set. Blend in mayonnaise. Fold in vegetables and cottage cheese. Pour into 4 cup lightly oiled ring mold. Chill until firm.

Almond-Lime Salad

Serves 8 to 10
For festive occasions

1 (6 ounce) packaged
   lime-flavored gelatin
1 cup hot water
1 cup pineapple juice
1 tablespoon lemon juice
Pinch of salt
½ cup mayonnaise

½ cup cottage cheese
½ cup sour cream
½ cup crushed drained
   pineapple
½ cup slivered almonds
¼ cup butter

Saute almonds in butter. Set aside. Dissolve gelatin in hot water. Add pineapple juice, lemon juice and salt. Mix together mayonnaise, cottage cheese, sour cream and crushed pineapple; add to gelatin mixture. Add almonds and butter to mixture and pour into 1½ quart lightly greased mold. Chill. For Christmas effect add 1 (3 ounce) package clear red gelatin poured on top of mold. When it is unmolded you will have a bright red base under your salad.

Apricot Salad

Serves 10

1 (16 ounce) can apricots,
drained
1 (1 pound 4 ounce) can
crushed pineapple, drained

1 (6 ounce) packaged
orange-flavored gelatin
2 cups hot water
1 cup reserved juice from
apricots and pineapple

In large bowl, add hot water to gelatin. Mix well. Add fruit juice,
apricots and pineapple. Pour into 13×9 baking dish. Chill until firm.
Frost with topping and sprinkle with chopped walnuts.

Topping:
1 beaten egg
½ cup sugar
3 tablespoons flour
1 cup reserved juice from
apricots and pears

2 tablespoons butter
1 package whipped topping
¼ cup chopped walnuts

Add egg, sugar and juice slowly to flour, in top of double boiler.
Cook until thick. Remove from heat and add butter. Beat together
and cool before folding in whipped topping.

Bing Cherry (Sherry) Ring

Serves 6 to 8

1 (1 pound 1 ounce) can bing
cherries
2 cups orange juice
1½ cups sherry

1 cup sugar
3 tablespoons unflavored gelatin
Nut meats

Mix the juice from the cherries with 1½ cups orange juice, sherry
and sugar. Bring to a boil. Soak gelatin in remaining orange juice.
Dissolve in the hot fruit syrup. When mixture begins to thicken,
pour into wet, 6-cup mold. Add cherries which have been stuffed
with pecans or other nut meats. Chill. Serve with fruit and
mayonnaise.

Ginger Ale Salad

Serves 6 to 8

1 (3 ounce) package
orange-flavored gelatin
1 cup ginger ale
¾ cup hot water

1 (11 ounce) can mandarin
oranges, drained
1 (1 pound 1 ounce) can pitted
bing cherries, drained
Slivered blanched almonds

Prepare gelatin, using hot water and ginger ale as liquid. Stir in oranges, cherries and almonds. Pour into mold. Chill until set. Unmold and garnish with lettuce.

Sea Foam Salad

Serves 8
For land lubbers, too

1 (3 ounce) package
lime-flavored gelatin
1 (1 pound, 13 ounce) can
pears, reserve juice

1 cup hot pear juice
1 (8 ounce) package
cream cheese, softened
1 cup heavy cream, whipped

Dissolve gelatin in hot pear juice. Cool. Mash pears into cream cheese. Add to gelatin. Whip cream and fold into gelatin mixture. Turn into lightly oiled 6-cup mold and chill.

Frozen Cranberry Salad

Serves 12 to 16
Also good as a luncheon dessert

1 (16 ounce) can whole
cranberry sauce
1 (8 ounce) can crushed
pineapple
2 tablespoons sugar

2 tablespoons mayonnaise
2 (3 ounce) packages cream
cheese, softened
2 cups heavy cream, whipped

Combine all ingredients. Freeze in 2-quart mold or dish. Unmold just before serving.

Orange Molded Salad

Serves 12
Ice cream makes the difference

2 (3 ounce) packages
    orange-flavored gelatin
2 cups boiling water
2 (6 ounce) cans frozen orange
    juice
1 pint vanilla ice cream

2 (11 ounce) cans mandarin
    oranges, drained
2 (11 ounce) cans crushed
    pineapple
2 cups miniature marshmallows

Dissolve gelatin in boiling water. Blend ice cream and juice
together. Add oranges, pineapple and marshmallows. Add to gelatin
mixture. Refrigerate until set. Serve with a fruit dressing or
whipped cream.

Sherried Grape Mold

Serves 6 to 8
Perfect for a New Year's buffet

¾ cup granulated sugar
2 envelopes unflavored gelatin
1 cup water
2 cups white wine

⅔ cup sweet sherry
3 cups seedless green or red
    grapes (about 1 pound)
¾ cup sour cream

Combine sugar, gelatin and water in a saucepan. Cook over low
heat, stirring constantly until sugar and gelatin are dissolved. Add
wine and sherry. Rinse and drain grapes. Place half of them in a
6-cup mold. Pour half the gelatin mixture over the grapes. Pour
other half into a bowl. Place both containers in refrigerator to chill.
Once the mixture in the bowl is slightly thickened, remove it from
refrigerator. Add sour cream and whip until fluffy. Fold in
remaining grapes. Pour into mold. Chill until firm. When ready to
serve, quickly dip the mold in hot water and invert onto platter.
Remove mold. Garnish with grape clusters.

Red, White and Blue Fruit Mold

Serves 15 to 20
"Hooray for the Red, White and Blue"

1st Layer:

2 (3 ounce) packages
   cherry-flavored gelatin
1½ cups boiling water
1½ cups peach and pear juice,
   combined

1 (16 ounce) can peach halves
1 (16 ounce) can pear halves
Cherries

Dissolve gelatin in boiling water and chill. Place drained fruit on bottom of 15×10½ pan with a cherry in center of each peach and pear half. Alternate peaches and pears. When gelatin is thickened, pour over the fruit. Set.

2nd Layer:

2 (3 ounce) packages
   lemon-flavored gelatin
1 (1 pound, 4 ounce) can
   crushed pineapple, drained
1 cup boiling water

1 cup pineapple juice
1 cup sour cream
1 (8 ounce) package
   cream cheese, softened

Dissolve gelatin with boiling water. Add pineapple juice. Refrigerate until thickened. Add sour cream, pineapple and cream cheese. When partially set, pour over first mixture. Set.

3rd Layer:

2 (3 ounce) packages black
   raspberry-flavored gelatin
2 (15 ounce) cans blueberries

1½ cups boiling water
1½ cups blueberry juice

Dissolve gelatin in boiling water. Add blueberry juice. Refrigerate. When thickened, add drained blueberries and pour over set pineapple mixture. Chill.

Strawberry Gelatin Salad

Serves 6

2 (3 ounce) packages
  strawberry-flavored gelatin
2 cups hot water
1 box frozen strawberries with
  juice

1 (13½ ounce) can crushed
  pineapple with juice
2-3 bananas, mashed
1 (8 ounce) carton sour cream

Dissolve gelatin in 2 cups hot water. Add thawed strawberries with juice, pineapple with juice, and mashed bananas. Pour half of mixture into 13×9 pan. Chill. When set, spread with sour cream. Chill rest of gelatin until slightly thickened. Pour over sour cream. Chill. Cut in squares to serve.

24 Hour Salad

Serves 6 to 10
A golden oldie

2 cups canned white cherries,
  halved and pitted
2 cups diced pineapple
2 cups mandarin orange sections
2 cups miniature marshmallows

2 eggs
2 tablespoons sugar
¼ cup light cream
Juice from 1 lemon
1 cup heavy cream, whipped

Combine well drained fruit and marshmallows. Beat eggs until light. Gradually add sugar, cream and lemon juice. Cook in double boiler until smooth and thick, stirring constantly. Cool. Fold in whipped cream. Pour over fruit mixture and mix lightly. Chill 24 hours. Do not freeze. Garnish with maraschino cherries and orange sections or with fresh mint and sweet seedless grapes.

Sweet & Sour Mandarin Salad

Serves 4

¼ cup sliced almonds
1 tablespoon plus 1 teaspoon
  sugar
¼ head iceberg lettuce
¼ head Romaine lettuce

2 medium stalks celery, thinly
  sliced
1 (11 ounce) can mandarin
  oranges, drained

Stir together almonds and sugar over low heat until almonds are well coated and brown. Cool and break apart. Set aside. Mix together next 4 ingredients. Chill.

Dressing:
¼ cup oil
2 tablespoons sugar
2 tablespoons vinegar

½ teaspoon salt
Dash pepper
Dash cayenne

Mix together in shaker bottle. Pour over salad ingredients and toss. Sprinkle almonds over top. Serve immediately.

Party Chicken Salad

Serves 4

1 (3 ounce) package
  lemon-flavored gelatin
1¾ cups boiling chicken
  consomme
Dash of white pepper
Dash of paprika
2 teaspoons vinegar
¼ cup mayonnaise

½ cup finely diced celery
1 tablespoon chopped pimiento
1 tablespoon chopped parsley
¼ cup crushed pineapple,
  drained
¼ cup coarsely chopped pecans
2 teaspoons sweet pickle relish
1½ cups diced, cooked chicken

Dissolve gelatin in boiling consomme. Add pepper, paprika, vinegar and mayonnaise; blend well. Chill until very thick. Then add remaining ingredients. Pour into a 1 quart mold. Chill until firm. Unmold on crisp lettuce.

Mrs. John DiBiaggio
Wife of President of University of Connecticut

Turkey Salad

Serves 18
A real crowd pleaser

12 cups cooked turkey, cubed
4 cups diced celery
3 (10 ounce) jars watermelon
   pickle, drained and chopped
1 medium chopped onion

3 cups salad dressing
4 teaspoons salt
2 teaspoons curry powder
¼ teaspoon pepper
4 cups chow mein noodles

Cook a turkey breast to yield 12 cups of meat. Cool. Mix all ingredients together except noodles. Add noodles just before serving.

In 1740 the sales force of Berlin tinsmith Edward Pattison were the first to be called "Yankee Pedlars."

Turkey Salad in Melon Ring

Serves 6
Perfect for a bride's luncheon

3 tablespoons lemon juice
4 cups cooked turkey, cut up
1 cup sliced celery
¾ cup chopped onion
1 teaspoon salt
½ teaspoon pepper

1 (2 ounce) jar sliced pimiento,
   drained
¼ cup roasted almonds
⅓ cup salad dressing
1 cup halved green grapes
2 melons

In bowl pour lemon juice over turkey. Add celery, onion, salt, pepper, pimiento, almonds, dressing and grapes. Toss together. Make slices of melon rings. Scoop out seeds. Place melon ring on lettuce. Spoon turkey mixture in center. Arrange extra grapes around ring.

Hot Turkey Salad

Serves 8 to 10

4 cups cooked turkey or
  chicken, cut up
2 (10¾ ounce) cans cream of
  mushroom soup
2 cups chopped celery

Sprinkling of lemon juice
Heaping tablespoon mayonnaise
2 tablespoons dry onion
1 (8 ounce) can water
  chestnuts, optional

Mix all ingredients together. Put in a 13×9 baking dish.

Topping:
½ cup butter or margarine   1 small package stuffing mix

Melt butter or margarine in saucepan. Stir in stuffing mix. Place on top of turkey mixture. Bake at 350° for ½ hour.

Pasta Twist & Broccoli Salad

Serves 8
"Must be served at room temperature"

½ pound Rotelle or macaroni
  twists
2 cups fresh broccoli, cut into
  flowerets
2 cups ½-inch cubed firm
  tomatoes
1 (6½ ounce) can tuna, packed
  in oil
Freshly ground pepper to taste

3 tablespoons red wine vinegar
½ cup olive oil
¼ teaspoon dried hot pepper
  flakes
½ cup finely chopped Italian
  parsley
½ cup thinly sliced red onion
¾ cup loosely packed fresh basil
Salt to taste

Cook pasta per directions for al dente. Drain and run quickly under cold running water. Drain well. Put in mixing bowl. Cook broccoli in boiling, salted water about 5 minutes until tender but not soft. Drain well. Add broccoli and remaining ingredients to pasta. Toss well. Serve at room temperature. Can be made day before. Refrigerate. Remove from refrigerator at least 4 hours before serving.

Pasta Primavera Salad

Serves 8
Summer supper or picnic lunch

Vinaigrette Dressing:
3 tablespoons Dijon mustard
3 tablespoons freshly squeezed
   lemon juice
4 garlic cloves, crushed

Salt and freshly ground pepper
   to taste
½ cup olive oil

Salad:
2 large sweet red peppers,
   seeded and cubed
4 cups fresh broccoli flowerets
1 pound Mozzarella cheese,
   cubed

6 large sliced pitted black olives
½ cup toasted pine nuts
1 pound fresh fettucini

Prepare vinaigrette dressing by combining mustard, lemon juice and garlic, salt and pepper in a bowl. Slowly add the oil, whisking constantly. To prepare salad, blanch peppers and broccoli in separate pans. Drain and rinse under cold water to retain crisp texture. Cook fettucini in 6 quarts boiling salted water for 2-4 minutes. Drain well. Combine vegetables, cheese, pasta, olives and dressing. This may be refrigerated overnight if desired. When ready to serve toss in pine nuts.

Rice and Lentil Salad

Serves 6

1 cup uncooked rice
1 cup uncooked lentils
¼ cup Italian parsley
1 small onion, chopped
2 scallions, chopped
¼ cup chopped pimiento

¾ cup olive oil
¾ cup red wine vinegar
1 tablespoon oregano
½ teaspoon garlic
Salt and pepper, to taste

Cook rice and lentils, separately, according to package directions. Mix with remaining ingredients. Chill.

Bulgur Salad (Tabbouleh)

Serves 8 to 10
Refreshing and nutritious

1 cup bulgur (fine cracked
   wheat)
3 cups boiling water
2 tomatoes, seeded and chopped
1 cucumber, peeled, seeded and
   diced
1 cup finely chopped parsley
½ cup finely chopped scallions

3 tablespoons finely chopped
   fresh mint or 3 teaspoons
   crumbled dried mint
¾ cup lemon juice
¾ cup olive oil
Salt and freshly ground pepper
Romaine lettuce leaves
Tomato wedges
Black olives

Put bulgur in a sieve and rinse with cold water. Then place bulgur
in a bowl and pour boiling water over it. Let soak for about one hour
or until bulgur has expanded and is light and fluffy. Thoroughly
drain off excess water. Add remaining ingredients except the
Romaine lettuce. Toss to blend thoroughly. Cover and chill well. To
serve, mound bulgur salad in center of large platter and garnish
with Romaine, tomato wedges and black olives. Note: Fine cracked
wheat or bulgur is available at specialty shops or health food stores.

Taco Salad

Serves 8 to 10
Good for a crowd

2 pounds ground beef
1 package taco mix
1 head lettuce
3 tomatoes
1 cucumber
1 green pepper

½ pound fresh mushrooms
1 avocado
1 package Hidden Valley Ranch
   dressing
1 bag corn chips

Brown ground beef and drain. Add taco mix and refrigerate. Cut
next 6 ingredients into bite-sized pieces. Put in large bowl. Top with
meat and prepared dressing. Sprinkle corn chips on top or serve
separately on the side.

Ham 'N Broccoli Salad

Serves 4 to 6

1 cup cooked elbow macaroni,
  drained and chilled
½ cup chopped celery
½ cup chopped green pepper
¼ cup chopped Spanish onion
1 cup chopped broccoli, cooked
  and chilled

⅔ cup mayonnaise
1 tablespoon sugar
¾ cup shredded Cheddar
  cheese
2 cups thinly sliced ham, cut in
  narrow strips

Layer salad bowl with first five ingredients. Spread mayonnaise over top. Sprinkle sugar on mayonnaise. Layer remaining ingredients. Refrigerate. Mix before serving on lettuce.

Marinated Roast Beef Salad

Serves 4
Spruce up your leftovers

½ pound cooked roast beef, cut
  in julienne strips
¼ cup chopped dill gherkins, or
  2 tablespoons sliced green
  olives
2 tablespoons chopped onion
¼ cup chopped celery
1 hard cooked egg, chopped

1 potato, cooked, peeled and
  diced
2 tablespoons beef broth
1 tablespoon olive oil
1 tablespoon tarragon vinegar
2 teaspoons Dijon mustard
Garlic, salt and pepper, to taste
¼ teaspoon Worcestershire
  sauce

In bowl, combine first 6 ingredients. In another bowl mix remaining ingredients. Toss meat mixture with dressing and sprinkle salad with chopped parsley. Chill.

Tadisch's Zinovich Salad

Serves 4
One of San Francisco's best.

1 head Boston lettuce	1½ cups frozen green peas
1 (8 ounce) can shrimp, or 8 ounces fresh or frozen shrimp	Russian dressing

Cook peas 2 minutes and chill. Tear lettuce into bite sized pieces. Toss with shrimp and peas. Spoon creamy Russian dressing over all. Close your eyes and you're on California Street listening to cable cars!

In Groton the world's first atomic-powered submarine, the Nautilus, was christened by First Lady Mamie Eisenhower in 1954.

Salmon Mousse

Serves 8
Try this as an appetizer

1 teaspoon chopped onion	1 cup mayonnaise, yogurt may be substituted
1 (1 pound) can salmon	1 cup sour cream
2 envelopes unflavored gelatin, dissolved in heated juice of salmon	2 hard cooked eggs
	2 teaspoons capers
	2 teaspoons stuffed olives

Combine all ingredients in food processor or blender. Put into fish mold. Chill. Unmold and surround with sliced cucumbers, tomato wedges and greens.

Shrimp Mousse

Serves 6

2 (4½ ounce) cans small shrimp or 1 (8 ounce) package frozen shrimp
1 (10¾ ounce) can tomato soup, undiluted
1 (8 ounce) package cream cheese

2 packages unflavored gelatin
½ cup cold water
½ cup chopped green peppers
½ cup chopped onion
1 cup mayonnaise

Heat soup to boiling. Remove from heat. Add cream cheese. Beat until creamy. Dissolve gelatin in cold water and add to mixture. Set slightly; add shrimp, vegetables and mayonnaise. Mix and pour into mold and chill. Unmold. Before serving top with mayonnaise or mayonnaise mixed with whipped cream.

German Tuna Salad

Serves 4

1 (7½ ounce) can solid white tuna, drained and flaked
2 hard cooked eggs, diced

1 large unpared apple, diced
2 stalks celery, diced

Dressing:
½ cup sour cream

½ cup mayonnaise

Mix tuna, eggs, apple, and celery together. Toss with dressing and chill at least 3 hours.

Aunt Glady's Salad Dressing

Makes 1 Quart
Everybody likes it

2 teaspoons salt
2 teaspoons paprika
2 teaspoons dry mustard
1 cup sugar

½ cup vinegar
2 teaspoons celery seed
2 cups vegetable oil
½ onion, grated

Mix all ingredients together. Shake well and refrigerate. Shake well before using on tossed salad or cabbage salad.

Low Calorie French Dressing

Makes 1 Pint
A favorite original recipe

4 tablespoons sugar
4 teaspoons salt
½ teaspoon pepper
1 teaspoon ground mustard seed
1 teaspoon paprika
½ teaspoon celery seed

1 teaspoon salad herbs
6 tablespoons salad oil
4 tablespoons red wine vinegar
8 tablespoons cider vinegar
1 garlic clove, cut into thirds
1 scant cup tomato juice

Mix all ingredients together except tomato juice and garlic clove. Pour dressing into pint size bottle. Add garlic and tomato juice. Shake well. Shake again before using. Keeps well in refrigerator.

Tomato French Dressing

Makes 1 cup
Especially good on cold meat

½ cup tomato juice
2 tablespoons vinegar
2 tablespoons finely chopped
   green pepper
1 teaspoon Worcestershire sauce

½ teaspoon salt
½ teaspoon dry mustard
1 garlic clove
¼ teaspoon liquid sugar
   substitute

Combine all ingredients in blender and puree. Keep refrigerated.

Gorgonzola Dressing

Makes 2 cups

½ cup milk
1½ cups mayonnaise
¼ teaspoon minced garlic
1 teaspoon minced onion

Dash salt
⅛ teaspoon paprika
½ to ¾ cup crumbled
Gorgonzola cheese

Combine all ingredients and chill for at least 8 hours before serving.

Grandma Miller's Salad Dressing

Makes 3½ Cups
Great on mixed salad

½ cup sugar
3 teaspoons salt
2 teaspoons dry mustard
1 medium onion, grated
2 teaspoons Worcestershire
sauce

1 cup vegetable oil
¾ cup cider vinegar
1 (10¾ ounce) can condensed
tomato soup
Dash cayenne or tabasco sauce

Combine above ingredients in bowl or large jar and mix or shake
until well blended. Stores for weeks in refrigerator. Shake just
before using.

Pennsylvania Dutch Salad Dressing

Makes 1½ cups

2 eggs, well beaten
¾ cup vinegar
½ cup water

½ teaspoon salt
2 heaping tablespoons sugar
5 strips bacon

Fry bacon until brown. Add rest of ingredients stirring constantly.
Do not boil. This dressing should be used hot and is especially good
for hot potato salad or on salad greens.

Fresh Fruit Topping

Serves 4 to 5
For fruit salad or dessert

½ cup sugar
1 egg, beaten
⅓ cup fresh orange juice

2 tablespoons fresh lemon juice
½ pint whipping cream,
  whipped stiff

Cook sugar, egg, orange and lemon juices together in double boiler, stirring often with wire whisk until thick. Cool and chill. (This can be done several days ahead). When ready to serve fold thoroughly into whipped cream. Spoon over fresh fruit.

Poppy Seed Dressing

Makes 3½ Cups

1½ cups sugar
2 teaspoons dry mustard
2 teaspoons salt
⅔ cup vinegar

3 tablespoons onion juice
2 cups salad oil, not olive oil
3 tablespoons poppy seeds

Mix first 4 ingredients in a blender. Add onion juice and then slowly add oil, continuing to beat until thick. Add poppy seeds and beat for a few minutes longer. Keeps well in refrigerator. (Onion juice can be obtained by putting onion in blender and then straining.) Superb on crisp greens with slices of avocados, grapefruit and orange sections

Sweet Dressing

Makes 1½ Cups

1 cup oil
½ cup vinegar
6 teaspoons sugar
1 teaspoon dry mustard
1 teaspoon paprika

1 teaspoon Worcestershire sauce
2 teaspoons salt
¼ teaspoon pepper
1 teaspoon celery seed
⅛ teaspoon garlic powder

Combine all ingredients and shake well.

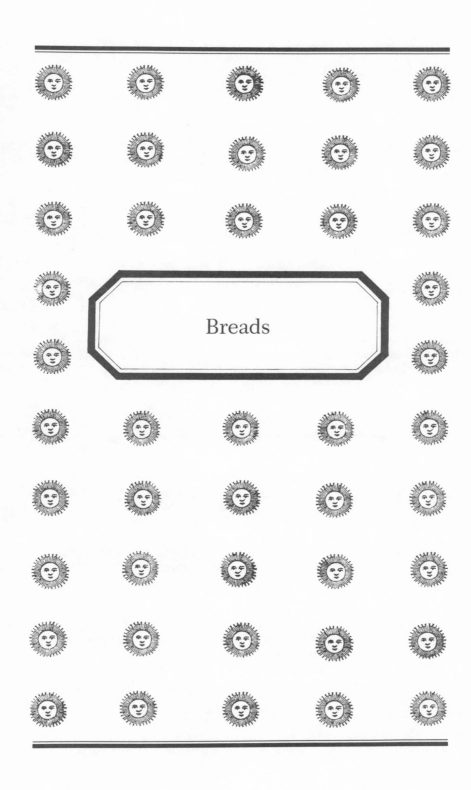

Breads

Plain or Cinnamon Rolls

Makes 2 Dozen

1 package dry yeast	1 cup scalded milk
1 teaspoon sugar	1 egg, beaten
⅓ cup hot water	4 cups flour
⅓ cup shortening	½ cup butter, melted
⅓ cup sugar	Cinnamon
1 teaspoon salt	½ to ¾ cup brown sugar

Preheat oven to 400°. Dissolve yeast and 1 teaspoon sugar in hot water. Set aside to rise. Add shortening, sugar and salt to scalded milk; cool add egg to yeast mixture. In large bowl combine milk mixture and egg mixture with flour. Dough will be sticky and moist. Cover bowl with a towel. Let rise 2-3 hours. About 1½ hours before serving, roll ½ the dough into a rectangle on floured board. For plain rolls, cut strips about 1-inch wide and tie in a knot. Cover, let rise 1½ hours. Then bake for 10 minutes on greased cookie sheet. For "sticky buns", drizzle ½ of melted butter over dough. Sprinkle with cinnamon and brown sugar. Roll lengthwise and cut in 12 pieces. Place in greased muffin tins; cover, let rise 1½ hours. Repeat with remaining dough.

Onion Rolls

Makes 1 Dozen

½ cup scalded milk	½ cup lukewarm water
¼ cup butter or margarine	1 egg
1 tablespoons sugar	¾ cup lightly browned onion
1½ teaspoons salt	3 cups flour
1 package dry yeast	

Preheat oven to 350°. Pour milk over butter, sugar and salt. Cool to lukewarm. Add the yeast dissolved in warm water. Blend in egg, onion and flour. Beat well. Cover and let stand in warm place for 15 minutes. Turn on floured board and roll or pat out to 9×12 rectangle. Cut into smaller rectangles. Fold corners toward center. Place on cookie sheet with folded corners underneath. Bake for 15 minutes.

Sticky Pecan Rolls

Makes 16
Iowa State Fair winner

Dough:

1 cup boiling potato water	½ teaspoon sugar
½ cup sugar	2 tablespoons warm water
½ cup butter	2 beaten eggs
1 teaspoon salt	4 cups sifted flour
1 package dry yeast	

Mix together boiling potato water, sugar, butter and salt. Cool to lukewarm. Soften yeast in warm water and sugar; add to first mixture. Add beaten eggs then 2 cups of sifted flour; beat well. Stir in remaining flour. Refrigerate overnight. Three hours before serving, butter two 9 inch pie pans. Prepare pans with syrup

Syrup:

½ cup brown sugar	1 teaspoon water
2 tablespoons butter	½ cup chopped pecans

Mix first three ingredients in saucepan. Heat until slightly boiled and well mixed. Pour into buttered pie pans. Sprinkle with pecans.

Filling:

¼ cup butter	Cinnamon
Sugar	Pecans, chopped

Roll out dough to 8×11. Sprinkle on sugar, cinnamon, pecans and thinly sliced pieces of butter. Roll up lengthwise cut in ½ inch slices. Place side by side in pie pans. Let rise in warm area 3 hours. Bake at 425° for 15 minutes.

When the first white man came to Connecticut in 1614 there were sixteen different Indian tribes of the Algonquian federation living in the territory. Indian life in Connecticut can be explored in museums at Montville, Somers, and Washington.

Blueberry Muffins

Makes 1 Dozen
Great with coffee for breakfast

½ cup butter or
   margarine, softened
1 cup sugar
2 eggs
2 cups unsifted flour
2 teaspoons baking powder

½ cup milk
1 teaspoon vanilla
2 cups blueberries
2 teaspoons sugar for topping
   (optional)

Preheat oven to 375°. Cream shortening and sugar until fluffy. Add eggs, one at a time, and mix until blended. Sift dry ingredients and add alternately with milk and vanilla. Mash ½ cup blueberries and stir in by hand. Add remaining blueberries whole and stir in by hand. Line muffin tins with cup cake liners and fill ⅔ full with batter. Sprinkle sugar on top of each muffin if desired. Bake for 25 minutes.

Cranberry Muffins

Makes 1 Dozen

1 cup fresh cranberries
½ cup chopped nuts
2 tablespoons sugar
2 cups flour
¼ cup sugar

1 tablespoon plus 1 teaspoon
   baking powder
½ teaspoon salt
1 egg, beaten
¾ cup milk
¼ cup butter, melted

Preheat oven to 400°. Toss cranberries and nuts with sugar; set aside. Combine flour, sugar, baking powder and salt. Mix well. Combine egg, milk and butter. Make a well in center of dry ingredients. Add liquid ingredients, cranberries and nuts, stirring until well blended. Spoon into greased muffin pans, filling ⅔ full. Bake for 25-30 minutes.

English Muffins in a Loaf

Makes 2 Loaves
Cut a slice and you have an English Muffin

6 cups unsifted flour
2 packages dry yeast
1 tablespoon sugar
2 teaspoons salt

¼ teaspoon baking soda
2 cups milk
½ cup water
Cornmeal

Preheat oven to 400°. Combine 3 cups flour, undissolved yeast,
sugar, salt and baking soda. Heat milk and water until very warm.
Add to dry ingredients and beat well. Stir in remaining flour to
make a stiff batter. Pour into two 8×4 greased loaf pans that have
been sprinkled with cornmeal. Sprinkle tops with cornmeal. Cover;
let rise in a warm place for 45 minutes. Bake for 25 minutes.
Remove from pans and cool.

Variations:
For garlic loaf: Add 2 tablespoons chopped parsley and 1½
teaspoons garlic powder to dry ingredients.

For sour cream and chive: Add 3 tablespoons freeze-dried chives to
dry ingredients. Use only 1½ cups milk, ½ cup sour cream (at room
temperature) with remaining flour.

For orange flavored: Add 2 tablespoons grated orange rind to dry
ingredients.

Betty's Brown Bread

Makes 4 Loaves
Delicious sweet bread for holidays

4 cups buttermilk
1 cup molasses
1 cup sugar
4 cups graham flour or whole
    wheat flour

1 cup white flour
1 cup corn meal
2 teaspoons salt
2 cups raisins

Preheat oven to 350°. Mix all ingredients together in large bowl.
Turn into 4 greased loaf pans. Fill about ½ full and bake for 1 to
1¼ hours.

Orange Blossom Muffins

Makes 1 Dozen

1 egg, slightly beaten
¼ cup sugar
½ cup orange juice
2 tablespoons salad oil

2 cups packaged biscuit mix
½ cup orange marmalade
½ cup chopped pecans

Preheat oven to 400°. Combine egg, sugar, orange juice and salad oil. Add biscuit mix. Beat vigorously 30 seconds. Stir in marmalade and pecans. Grease muffin pans or line with paper bake cups. Fill ⅔ full. Sprinkle with spicy topping. Bake for 20-25 minutes or until done.

Spicy Topping:
¼ cup sugar
1½ tablespoons flour
½ teaspoon cinnamon

¼ teaspoon nutmeg
1 tablespoon butter or margarine

Combine first four ingredients. Cut in butter until crumbly.

Make Ahead Bran Muffins

Makes 4-5 Dozen
A real time saver

1 quart buttermilk
8 teaspoons baking soda
1½ cups cooking oil
½ cup molasses
4 eggs, beaten

5½ cups flour
1 teaspoon salt
2½ cups sugar
2 cups bran cereal
3 cups bran flakes cereal

Preheat oven to 375°. Mix buttermilk and baking soda. Add oil, molasses and eggs. Stir well. Add dry ingredients, stirring well. Store in covered container in refrigerator and use as needed. Fill greased muffin tins ½ full. Bake for 15-20 minutes.

Pineapple Muffins

Makes 2 Dozen
A tasty variation of a bran muffin

½ cup sugar
⅓ cup shortening
⅓ cup honey
2 eggs, slightly beaten
1⅓ cup bran
1⅓ cup flour

2 teaspoons baking soda
½ teaspoon salt
1 cup evaporated milk
1 cup crushed pineapple, well
    drained

Preheat oven to 350°. Cream sugar, shortening and honey together.
Add to remaining ingredients and mix lightly with a spoon. Fill
greased muffin tins ⅔ full. Bake for 25 minutes, or cover pans with
wax paper and store in refrigerator overnight and bake in the
morning.

Apple Butter Bread

Makes 1 Loaf

1½ cups plus 2 tablespoons
    flour
2 teaspoons baking powder
½ cup brown sugar
1 teaspoon cinnamon
½ teaspoon nutmeg
½ teaspoon salt
1 egg

4 tablespoons butter, melted
½ cup apple butter
¼ cup milk
¼ cup cider
½ cup white raisins soaked in
    2 tablespoons brandy or
    orange juice

Preheat oven to 350°. In large bowl mix in flour, baking powder,
sugar, spices and salt. Make a well in center and add egg, butter,
apple butter, milk and cider. Mix quickly. Add drained raisins. Pour
into well greased loaf pan, ring mold or Bundt pan. Bake 45
minutes.

Applesauce Pumpkin Bread

Makes 2 Loaves

⅔ cup shortening
1⅓ cups sugar
1⅓ cups honey
4 eggs
1 cup applesauce
1 cup pumpkin
3⅓ cups flour
2 teaspoons baking soda

½ teaspoon baking powder
1½ teaspoons salt
1 teaspoon cinnamon
½ teaspoon mace
½ teaspoon nutmeg
⅔ cup apple juice
1 cup chopped walnuts
½ cup raisins

Preheat oven to 350°. Cream shortening, sugar and honey. Add eggs, one at a time, beating after each addition. Stir in applesauce and pumpkin. Sift dry ingredients. Add alternately with apple juice. Stir in nuts and raisins. Turn batter into 2 greased loaf pans. Bake 1 hour.

Apricot Raisin Nut Bread

Makes 1 Loaf

½ cup dried apricots
Boiling water
1 large orange
½ cup raisins
2 tablespoons butter or
    margarine
1 cup sugar

1 teaspoon vanilla
1 egg
½ cup chopped nuts
2 cups sifted flour
2 teaspoons baking powder
½ teaspoon baking soda
¼ teaspoon salt

Preheat oven to 350°. Cover apricots with boiling water and soak about ½ hour. Squeeze juice from orange and add enough boiling water to make 1 cup; set aside. Save skin. Put drained apricots, cut up orange skins and raisins through food processor; chop lightly. Cream butter and sugar; add vanilla. Beat in egg, add fruit and nuts. Stir in dry ingredients alternating with juice. Pour in greased 9×5 pan and bake for 50-60 minutes.

Banana Bread

Makes 1 Loaf
Good with luncheon salads

½ cup butter, softened
1 cup sugar
2 eggs
2 cups flour
1 teaspoon baking soda

3 ripe mashed bananas
3 tablespoons sour cream or
  milk
½ cup chopped nuts

Preheat oven to 350°. Cream butter, sugar and eggs well. Add flour, baking soda, mashed bananas and sour cream until well blended. Add chopped nuts. Pour into well greased and floured 9×5 loaf pan. Bake for 1-1¼ hours or until tester is dough free. Cool and wrap in foil for 24 hours.

Dinner Rolls

Makes 4 Dozen

4 to 4½ cups flour
2 packages dry yeast
3 tablespoons sugar
1 teaspoon salt

½ teaspoon baking soda
1¼ cups buttermilk
½ cup water
½ cup shortening

Preheat oven to 400°. In large bowl combine 1½ cups flour, yeast, sugar, salt and baking soda. In saucepan, heat buttermilk, water and shortening until warm (shortening does not need to melt). Add to flour mixture. Blend at low speed, then beat 3 minutes at medium speed. By hand, stir in remaining flour, enough for firm dough. Knead for 5 minutes. Place in greased bowl, turn to grease top. Cover and let rise in warm place until almost doubled, about 20 minutes. Divide dough into 48 pieces and form into balls. Place on greased cookie sheet. Bake 15-20 minutes. Remove from pan, brush with butter. Cool on racks.

Boston Brown Bread

Makes 2 Loaves
High fiber-no sugar

1 cup whole wheat flour
1 cup rye flour
¼ cup corn meal
2 tablespoons raw wheat germ
  (optional)
2 tablespoons unprocessed bran
  (optional)

2 teaspoons baking soda
¼ teaspoon sea salt
2 eggs, beaten
1½ cups skim milk
½ cup molasses
½ to 1 cup seedless raisins

Preheat oven to 325°. Combine all ingredients in large bowl. Mix well. Pour into 2 greased 1 pound coffee cans. Bake for 70 minutes. Turn out on wire racks to cool. Freezes well.

Cheddar, Bacon and Olive Bread

Makes 1 Loaf or 12 Muffins
A bread with character

2½ cups flour
2½ teaspoons sugar
2 teaspoons baking powder
½ teaspoon baking soda
1 teaspoon salt
1 teaspoon dry mustard
Dash cayenne pepper
¼ cup butter, softened

1 cup shredded sharp Cheddar
  cheese
1 egg
1 cup buttermilk
1 teaspoon Worcestershire sauce
6 slices bacon, crisply cooked
  and crumbled
1 cup coarsely chopped, pitted
  black olives

Preheat oven to 375°. Mix flour, sugar, baking powder, baking soda, salt, mustard and pepper. Cut in butter with fork until mixture resembles coarse meal. Stir in shredded cheese. Combine egg, buttermilk and Worcestershire sauce. Make a well in flour mixture and pour in liquid; mix until moistened. Stir in bacon and olives. Turn into a greased 9×5 loaf pan. Bake for 30-40 minutes. Turn out of pan and cool on wire rack. To make muffins, fill well greased muffin pans. Bake for 20-25 minutes.

Christmas Rye Bread (Vörtlimpa)

Makes 2 Loaves
God Jul

1½ cups stout
1 tablespoon finely ground anise
1 tablespoon finely ground
   fennel
2 tablespoons shortening
½ cup dark corn syrup
Grated rind of one orange

¼ cup sugar
½ teaspoon salt
4 cups sifted all purpose flour
2 cups sifted medium rye flour
1 package dry yeast
¼ cup warm water
Hot water

Preheat oven to 350°. Combine stout, anise, fennel and shortening in saucepan, heat to lukewarm. Pour into large mixing bowl and add syrup, orange rind, sugar and salt. Mix well. Add 2 cups all purpose and 1 cup rye flour. Beat until smooth. Dissolve yeast in warm water and add to first mixture. Beat until thoroughly mixed. Add remaining flour. Turn dough out on lightly floured pastry cloth. Knead until smooth and elastic. Place in greased bowl, turning to grease top; cover and let rise until double in bulk, 1½ to 2 hours. Punch down and let rise again until double in bulk, 1 to 1½ hours. Shape into 2 loaves about 12 inches long, place on greased cookie sheet or in three 9×9 round greased pans. Let rise until double in bulk, about 1 hour. Perforate each loaf 5 or 6 times with fork. Bake 45-50 minutes. Remove from oven and brush top of loaves with hot water.

Herb Bread

Makes 1 Loaf
Good toasted with a thick soup

3 cups unbleached flour
3 teaspoons salt
4½ teaspoons baking powder
3 tablespoons sugar

1 tablespoon herb blend, fine or
   robust
1 (12 ounce) can beer, room
   temperature

Preheat oven to 325°. Mix flour, salt, baking powder, sugar and herb blend. Stir in beer. Grease a 9×5 loaf pan. Sprinkle with cornmeal. Turn batter into pan and bake for 65 minutes. Bread will be pale in color and very rough on top. Turn out and cool on rack.

Dill Casserole Bread

1 Round Loaf
Grandma's best bread

1 package dry yeast
¼ cup warm water
1 cup creamed cottage cheese
2 tablespoons sugar
1 tablespoon instant minced
   onion

2 tablespoons dill seed
1 tablespoon butter, melted
1 egg, unbeaten
2¼ to 2½ cups sifted flour
1 teaspoon salt
¼ teaspoon baking soda

Preheat oven to 350°. Add yeast to warm water. When dissolved, add cottage cheese heated to lukewarm. Stir in sugar, onion, dill, butter and egg. Sift salt and baking soda with flour and gradually add to dough. Knead for 10 minutes and let rise in greased bowl in warm place until double in bulk. Punch down and place in 1½ quart round, ovenproof casserole. Let rise again 30-40 minutes. Bake for 40-45 minutes.

Nutty Orange Bread

Makes 1 Loaf

1 egg
Zest from orange, grated
¾ cup orange juice
2 cups flour
½ cup sugar
2 teaspoons baking powder

½ teaspoon baking soda
½ teaspoon salt
¾ cup chunky peanut butter
¼ cup butter
¼ cup chopped peanuts

Preheat oven to 350°. Grease an 8×4 loaf pan. Combine egg, orange zest and juice. Set aside. In medium bowl combine flour, sugar, baking powder, baking soda and salt. Add peanut butter and butter. Using a pastry cutter (or two knives) cut peanut butter and butter into the flour until it resembles coarse meal. Add liquid ingredients and stir just until moistened. Turn into prepared pan. Sprinkle chopped peanuts on top. Bake for 1 hour or until a toothpick inserted in center comes out clean. Cool in pan on a rack for 10 minutes. Remove from pan and cool completely.

Nutritious Breakfast Bread

Makes 2 Loaves

1 cup flour
1 cup whole wheat flour
½ teaspoon salt
½ teaspoon baking soda
2 teaspoons baking powder
⅔ cup non-fat dry milk powder
⅓ cup oatmeal
½ cup brown sugar
½ cup unsalted chopped
  peanuts

¼ cup chopped walnuts
½ cup raisins
⅓ cup chopped prunes
3 eggs
½ cup vegetable oil
½ cup molasses
¾ cup orange juice
1 cup mashed bananas

Preheat oven to 325°. Combine flour, salt, baking soda, baking powder, dry milk, oatmeal, sugar, nuts, raisins and prunes in large bowl. Blend thoroughly with fork. Beat eggs until foamy. Add oil, molasses, orange juice and bananas. Add mixture to dry ingredients. Stir until all flour is moistened. Pour into two 8×4 greased loaf pans. Bake for 1 hour. (For muffins fill greased tins ⅔ full, bake at 350° for 20 minutes). Cool slightly before removing from pan. You may substitute raw chopped apples, grated carrots, applesauce or grated zucchini for bananas.

Honey Walnut Bread

Makes 1 Loaf

1 cup milk
1 cup honey
½ cup sugar
¼ cup butter, softened
2 egg yolks

2½ cups sifted flour
1 teaspoon salt
1 teaspoon baking soda
½ cup walnuts

Preheat oven to 350°. Scald milk and honey. Add sugar and stir over medium heat until sugar dissolves. Cool mixture. Beat in butter and egg yolks. Add dry ingredients and beat well. Add nuts. Pour into greased and floured bread pan. Bake for 1 hour. Cool 15 minutes in pan. Cool on rack. Serve thinly sliced with butter or cream cheese and preserves.

Irish Raisin Bread

Makes 1 Loaf
Leprechauns' Favorite

4 cups flour
3 teaspoons baking powder
1 teaspoon baking soda
½ cup sugar
1 teaspoon salt

1 cup raisins
3 tablespoons caraway seeds
3 eggs, well beaten
1½ cups milk
3 tablespoons oil

Preheat oven to 350°. Sift flour, baking powder, baking soda, sugar and salt together in large bowl. Add raisins and caraway seeds. Blend eggs, milk and oil. Make a hole in flour mixture and pour in liquid mixture, stirring until smooth. Bake for 1 hour in large round, greased pan. Brush beaten egg yolk over the top for shine and crust.

Lemon Bread

Makes 1 Loaf
Lovely hostess gift

⅓ cup shortening
1⅓ cups sugar
2 eggs
1½ cups sifted flour
1½ teaspoons baking powder

¼ teaspoon salt
½ cup milk
½ cup chopped nuts
Grated rind and juice of one
    lemon

Preheat oven to 350°. Beat together shortening and one cup of sugar until light and fluffy. Add eggs, one at a time, beating well after each one. Sift dry ingredients together and add alternately with milk to the sugar mixture, beating well after each addition. Add nuts and lemon rind. Turn batter into greased 8×4 inch loaf pan. Bake for 50-60 minutes. Blend remaining sugar and lemon juice. Pour over bread as soon as it comes from the oven. Cool in pan.

Healthy White Bread

Makes 3 Loaves
Delicious toasted

5½ to 6½ cups bread flour
½ cup rye flour
½ cup whole wheat flour
½ cup wheat germ
1 cup non-fat dry milk powder
3 packages dry yeast
1 tablespoon salt

3 cups warm water
⅓ cup butter or
    margarine, softened
⅓ cup honey
1 tablespoon dark molasses
1 egg
Melted butter

Preheat oven to 350°. Blend 2 cups bread flour, milk powder, yeast and salt in mixer. Pour in 2 cups water and beat for 3 minutes. Add butter, honey, molasses and egg. Add 3 cups bread flour, rye flour, whole wheat flour and wheat germ. Add remaining bread flour to make a stiff dough that does not stick to sides. Beat well 5 minutes. Turn out on lightly floured board. Knead in more flour until smooth. Place in greased bowl. Brush lightly with melted butter. Cover with dish towel. Let rise in warm place until doubled in size, 1 to 1½ hours. Punch dough down. Turn out on lightly floured board and knead gently to remove air bubbles. If too sticky add a little more flour. Divide into 3 sections. Shape into loaves. Place in three greased 9×5 loaf pans. Lightly brush with melted butter. Cover with dish towel. Let rise in warm place until doubled in size, 40-45 minutes. Bake for 40-45 minutes or until golden brown and loaves sound hollow when thumped.

Variations:
For onion and garlic bread: Add 1½ cups finely chopped onions, 3 medium size garlic cloves, minced. Because of the large amount of water in onion and garlic more flour may be needed. Makes 3 loaves.

For pepperoni bread: Add one pepperoni and one hot pepper. Steam pepperoni about 30 minutes then cut lengthwise into 6-8 long strips, then cut strips into ¼ inch pieces. Finely chop hot pepper. Add both pepper and pepperoni to the bread dough. Makes 3 loaves.

For healthy raisin and nut bread: Add 1 tablespoon molasses, 1 cup raisins, 1 cup chopped mixed nuts, ¼ cup chopped dried apricots or other dried fruit.

Rhubarb Bread

Makes 2 Loaves
Very good-tart

½ cup brown sugar
⅔ cup oil
1 egg
1 cup buttermilk
1 teaspoon salt
1 teaspoon baking powder

1 teaspoon baking soda
1 teaspoon vanilla
2 ¾ cups flour
1½ cups diced rhubarb
½ cup chopped walnuts

Preheat oven to 325°. Mix ingredients in order given. Pour into two 8×4 buttered and floured loaf pans, ⅔ full. Bake for 50 minutes. For muffins, spoon into buttered and floured muffin cups. Bake at 325° for 20 minutes.

Rhubarb Coffee Cake

Serves 12 to 15

2 cups sifted flour
1¼ cups sugar
1 teaspoon baking soda
1 teaspoon salt
1 teaspoon cinnamon
¼ teaspoon allspice

¼ teaspoon powdered cloves
2 eggs
½ cup oil
⅓ cup milk
2 cups fresh rhubarb, cut in
    1-inch pieces

Preheat oven to 350°. Sift dry ingredients together in mixing bowl. Combine eggs, oil and milk in another bowl and beat. Add dry ingredients. Fold in rhubarb and turn into a greased 13×9 pan. Spoon topping over batter and bake for 50 minutes.

Topping:
⅔ cup flour
½ cup brown sugar
4 tablespoons butter, softened

¾ cup flaked coconut
¼ cup chopped nuts

Blend together flour, brown sugar and butter. Add coconut and chopped nuts.

Spoon Bread

Makes 1 Loaf

2 cups milk
1 cup cornmeal
4 tablespoons butter

1 teaspoon salt
4 egg yolks, beaten
4 egg whites, beaten

Put milk into top of double boiler and heat over boiling water until almost boiling. Slowly add cornmeal, stirring constantly and cook until mixture is smooth and thick, about 1 minute. Add butter and salt and set aside to cool slightly. Beat egg yolks well and stir into cornmeal mixture. Beat egg whites until stiff, but not dry, and ·slowly fold into cornmeal mixture. Pour batter into a well-buttered 2 quart casserole and bake at 375° for 35-40 minutes. It will be brown on top and light and puffy. Serve from casserole with a spoon and top with a large dollop of butter.

Jewish Coffee Cake

Makes 1 Cake

1½ cups butter
1½ cups sugar
5 eggs
½ teaspoon salt
1½ teaspoons baking soda

3 teaspoons baking powder
3¾ to 4 cups flour
1½ cups sour cream
1½ teaspoons vanilla
1½ teaspoons almond extract

Topping:
¾ cup chopped nuts
1 tablespoon cinnamon

¾ cup sugar

Preheat oven to 375°. Cream butter and sugar. Add eggs, one at a time and beat well. Mix dry ingredients. Alternate with sour cream. Add vanilla and almond. Put half the batter in greased tube pan. Spread with half of topping. Then add remaining batter. Spread remaining half of topping. Bake for 55 minutes.

Strawberry Bread

Makes 2 Loaves
Terrific with cream cheese and salad for a light lunch

2 (10 ounce) packages frozen
  strawberries, thawed
4 eggs
1¼ cup salad oil
3 cups flour

2 cups sugar
3 teaspoons cinnamon
1 teaspoon baking soda
1 teaspoon salt
1 cup chopped nuts

Preheat oven to 350°. Grease and flour two 9×5 loaf pans. In bowl combine strawberries, eggs and oil. In separate bowl combine flour, sugar, cinnamon, baking soda, salt and nuts. Add strawberry mixture to dry ingredients and stir until blended. Pour batter into pans. Bake 1 hour or until toothpick inserted in center comes out clean.

Zucchini Nut Bread

Makes 2 Loaves
Everyone's favorite

3 eggs, beaten
1 cup oil
1½ cups sugar
2 cups grated zucchini,
  unpeeled
2 teaspoons vanilla
3 cups flour
1 teaspoon salt
1 teaspoon baking soda

¼ teaspoon baking powder
1½ teaspoon cinnamon
Dash nutmeg
Dash cloves
1 cup chopped nuts
¾ cups raisins or chopped dates
Grated rind of 1 orange
  (optional)

Preheat oven to 350°. Mix eggs, oil, sugar, zucchini and vanilla. Sift together dry ingredients. Add to egg mixture. Stir in nuts and raisins. Pour into two greased 9×5 loaf pans and bake for 50-60 minutes, until bread sounds hollow when tapped on top. Turn out onto wire rack to cool after 10 minutes.

Cranberry Swirl Coffee Cake

Make 1 Cake

½ cup shortening
1 cup sugar
2 eggs
1 teaspoon baking soda
1 teaspoon baking powder
2 cups flour
½ teaspoon salt

1 cup sour cream
2 teaspoons vanilla or almond
flavoring
1 (7 ounce) can whole cranberry
sauce
⅓ cup chopped nuts

Preheat oven to 350°. Cream shortening and sugar. Gradually add unbeaten eggs, one at a time, using mixer at medium speed. Reduce speed and add sifted dry ingredients, alternating with sour cream, ending with dry ingredients. Add flavoring. Grease and 8-inch tube pan. Put layer of batter in pan. Swirl some cranberry sauce on batter. Add remaining batter and swirl remaining cranberry sauce on top. Sprinkle with nuts. Bake for 55 minutes.

Topping:
¾ cup confectioners' sugar
½ teaspoon vanilla or almond
flavoring

1 tablespoon warm water

Cool cake in pan 5-10 minutes before removing. Mix all ingredients and spread over top of cake. Let topping drizzle over sides.

Mom's Biscuits

Makes 8
The best shortcake biscuit

2 cups flour
1 teaspoon baking soda
2 teaspoons cream of tarter

2 heaping tablespoons
shortening
Milk

Preheat oven to 375°. Sift flour, baking soda and cream of tarter together in a bowl. Add shortening and mix well. Add just enough milk (about 1 cup) to work in flour mixture. Place dough on floured board and roll or flatten to about ½ inch thick. Use floured biscuit cutter or tumbler about the same size to cut out biscuits. Place in pan and bake for 20-30 minutes or until browned.

Swedish Tea Ring

Makes 1 Loaf
A must for holiday baking

3¼ to 3½ cups flour
1 package dry yeast
1 cup milk
6 tablespoons butter or
  margarine

⅓ cup sugar
½ teaspoon salt
1 egg
Confectioners' sugar

Preheat oven to 375°. In large mixing bowl combine 2 cups of flour and yeast. In saucepan heat together milk, butter, sugar and salt until just warm, stirring constantly until butter almost melts. Add to dry mixture. Add egg and beat at low speed of electric mixer for ½ minute, scraping bowl constantly. Beat 3 minutes at high speed. By hand, stir in enough of the remaining flour to make a soft dough. Knead on lightly floured surface until smooth, 3-5 minutes, adding a small amount of additional flour if too sticky. Shape into a ball. Place in a greased bowl, turning once to grease surface. Cover and let rise in warm place until doubled, about 1 hour. Punch dough down. Let rest 10 minutes. Roll into an 18×12 inch rectangle. Spread with Almond Filling. Roll lengthwise, jelly roll fashion. Pinch to seal edge. Place seam side down and form into a ring on a greased 15-inch round baking sheet. Cut with kitchen shears every ½ inch to within ½ of bottom. Gently pull slices alternately to the left and to the right. Let ring rise in a warm place until nearly doubled, about 45 minutes. Bake for 15-20 minutes. While still hot, sprinkle with confectioners' sugar.

Almond Filling:
2 tablespoons butter
⅓ cup sugar

¼ cup ground almonds
¼ teaspoon almond extract

Cream butter until light and fluffy, gradually adding sugar. Stir in almonds and extract.

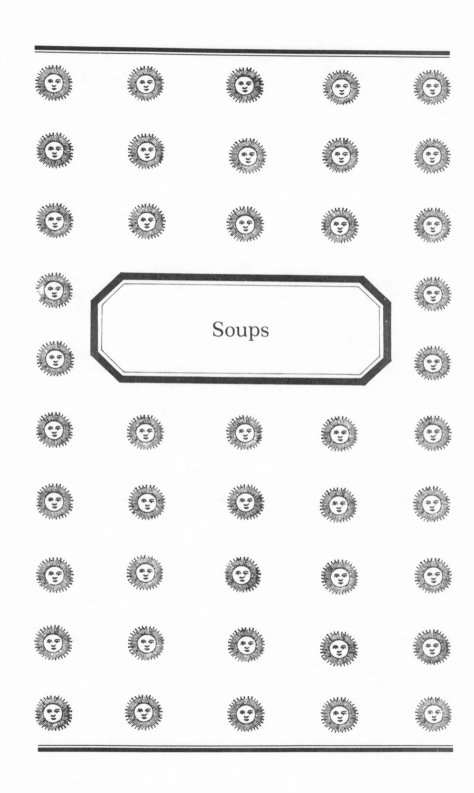

Soups

Chilled Broccoli Soup

Serves 8
Delicious and low in calories

3 tablespoons butter or
  margarine
1 cup chopped onion or scallions
1 (1½ pounds) bunch broccoli
1 cup raw, peeled, diced
  potatoes

6 cups chicken broth
Salt and pepper, to taste
⅔ cup fresh parsley leaves
1 cup half and half

Wash and trim broccoli. Reserve 1 cup flowerets; chop remaining broccoli. In covered dutch oven saute onions in butter over low heat until soft but not brown. Add broccoli, potatoes and broth to onions. Bring to a boil and season with salt and pepper. Simmer, covered, about 20 minutes. Set aside to cool. Blanch reserved flowerets with parsley in boiling salted water, about 3 minutes; drain. Set aside 8 tiny flowerets. Refrigerate for garnish. Drain vegetables; reserve broth. Puree vegetables in food processor or blender until smooth with slight texture. Add blanched broccoli and parsley leaves which gives the soup a brilliant color. Puree again for a few seconds and return to broth. Chill soup several hours or overnight. Before serving, combine soup and milk; check seasoning. Garnish with reserved flowerets. (May be made with watercress, spinach, sorrel, zucchini or a combination).

Chilled Cantaloupe Soup

Serves 12
A great beginning to summer

6 cantaloupes
¾ cup dry sherry

¾ cup sugar
1½ cups orange juice

Cut cantaloupes in half. Scoop pulp from each cantaloupe; leave shells ½-inch thick. Cut thin slice from bottom to make stable. Combine pulp and rest of ingredients in blender. Process until smooth. Chill thoroughly. Pour into shells when ready to serve. Garnish with sprig of mint.

Cream of Cucumber Soup

Serves 4

4 cups of pared, seeded, sliced
   cucumbers
1 onion, sliced
¼ cup butter
4 (¾ ounce) cans deviled
   chicken

1 cup light cream or milk
1 teaspoon salt
¼ teaspoon pepper
¼ teaspoon nutmeg

Saute cucumber and onion in butter for 8-10 minutes or until
transparent. Blend in food processor or blender. Add chicken, cream
and seasonings. Blend 1 minute or until smooth. Chill at least 4
hours if serving cold. Can be served hot or cold.

Gazpacho

Serves 6
Cold Spanish Soup

5 ripe tomatoes, peeled and
   seeded
1 cucumber, peeled and seeded
1 green pepper, seeded
1 garlic clove
3 scallions
1 teaspoon parsley
1 teaspoon basil
1 teaspoon thyme
1 teaspoon tarragon

1 teaspoon rosemary
1 tablespoon safflower oil
1½ tablespoons wine vinegar or
   3 tablespoons lemon juice
2 cups chilled tomato juice
1 teaspoon chili powder
½ bunch watercress (optional)
Salt and pepper, optional
Croutons for garnish

Place all ingredients (except tomato juice) in blender or food
processor and coarsely chop. Add tomato juice. Season to taste.
Serve chilled with croutons. Decorate with watercress.

Fresh Strawberry Soup

Serves 6

2 pints fresh strawberries,   1 cup red wine
  hulled, cut in half   ½ cup sugar
1 tablespoon cornstarch   1 cup sour cream
1 cup orange juice   Mint leaves for garnish

Place half the strawberries in food processor or blender and spin.
Add remaining berries and puree. Blend cornstarch with ¼ cup of
orange juice in 2-quart saucepan; add remaining orange juice, red
wine, sugar and pureed strawberries. Heat just to boiling over
medium heat, stirring frequently. Remove from heat. Stir in sour
cream with whisk. Cover and refrigerate until cold. Garnish with
mint leaves.

*Repertory theater covers the main season at the American Shakespeare Theater in
Stratford. Ballets, concerts, and operas are presented in the off-season months.*

Cold Watercress and Leek Soup

Serves 4

1 bunch leeks, white part only,   3 cups water
  sliced   1 teaspoon salt
1 bunch watercress, stems   1-2 tablespoons dried basil
  removed   2 cups plain yogurt
3 chicken bouillon cubes

Combine all ingredients except yogurt and boil until tender, about
15 minutes. Cool. Put into blender and puree. Add yogurt and serve
chilled.

Zucchini Soup

Serves 6

2 pounds zucchini (about 5 small zucchini, do not use large zucchini)
5 tablespoons finely chopped shallots

4 tablespoons butter
4 cups chicken broth
1½ teaspoons curry powder
1 teaspoon salt

Wipe zucchini clean. Slice across in ¼-inch slices. Melt butter in large skillet and as soon as it is foaming put in the zucchini and shallots. Cover and saute for 10 minutes, stirring frequently to prevent scorching. The zucchini should be soft, but not browned. Put half of the zucchini and shallots in a blender with half of the liquid, curry powder and salt. Blend for 1 minute. Repeat with rest of the ingredients. Combine both batches in a bowl and keep warm. Reheat if serving hot (with croutons) or refrigerate and serve cold with chives sprinkled on top.

Katharine Hepburn
Four time Academy Award Winning Actress

Carrot Soup

Serves 4

3 tablespoons butter
1 pound carrots, peeled and sliced
1 small onion, quartered
1 medium potato, peeled and cubed

½ teaspoon salt
Dash pepper
½ teaspoon sugar
3 cups beef broth
1 tablespoon chopped parsley

Melt butter in soup pot. Add carrots, onion, potato, salt, pepper and sugar. Cover and cook over medium heat for 15 minutes. Add broth and bring to a boil. Lower heat; cover and simmer for 15 minutes. Let cool. Puree in blender. Serve hot. Garnish with parsley.

Black Bean Soup

Serves 6 to 8

1 pound black beans	10 cups water
1 large green pepper, seeded and chopped	

In soup pot soak beans and green pepper in water overnight. Simmer for 45 minutes until softened.

⅔ cup olive oil	½ teaspoon pepper
1 large onion. chopped	¼ teaspoon oregano
4 garlic cloves	1 bay leaf
1 large green pepper, seeded and chopped	2 tablespoons sugar
4 teaspoons salt	2 tablespoons vinegar
	2 tablespoons white wine

Saute onion, garlic and green pepper in oil. Add 1 cup cooked beans and mash. Pour contents of frying pan back into pot. Add salt, pepper, oregano, bay leaf and sugar. Simmer for 1 hour. Add vinegar and white wine. Simmer 1 hour until thick. If soup does not thicken, remove cover. Before serving 2 tablespoons olive oil may be added. Serve with rice. Garnish with finely chopped onions and eggs.

Crab Meat Soup

Serves 6
So simple but delicious

½ cup minced onion	2 soup cans water
2 tablespoons butter or margarine	1 bay leaf
2 (10¾ ounce) cans tomato soup	1 (7 ounce) can drained crab meat
	½ soup can dry sherry

Saute onions in butter and set aside. Heat soup and water. Add onion and bay leaf. Simmer 10 minutes. Add crab meat and sherry. Stir and serve.

Beer-Cheese Soup

Serves 8

8 slices bacon
1 medium onion, chopped
1 stalk celery, chopped
1 leek, or several scallions,
   chopped
1 cup oats

Salt and pepper, to taste
6 cups chicken stock
4 cups beer
8 ounces Gruyere or Cheddar
   cheese, grated
½ cup cream or half and half

Fry bacon for 3 minutes; coarsely chop. Saute onion, celery and leek or scallions in bacon fat for 5 minutes. Transfer to large soup pot and add oats, salt and pepper, chicken stock and beer. Simmer 40 minutes; cool. Pour into blender container a portion at a time, and blend until smooth. Return to pot and add shredded cheese. Cook over low heat until cheese is melted. Stir in cream or half and half.

Chicken Corn Soup

Serves 6 to 8
An old-time favorite

1 quart chicken broth
1 small onion, chopped
1 celery stalk, chopped
2 hard-cooked eggs

1 (10 ounce) package frozen
   fresh corn or canned corn
1 cup cooked, diced chicken
1 cup cooked fine noodles
2 tablespoons chopped parsley

Combine all ingredients. Simmer for 1 hour.

Garbanzo and Sausage Soup

Serves 4
Perfect on a cold winter's night

½ pound hot Italian sausage
2 medium onions, chopped
2 celery stalks, chopped
2 garlic cloves, minced
1 (20 ounce) can chick peas
3 cups chicken stock
1 bay leaf

10 peppercorns
½ teaspoon Worcestershire
   sauce
½ teaspoon paprika
1 large potato, peeled and diced
Salt (optional)
Garlic croutons

Poach sausage in boiling water for 5 minutes. Drain. Cut into
1-inch pieces. Cook sausage pieces in large saucepan until some fat
is rendered. Add onions, celery and garlic and saute until the onion
is wilted. Add garbanzo beans, chicken stock, bay leaf, peppercorns,
Worcestershire sauce, paprika and potato. Bring to a boil. Reduce
heat, cover and simmer for 30 minutes or until potato is tender.
Serve hot with garlic croutons.

Mushroom-Broccoli Chowder

Serves 6

1 (14½ ounce) can chicken
   broth
½ (10 ounce) package frozen
   chopped broccoli
1½ cups sliced fresh
   mushrooms
½ cup chopped onion

2 tablespoons butter
2 tablespoons flour
½ teaspoon salt
⅛ teaspoon pepper
1½ cups milk or half and half
1 (8 ounce) can whole kernel
   corn, drained (optional)

In small saucepan bring broth and broccoli to boiling. Reduce heat.
Cover and simmer 5 minutes. Set aside. In larger pan cook
mushrooms and onion in butter. Blend in flour, salt and pepper.
Add milk. Cook and stir until thickened, about 2 minutes. Add
broccoli, broth and corn, if desired. Heat through and serve.

Lentil Soup

Serves 8 to 10

1 cup lentils
5 cups water
2 cups tomato juice or
  1 (1 pound) can crushed
  tomatoes
1 large onion, chopped
1 tablespoon Worcestershire
  sauce
2 teaspoons beef bouillon
Salt and pepper, to taste
1 teaspoon crushed garlic

1 bay leaf
½ cup chopped parsley
1-2 carrots, sliced
1-2 celery stalks, sliced
½ teaspoon thyme
2 potatoes, cubed (optional)
1 (10 ounce) package frozen
  green beans (optional)
1 (10 ounce) package frozen
  chopped spinach (optional)

Rinse lentils. In saucepan combine all ingredients except vegetables. Cover and simmer 1 hour. Add vegetables, if desired, and simmer ½ hour more until done.

Sweet Potato Soup

Serves 8

4 cups peeled sweet potatoes,
  cut into chunks
3 cups thickly sliced leeks or
  onions
3 carrots, cut into chunks
3 celery stalks, sliced into large
  chunks
2 quarts water

Sea salt, to taste
Freshly ground pepper, to taste
¼ cup milk
2 tablespoons toasted sesame
  seeds
1 tablespoon caraway seeds
½ teaspoon tarragon
1 tablespoon margarine

Place sweet potatoes, leeks, carrots, celery and water in large pot. Add salt and pepper. Bring to a boil. Cover and simmer 40 minutes. Soup will be lumpy. With a slotted spoon, remove half of carrots, celery and some firmer potato chunks and reserve. Puree remainder of soup in food processor or blender until smooth. Return to pot and add reserved vegetables, milk, sesame seeds, caraway seeds, tarragon and margarine. Reheat. Serve immediately.

Viennese Soup with Dumplings

Serves 4

Dumplings:
2 tablespoons butter
1 egg
¼ teaspoon salt

⅛ teaspoon nutmeg
6 tablespoons cream of wheat
1 teaspoon cold water

Soup:
4 cups beef broth
1 cup peas

1 cup sliced mushrooms
1 tablespoon chopped chives

Cream butter. Add rest of dumpling ingredients. Let stand 2 hours. Heat broth. Using a teaspoon form small balls from the cream of wheat mixture. Simmer in broth for 10 minutes. Add mushrooms and peas and simmer 10 minutes. Add chives.

Zucchini Sausage Soup

Makes 3½ Quarts

1 pound Italian sweet or hot
  sausage
2 cups celery, sliced in ½-inch
  pieces
2 pounds zucchini, sliced in
  ½-inch pieces
1 cup chopped onion
2 (28 ounce) cans tomatoes
2 teaspoons salt

1 teaspoon Italian seasoning
1 teaspoon oregano
1 teaspoon sugar
½ teaspoon basil
¼ teaspoon garlic powder
1 cup red wine
½ cup water
2 green peppers, cut in ½-inch
  pieces

Remove casings from sausage. Brown in large Dutch oven. Drain off excess fat. Add celery and cook 10 minutes, stirring occasionally. Add all remaining ingredients except peppers. Simmer, covered for 20 minutes. Add pepper and cook, covered for 10 minutes. Longer cooking improves the flavor. Can be served with grated cheese on top.

New England Clam Chowder

Serves 8 to 10
Perfect for an Autumn day in Connecticut

5-7 pounds quahogs
2 large onions, sliced
½ pound salt pork (all fat) cut
  very fine
2 celery stalks, finely minced
2 carrots, finely minced

3 potatoes, diced
1 tablespoon chopped parsley
½ teaspoon thyme
2 bay leaves
Fresh ground pepper

Fry pork until brown and drain on paper towel. Add onion and saute until golden. Wash clams and heat in small amount of water until shells open, about 5 minutes. Finely chop in food processor or blender (if using blender, add some broth). Put pork, onion and broth in kettle. Add water and/or clam juice to make 8 cups (use 2 to 1 water to clam juice). Add all vegetables and simmer.

Roux:
1 tablespoon butter
1 tablespoon flour

1 tablespoon Worcestershire
  sauce
Dash tabasco

Prepare roux by melting butter slowly and gradually add flour, sprinkling it in and stirring constantly until a nice delicate brown. Stir in Worcestershire sauce and tabasco. Add to clam chowder and serve.

Clam Chowder

Serves 8 to 10

2 medium chopped onions
3 tablespoons butter or
  margarine
2 (10 ounce) cans baby clams,
  with juice

6 medium potatoes, peeled and
  diced
1 cup water
6 cups milk
Salt, pepper, parsley

Cook onion in butter until golden. Add clams, clam juice, potatoes and water. Simmer until potatoes are cooked, about 45 minutes. Add milk and simmer ½ hour. Do not boil. Season to taste and enjoy with oyster crackers.

Senegalese Soup

Serves 6
Some like it hot, some like it cold

3½ cups chicken stock
1 cup finely chopped, cooked
   chicken

½ teaspoon curry powder
4 egg yolks
2 cups cream or half and half

Bring chicken stock to a boil and add chicken and curry powder.
Beat the egg yolks. Add slowly to pot so as not to curdle. Then
blend with cream. Add to the stock stirring constantly over low heat
until just thickened. Water chestnuts or celery may be added
toward the end for crunchiness.

Seafood Mediterranean

Serves 6 to 8
Easy, elegant bouillabaisse

3 garlic cloves, minced
½ cup oil
1 cup dry white wine
2 cups canned Italian plum
   tomatoes
1 teaspoon oregano
2 bay leaves

1½ teaspoons salt
½ teaspoon pepper
1 cup chopped parsley
3-4 pounds fish, shellfish or
   lobster, the greater the variety
   the better

In deep pot saute garlic in oil for 1 minute. If using lobster, add
pieces and cook 3 minutes. Add wine, tomatoes, oregano, bay
leaves, salt and pepper. Cover and simmer 5 minutes. Add fish and
cook until easily pierced with knife, about 8 minutes, until shellfish
have opened and shrimp are pink. Stir in parsley. Serve in soup
bowls with French bread. (Sauce can be made ahead if lobster is
not used. Fish can be added shortly before serving time.)

Pesto Vegetable Soup

Serves 6 to 8

½ cup dried white beans
2 large carrots, diced
2 medium potatoes, diced
1 small zucchini, diced
1 yellow squash, diced
1 leek, trimmed, split and
   chopped
1 pound tomatoes, peeled,
   seeded and diced

1 celery stalk
Parsley sprigs
1 bay leaf
Salt and pepper, to taste
¼ cup fresh basil
3 garlic cloves
1 cup Parmesan cheese, plus
   extra for the table
⅓ cup olive oil

Place beans in heavy pot with enough water to cover by 2 inches. Bring to a boil and simmer for 1 hour. Drain. (This can be done day before). Place beans, carrots, potatoes, zucchini, yellow squash, leek and tomatoes in large pot. Tie the celery, parsley and bay leaf together with a string to make a bouquet garni. Add to the pot. Add enough water to cover (about 2½ quarts). Add salt and pepper to taste. Bring to a boil, lower heat and simmer 1 hour or until the vegetables and beans are very tender. In food processor or blender, puree the basil, garlic and cheese. Slowly add the oil until a paste forms. This is the pesto. Remove the bouquet garni. Discard. To serve, remove soup from heat. Stir in the pesto. Taste for seasonings and serve immediately. Sprinkle each bowl with grated Parmesan cheese. Do not reheat after adding the pesto.

At Naugatuck in 1939 Charles Goodyear's lab pot boiled over spilling a mess of rubber and sulphur onto a red-hot stove. The result was vulcanized rubber.

Pasta, Cheese & Eggs

Pasta

Makes 1 Pound

3 eggs
2 tablespoons oil

2 teaspoons salt
2 cups unbleached flour

Process to ball in food processor. If ball does not form, add a few drops oil. Wrap in plastic wrap and let set at room temperature for ½ hour. Using handcranked pasta maker, roll pasta to finest setting for delicate creamy sauces and heavier for robust, hearty sauces. Allow to dry a few minutes on rack or in layers of cloth toweling (until smooth and no longer tacky). Cut and either cook immediately, 3-5 minutes, or dry to cook later.

Ditalini and Spinach

Serves 4
No baking—quick and easy

45 ounces tomato sauce
1 cup water
Garlic powder
Parsley
Crushed red peppers,
Black pepper,

1 (10 ounce) package frozen
  chopped spinach
⅓ cup butter or margarine
1 (20 ounce) can cannellini
  beans (white kidney beans)
1 pound package ditalini, cooked
  and drained.

Place sauce in saucepan and season to taste with garlic, parsley, red pepper and black pepper. Add frozen spinach and cover. Cook over medium-high heat until spinach is completely defrosted, stirring occasionally. Add butter and simmer, covered, for ½ hour. Add cannellini beans and simmer until ready to serve. To ditalini add ¾ of sauce and stir. Allow to stand 10 minutes (pasta will absorb sauce and expand). Spoon into individual serving dishes and cover each with some of the remaining sauce. Serve with grated cheese, salad and garlic bread.

Fettuccini with Peas and Bacon

Serves 6

½ cup butter
6 shallots, minced
½ pound mushrooms, sliced
1½ cups whipping cream
½ package frozen tiny peas
½ pound bacon, cooked until crispy then chopped

1½ cups freshly grated Parmesan cheese
1 pound fettuccini, cooked al dente, drained
Salt and freshly ground pepper
Additional Parmesan cheese

Heat butter in large skillet. Add shallots and saute until soft. Add mushrooms. Increase heat to high and cook until mushrooms are very lightly browned. Add cream and let boil 2 minutes. Stir in peas and cook one more minute. Reduce heat to low, blend in fettuccini, cheese and bacon and toss until heated and sauce clings to pasta. Adjust consistency with cream. Season to taste with salt and pepper. Pass additional cheese if desired.

Linguine with Quahog Sauce

Serves 6
A quick, easy and hearty treat for seafood lovers.

1 dozen fresh quahogs (more if you have them)
¼ cup olive oil
3-4 garlic cloves, sliced or crushed

¼ teaspoon dried oregano
2 shakes red seed pepper
Fresh Italian parsley, chopped
1 pound linguine

Wash quahogs in cold water to remove sand. Open, reserving liquid in separate container, and then cut into smaller pieces with scissors. In one quart saucepan, saute garlic in olive oil until golden. Add reserved liquid from quahogs, oregano, pepper and parsley. Simmer, covered, approximately 10 minutes. Add chopped quahogs and bring to a boil; cover, turn off heat, letting mixture set for 15 minutes. Meanwhile, cook linguine al dente according to package directions. Drain and place in serving dish. Pour quahog sauce mixture over linguine and serve. (Canned clams can be substituted for quahogs).

Gloria's Spinach Lasagna

Serves 6 to 8
No precooking of noodles

½ cup water

½ pound lasagna noodles,
   uncooked

Sauce:
1 (29 ounce) can tomatoes,
   crushed
1 tablespoon Italian seasoning

1 tablespoon minced onion,
1 garlic clove, minced
1 teaspoon salt

Spinach-Cheese Mixture:
1 pound cottage cheese or
   Ricotta
½ cup Parmesan cheese

8 ounces Mozzarella cheese
1 (10 ounce) package frozen
   chopped spinach, thawed

Mix sauce ingredients together. Mix cheeses and spinach together.
In baking pan layer in following order: water, 3-4 spoonfuls of
sauce, ½ of the lasagna noodles, part of sauce, ½ spinach-cheese
mixture, remaining noodles, part of sauce, remaining
spinach-cheese mixture, remaining sauce. Cover with Mozzarella.
Bake, covered, at 375° for 45 minutes. Uncover and bake another 20
minutes more.

Company Eggs

Serves 6 to 8

2 cups grated Cheddar cheese
Butter
1 cup light cream or half and
   half

2 teaspoons mustard
½ teaspoon salt
¼ teaspoon pepper
12 eggs, lightly beaten

Spread cheese in 3-quart square pan. Dot with butter. Combine
cream, mustard, salt and pepper. Pour ½ mixture over cheese. Then
add eggs and remaining cream mixture. Bake at 350° for 35-40
minutes or until set.

Hay and Straw

Serves 6 to 8
The green (hay) and yellow (straw) noodles make a pretty and delicious dish

2 tablespoons finely chopped
  onion
¾ pound fresh mushrooms,
  sliced
6 tablespoons butter

½ pound cooked ham, cut in
  ¼-inch cubes
¾ cup heavy cream
1 pound fettucini noodles
1 pound spinach noodles
1 cup grated Parmesan cheese

Saute onion in 3 tablespoons butter until golden. Add mushrooms and cook 3 minutes after juices from mushrooms come to the surface. Stir often. Add ham and cook 1-2 minutes. Add remaining butter and cream. Cook until cream thickens slightly. Salt and pepper, to taste. Meanwhile, cook both types of noodles in separate pans (the green cooks more quickly). Cook until al dente. Drain. Add sauce and ½ of the Parmesan cheese and toss. Serve immediately with remaining cheese on the side.

Marion E. Morra
co-author "Choices"

Noodle Pudding

Serves 12

1 pound medium noodles
¼ cup butter
¼ pound Muenster cheese
2 large eggs, beaten
½ cup milk
½ cup sugar

⅛ pound cottage cheese
¼ pound whipped cream cheese
½ cup sour cream
½ cup raisins
Cinnamon, optional
½ teaspoon vanilla

Cook noodles 5 minutes in boiling water with 1 teaspoon salt. Drain well. Cut butter and Muenster cheese in small pieces. Add remaining ingredients to hot noodles. Pour into well greased 13×9 baking dish. Bake at 350° for 1 hour or until top is golden brown. Can be served hot or cold for brunch, lunch or dinner. Cut in square pieces.

Manicotti

Makes About 24

1 cup milk	6 eggs, beaten
1½ cups flour	½ teaspoon salt

Stir milk into flour, gradually until smooth. Add beaten eggs and salt. Continue stirring. Batter will be consistency of pancake batter. To make shells for manicotti, brush oil over bottom of 6-inch skillet and heat. Pour ½ cup batter into pan. Tilt pan back and forth so that it is evenly distributed. When batter is set, turn pancake over and cook until set. Slide off onto a warm dish as you make them.

Filling:

3 pounds Ricotta cheese	2 eggs
½ pound Mozzarella cheese, grated	½ cup Parmesan cheese
1 tablespoon chopped parsley	Salt and pepper

Combine all ingredients and stuff each shell, using about 2 tablespoons for each. Place filling to one side of shell and roll gently. Place shells in baking dish and top with your favorite sauce. Sprinkle Parmesan cheese over top and bake at 350° for 30 minutes.

Colonel Thomas Fitch, of Norwalk, helped create a popular tune as old as this country "Yankee Doodle." Lacking any semblance of a uniform each of his troops stuck a chicken feather in his hatband. A British surgeon extemporized the lines, "Stuck a feather in his hat and called it macaroni." Macaroni was the slang of the day for a dude or dandy.

Pasta Primavera

Serves 6 to 8

½ cup butter, unsalted
1 medium onion, minced
1 large garlic clove, minced
1 pound thin asparagus,
    trimmed and diagonally cut
½ pound mushrooms, thinly
    sliced
1 small carrot, thinly sliced
1 medium zucchini, sliced
½ of small cauliflower, flowerets
1 cup whipping cream
½ cup chicken broth

2 tablespoons chopped fresh
    basil, or 2 teaspoons dried
    basil
1 cup frozen tiny peas, thawed
2 ounces prosciutto or cooked
    ham, chopped
5 green onions, chopped
Salt and fresh ground pepper
1 pound fettuccini or linguine,
    cooked al dente, thoroughly
    drained
1 cup Parmesan cheese

Saute butter, onion and garlic until onion is soft. Mix in asparagus, mushrooms, carrots, zucchini and cauliflower, stir-fry for 2 minutes. Remove a few vegetables and reserve for garnish. Add cream, broth and basil and allow to boil about 3 minutes. Stir in peas, ham and green onion; cook 1 minute longer. Season. Add pasta and cheese, tossing until thoroughly combined and heated through. Turn onto a large serving platter and garnish with reserved vegetables. Serve immediately. Note: Variation—1 pound cooked shrimp can be added to cooked ham.

America's first school of law was founded in Litchfield by Tapping Reeve in 1774.

Jumbo Shells and Meat Filling

Serves 6

1 package jumbo shells	3 slices bread, diced
1½ pounds ground beef	½ cup milk
1 tablespoon butter, or oil	1 tablespoon chopped parsley
1 egg	Salt and pepper
½ pound Mozzarella cheese,	1 quart spaghetti sauce
diced	Grated Parmesan cheese

Brown meat. Add egg, cheese, bread, milk, parsley, salt and pepper; blend well. Parboil shells 6 minutes. Remove from water with strainer. Spoon and stuff immediately with meat mixture. Cover bottom of baking dish with spaghetti sauce. Arrange filled shells side by side in a single layer, making sure shells fill dish. (If this is not possible, use two smaller dishes). Cover with remaining sauce and bake at 350° for 30 minutes. Sprinkle with Parmesan cheese. Serve piping hot.

Buffet Ham and Cheese Souffle

Serves 8

8 slices soft white bread,	½ pound boiled ham, sliced thin
trimmed and cubed	2 cups milk
1 pound Swiss or Cheddar	6 eggs, separated
cheese, shredded	Butter

Spread bread cubes in bottom of well buttered, 10×6 baking dish. Layer cheese over bread cubes. Add ham. Beat egg whites until frothy, then add lightly beaten yolks. Add to milk and pour mixture over all. Season with salt and pepper and a dash of nutmeg. Place in refrigerator overnight. The next day dot with butter and bake, uncovered at 325° for 30 minutes.

Eve Potts
co-author "Choices"

Pastitsio

Serves 16
Popular main dish of Greece

1 (#2) box ziti	1¼ pound ground beef
5 heaping tablespoons flour	1 large onion
1 cup butter	Salt and pepper
½ gallon milk, warmed	Dash cinnamon
7 eggs, beaten	1 tablespoon tomato paste
1½ cups grated cheese	

Cook and drain ziti according to package directions.

Cream Sauce:
Blend flour in melted butter until smooth. Add warm milk gradually, stirring constantly until thickened. Remove from heat. Add eggs and cheese. In skillet, brown meat with onion in butter, salt, pepper and cinnamon. Add stick of cinnamon while cooking if you like. Add tomato paste and let simmer. After meat is cooked, mix with ziti and add ½ of cream sauce. Mix and add cheese to taste. Put in buttered 16×11 baking dish. Put remaining cream sauce on top. Bake at 350° for 1 hour or until light golden brown. Allow to set for 15 minutes before cutting into serving pieces. This may be made day ahead and reheated in oven before serving.

William Gillette built a reputation portraying Sherlock Holmes on the stage. He proved himself in another field when he directed the construction of a castle he designed himself. Perched on top of a hill, alongside the Connecticut River in Hadlyme, Gillette Castle took five years to fashion out of white oak and native stone.

Spaghetti with Mussels, Scallops, Shrimp

Serves 6 to 8

3 tablespoons light olive oil
1 large onion, minced
2 garlic cloves, minced
¼ cup dry white wine
½ teaspoon dried basil or 1½
    tablespoons fresh basil
1 teaspoon dried marjoram or 1
    tablespoon fresh marjoram
1½ cups canned tomatoes, well
    drained

1½ pounds mussels, scrubbed
    and debearded
1 pound sea scallops, halved
1 pound large shrimp, peeled,
    deveined and butterflied
Salt and freshly ground pepper
1 pound spaghetti, cooked al
    dente

Heat oil in 5-quart saucepan over medium-high heat. Add onion and
saute until lightly golden. Add garlic and saute an additional 30
seconds. Stir in wine, basil and majoram and cook 1 minute. Add
tomatoes, increase heat and boil 5 minutes. Reduce heat to
medium, add mussels or clams. Cover and cook until shells open,
about ½ inch, approximately 5 minutes. Add scallops and shrimp.
Cover and cook an additional 2-3 minutes, until scallops and shrimp
are barely firm. Season to taste with salt and pepper. Add spaghetti
and toss gently to mix.

Mass production of American timepieces originated in Bristol. Millions of clocks and
watches have been produced there since the industry was established in the
nineteenth century. Bristol is the site of America's finest Clock and Watch Museum.

Spinach Pasta Pinwheels

Serves 8

Sauce:

¼ cup butter
¼ cup flour
4 cups milk
⅔ cup grated Parmesan cheese
1 (10 ounce) package frozen chopped spinach, thawed and well drained

4 garlic cloves, crushed
¼ cup chopped parsley,
2 teaspoons basil
½ teaspoon salt
⅛ teaspoon pepper

In medium saucepan melt butter. Add flour and stir until smooth. Slowly add milk and continue to cook stirring occasionally, until mixture comes to a boil and thickens. Remove from heat. Stir in cheese until melted. Pour 2 cups sauce into blender or food processor. Add remaining sauce ingredients, cover and blend or process until well blended. Pour into remaining sauce in saucepan. Stir to combine. Reserve 1 cup of sauce for pasta filling, set rest aside.

Filling:

2 tablespoons butter
½ cup chopped onion
1 pound ground beef
2 garlic cloves, crushed
2 (10 ounce) packages frozen chopped spinach, thawed and well drained

1 (15 ounce) container Ricotta cheese
⅓ cup grated Parmesan cheese
1 teaspoon basil
1 teaspoon salt
⅛ teaspoon pepper

16 curly edge lasagna noodles

2 tablespoons salad oil

In large skillet, melt butter. Add onion and saute until tender. Add beef and cook, stirring occasionally, until browned. Remove from heat and stir in reserved cup of sauce and remaining filling ingredients. Grease an 8-inch round baking dish. Place 1 cup sauce in dish. Set aside. Cook noodles according to package directions, adding 2 tablespoons oil to the water. Drain and cool. As soon as you can handle, separate noodles and place in single layer on flat surface. Spread ⅓ cup beef mixture on each noodle to within 1-inch at one end. Roll up from the filled end, jelly-roll fashion. Lightly press uncovered portion against noodle to adhere. Place rolls upright in baking dish. Bake in preheated 350° oven for 1 hour. Heat remaining sauce and serve.

Curried Shrimp and Crabmeat Crepes

Serves 12

Crepe Batter:

1¼ cups flour
½ teaspoon salt
2 whole eggs
2 egg yolks

1 cup milk
¾ cup water
3 tablespoons butter, melted

Sift flour and salt together. Beat eggs and yolks and combine with milk and water. Add gradually to flour. Beat until batter is smooth. Add melted butter. Allow to stand in refrigerator at least 2 hours before making crepes.

Shrimp-Crabmeat Filling:

¼ cup butter
4 shallots, finely chopped
½ pound fresh cooked shrimp, chopped
½ pound fresh cooked crabmeat or any desired seafood
6 mushrooms, thinly sliced

Salt and pepper
2 tablespoons curry powder, or to taste
3 cups Bechamel sauce
Gruyere cheese, grated
Parmesan cheese, grated

Melt butter in saucepan. Saute shallots until soft. Add shrimp, crabmeat, mushrooms and salt and pepper to taste. Cook, covered, 5-10 minutes, until completely heated through. Add curry powder to sauce and taste for seasoning. Reserve 1 cup Bechamel sauce. Mix remainder into seafood mixture and gently heat.

Prepare crepes. Spread with seafood mixture and gently roll up. Place in greased serving dish, seam side down. Spoon remaining sauce over centers of crepes. Top with sprinkling of grated cheeses and brown under broiler.

Makes 3 Cups

Bechamel Sauce:

6 tablespoons butter
4½ tablespoons flour
2 cups hot whipping cream
1 cup white wine

¾ teaspoon salt
Dash pepper
Dash nutmeg
2 sprigs parsley

Melt butter in saucepan over medium heat. Add flour gradually and stir 1 minute. Slowly add hot cream, then wine, stirring constantly. Season with salt, pepper and nutmeg. Add parsley. Bring to a boil, reduce heat and simmer 10 minutes. Remove parsley.

Ruth Henderson's Sunday Lunch for 12

This is a typical Sunday lunch from the Vogtland, the part of Germany from which Mrs. Henderson comes. The menu is designed for a relaxed meal and the dishes keep warm easily on a large Sterno warming unit or electric hot tray. These dishes should be served with a green salad and an appropriate dessert.
The fricassee and berry sauce can be made a day ahead "I prefer to make the Eierkuchen on the morning of the luncheon, but they also can be made the day before and refrigerated, and will only be a little less light."
The rolled, leftover Eierkuchen are delightful sliced very thin and dropped in a good broth, served with finely chopped parsley on top.

German Pancakes (Eierkuchen)

Makes 24 Pancakes

5 cups flour
½ teaspoon salt
12 eggs

5 cups milk
1½ pound butter, melted

Sift flour in a 5-quart bowl with salt. Make a well in center. Beat eggs in a second 5-quart bowl. Add milk and blend. Transfer to a measuring cup. Pour egg mixture slowly into well while stirring continuously with a mixing spoon. Finish blending with whisk. (Do not use whisk in the beginning because batter is too thick.) Let stand at room temperature for approximately 1 hour. Stir again before using. Heat a generous ounce (2 tablespoons) butter in a 10-inch omelet pan over high heat. Use an ounce of melted butter for each Eierkuchen. Pour ½ cup batter in pan and reduce heat to medium. Cook until golden brown on both sides, turning once. Slide onto a dinner plate. While next Eierkuchen is cooking, roll up the first one and place in an 18-inch, deep oven-to-table baking dish. The pancakes must be rolled while still warm and flexible. Continue in this manner until all batter is used. Cover dish with foil and reheat pancakes in a 250° oven before serving.

Ruth Henderson

Chicken and Ham Fricassee

Serves 12

Ingredients for poaching
  chicken:

6 cups water
2 whole carrots
1 shallot, peeled
1 stalk celery
4 sprigs fresh sage or 1 teaspoon
  dry sage

4 sprigs fresh marjoram or 1
  teaspoon dry leaf
4 chicken breasts, skinned and
  boned

Bring all poaching ingredients to a boil in a 5-quart pot. Add chicken breasts and simmer 15 minutes or until cooked. Remove breasts. Cool and dice. Strain broth and reserve.

Ingredients for Fricassee:

½ cup butter
½ cup flour
5 cups broth from poaching
Juice of ½ lemon
Diced chicken
3 cups baked ham, diced

1 cup prosciutto or Westphalian
  ham, diced
1 (15 ounce) can early June
  peas
1 (15 ounce) can asparagus tips
¼ cup parsley, finely chopped

Melt butter in large saute pan over medium heat. Add flour. Cook and stir until roux is golden yellow. Add broth and whisk until smooth. Bring to a boil and simmer on very low heat for 5 minutes. Add lemon juice, diced chicken, ham and prosciutto and simmer 5 minutes more. Do not add salt. The saltiness of the ham should be plenty. Add vegetables and simmer again for 5 minutes (15 minutes total). Serve in a pottery casserole or the pot you cook it in. Sprinkle with chopped parsley just before serving as sauce for German pancakes. Note: Fresh steamed vegetables, or several varieties of mushrooms may be substituted for meats. This is the kind of dish everyone can put his personal stamp on.

Ruth Henderson

Four Berry Sauce

Serves 12

½ lemon with zest
3 cups sugar
1½ cups each blackberries, raspberries, currents and gooseberries, preferably fresh
or frozen without sugar. If the berries are frozen in syrup, cook them only with sugar to taste
1½ ounces good brandy

Wash the lemon. Cut into pieces and put in a food processor with 1 cup of the sugar. Process with the steel knife until lemon is finely ground. Combine berries with other sugar and lemon in a heavy pan and cook over medium heat stirring frequently until juice appears. Then simmer approximately 1 hour or until desired sauce texture is reached, still stirring frequently. Skim foam, add brandy and thereafter do not let boil. If necessary, reheat gently to below the simmer before serving as a sauce for German pancakes.
Note: Hot applesauce or plain cinnamon and sugar can be substituted for berry sauce.

Ruth Henderson
Mrs. Skitch, Henderson, wife of composer-conductor

Olga's Hot Cakes

Makes 18

2 eggs, slightly beaten
1¼ cups milk
1 cup sour cream
2 tablespoons sugar
¾ teaspoon salt
1½ cups flour
4 teaspoons baking powder
½ teaspoon baking soda

Combine eggs, milk, sour cream, sugar and salt. Sift flour, baking powder and baking soda. Add to milk mixture. Stir to mix; do not beat. Bake on ungreased griddle. Batter may get thick as it stands. Add a little milk to thin slightly.

Sourdough Pancakes

Serves 4 to 6
Delicious with blueberries

2 cups sour dough starter (room temperature, left out overnight)
2 tablespoons honey

1 egg, beaten
5 tablespoons oil
½ cup wheat germ
1 teaspoon baking powder

Add honey, egg and oil to starter dough using wooden spoon. Stir in wheat germ. Make paste of baking powder by adding a little water. Stir into batter. Pour batter on hot griddle. Serve with butter, syrup.

Recipe for Sourdough Starter:
1 small package yeast
¼ cup water
1 cup flour

2 tablespoons sugar
1 cup unsalted potato water, from boiled potatoes

Mix together in bowl (large enough to leave room for expansion) or crock using a wooden spoon—never use metal. Mixture should have ploppy consistency. Let rise at room temperature open to air for 48 hours. Refrigerate covered. To reactivate, mix in liquid on top. Add flour first , usually a cup or two. Add enough warm water to make a ploppy mixture. Let stand at room temperature 12 hours. Always make enough starter so that 2 cups can be left behind for next use.

Connecticut's little known contributions to civilization include such diverse essentials as friction matches, sewing machines, safety fuses, cork screws, mechanical calculators, pay telephones, micrometers, pins and needles, player pianos, automatic fire sprinklers, canned condensed milk and lollipops.

Classic Omelet

Serves 2

6 eggs
½ teaspoon salt
Dash pepper

3 tablespoons butter or
margarine

In small bowl, beat eggs, salt, pepper and 2 tablespoons cold water. In 10 inch skillet over medium heat, melt butter, tilting skillet to grease sides. Pour eggs into skillet; let set around sides. With metal spatula, gently lift edges as they set, tilting skillet to allow uncooked portion to run under omelet. Shake skillet occasionally to keep omelet moving freely in pan. When omelet is set but still moist on the surface, increase heat slightly to brown bottom of omelet. Place filling in center and with spatula, fold omelet in half; slide onto heated platter.

Smoked Oyster Omelet

Serves 2
Unusual and delicious

6 eggs for scrambling or 2
(3-egg) omelets
6 tablespoons smoked, chopped
oysters
¼ cup chopped tomato
2 tablespoons chopped parsley
1 teaspoon lemon juice
2 tablespoons thinly sliced water
chestnuts

¼ cup chopped scallions
¼ cup sliced mushrooms
1 tablespoon butter
¼ cup white wine
Garnish:
¼ cup sour cream
2 tablespoons chopped tomato
1 teaspoon chopped parsley

Combine oysters, tomato, parsley, lemon juice and water chestnuts in small bowl. Set aside. Saute scallions in butter until soft. Add wine. Reduce liquid to half by cooking over medium heat. Add scallion-mushroom mixture to oysters. Prepare omelet. Place half of mixture in center of each omelet. Fold in half or into thirds. Serve on a warm plate. Combine sour cream, tomato and parsley for garnish. Place in a small serving dish.

Creamy Cheese and Vegetable Omelet

Serves 2

4 tablespoons butter
¼ cup chopped onion
2 tablespoons diced green
  pepper
½ small garlic clove, minced
¼ pound mushrooms, thinly
  sliced
4 eggs

2 tablespoons water
¼ teaspoon salt
⅛ teaspoon pepper
1 ounce cream cheese, cut into
  small pieces
2 ounces Monterrey Jack or
  Cheddar cheese, shredded

In 10-inch skillet melt 1 tablespoon butter over medium heat. Add
onion, green pepper and garlic. Cook 5 minutes or until soft. Add
mushrooms. Cook 2 minutes or until tender. Remove vegetables
from skillet. Drain on paper towels. In medium bowl with fork, mix
eggs, water, salt and pepper until blended but not frothy. Stir in
cream cheese. Heat remaining butter in hot skillet. When melted
and browned pour in egg mixture. As eggs set, carefully push
cooked portion toward center, allowing uncooked portion to flow to
sides and bottom, tilting pan if necessary. When eggs are set, but
top is still moist and creamy, sprinkle shredded cheese over half of
omelet. Remove pan from heat. Spoon vegetable mixture over
cheese. Using a spatula, lift one side of omelet and fold over filling.
Slide omelet out onto a warm plate and serve.

Asparagus Souffle

Serves 6

¼ cup butter
8 eggs

1 can asparagus soup, undiluted
  (tomato or mushroom soup
  may be substituted)

Butter 9 inch round baking dish. Mix eggs with can of undiluted
soup. Pour this into the mold and bake at 350° for ½ hour or until
brown and high. Serve with crusty warm bread. Note: Instead of
soup use 1 cup fresh strawberries and ½ cup sour cream. Perfect
for summer time.

Fluffy Orange Pancakes

Serves 4
Light, melt-in-mouth pancakes

1½ cups flour
2 teaspoons baking powder
½ teaspoon salt
3 tablespoons sugar
2 eggs, separated

1 cup milk
½ cup orange juice
3 tablespoons butter, melted
  or oil
1 tablespoon grated orange peel

Sift flour with baking powder, salt and sugar into bowl. In another bowl lightly beat egg yolks and beat in milk, orange juice, butter and orange peel. Add liquid to dry ingredients and stir until well blended. Beat egg whites until soft peaks form and fold into batter. Bake on hot, lightly greased griddle. Serve with orange butter and fresh or frozen strawberries or peaches.

Orange Butter:
Mix ½ cup softened butter, 1 cup confectioners' sugar and 2 tablespoons grated orange peel.

Christmas Souffle

Serves 6
Bakes while you open your gifts

8 slices whole wheat or white
  bread, regular sliced
Butter
1 cup shredded Swiss or
  Cheddar cheese
6 eggs, beaten
3 cups milk

½ teaspoon dry mustard
1 tablespoon Worcestershire
  sauce
½ teaspoon salt
½ teaspoon curry powder,
  optional

Lightly butter the bread and break into cubes. In ungreased 2-quart casserole, alternate layers of bread and cheese. Mix remaining ingredients and pour over bread. Do not mix. Cover and refrigerate up to 2 days. Bake uncovered at 350° for 1 hour. Test with sharp knife.

Grits Souffle

Serves 6
A flavor from the South

2 cups milk
½ cup instant grits
1 teaspoon salt
½ teaspoon baking powder

2 tablespoons butter, melted
½ teaspoon sugar
3 eggs, separated

Grease 1½ quart casserole dish or souffle dish. Scald milk, add grits and cook until thick, stirring constantly. Add salt, baking powder, butter and sugar. Mix well. Beat egg yolks and add to grits. Whip egg whites until they form soft peaks. Fold into mixture. Pour into prepared baking dish. Bake at 375° for 30 minutes. Serve hot. Just before folding in the egg whites, ½ cup grated sharp cheese and a dash of tabasco sauce can be added to make an excellent variation of the above recipe.

Rice and Artichoke Quiche

Serves 6 to 8

1 cup brown rice
2 ⅔ cups chicken broth, canned
  or fresh
1 cup chopped kielbasa
1 medium onion, chopped
1 medium green pepper,
  chopped

1 (14 ounce) can artichoke
  hearts, drained, and cut in
  half
1½ cups Cheddar cheese
2 eggs
1 can cream of mushroom soup
Sliced pimientos for garnish

Cook rice in chicken broth until tender. Cool. Combine kielbasa, onion and green pepper. Heat over low heat. Set aside. Press rice into buttered quiche or 10-inch pie plate. Layer meat mixture, artichokes and cheese. Combine eggs and soup. Pour over quiche. Bake, uncovered at 350° for 50 minutes. Cool slightly. Make design of your choice with pimientos. Cut into wedges. Can be made ahead. Refrigerate. Bring to room temperature before baking.

Baked Eggs in Tomatoes

Serves 4
Brunch or for a different breakfast

4 large firm yellow or red
  tomatoes
Salt and pepper
1 garlic clove, finely chopped
4 eggs
2 teaspoons tomato puree

2 tablespoons heavy cream
2 tablespoons grated Parmesan
  cheese
4 slices bread
2 tablespoons butter
2 teaspoons olive oil

Wash, dry and slice tops off tomatoes. Scoop out all the inside pulp. Sprinkle insides with salt and pepper and turn shells upside down to drain for 30 minutes. When drained, dry tomato cups and sprinkle the inside with chopped garlic. Break one egg into each shell. If tomatoes are small, only add the egg yolk, reserving whites for another use. Season again. Blend tomato puree with cream and spoon over eggs. Sprinkle with cheese and place tomatoes in a buttered baking dish. Bake at 350° for 15-20 minutes or until eggs are set. While eggs are cooking, cut bread into rounds. Heat butter and oil in a skillet and saute bread on both sides until crisp and golden brown. Once eggs are set, arrange one tomato on each toast round. Serve immediately, sprinkled with fresh chopped parsley or basil.

Swiss Baked Eggs

Serves 6

½ pound Swiss cheese
1 cup heavy cream
6 eggs

¼ teaspoon salt
⅛ teaspoon pepper
Dash paprika

Line buttered 9-inch pie plate with cheese slices. Pour in heavy cream. Slip eggs side by side. Sprinkle with salt and pepper. Dash paprika. Bake at 425° for 15 minutes or until eggs are done as you like. Serve on toast or rice.

Eggs Somerset

Serves 4

4 English muffins, split and toasted
1½ cups shredded Swiss cheese
2 tablespoons butter
2 tablespoons chopped green onions and tops,
2 tablespoons flour
½ teaspoon salt

Dash nutmeg
1 cup half and half
1 (6 ounce) package crabmeat
1 tablespoon dry sherry
8 eggs, poached
4 slices bacon, cooked and crumbled

Sprinkle 3 tablespoons of cheese on each muffin. Set aside. Melt butter in pan; add onions and saute. Stir in flour, salt and nutmeg. Add milk and crabmeat, stirring. Cook until thick, stir in sherry. Set aside. Poach eggs. Place on muffins. Spoon sauce mixture over each. Sprinkle with bacon. Serve.

Italian Brunch

Serves 6

½ pound Italian sweet sausage
2 tablespoons olive oil
1 cup peeled and diced potatoes
½ cup thinly sliced onion
¼ cup chopped green pepper

1 cup peeled, seeded and diced tomatoes
8 eggs
¼ cup cream
Salt and pepper

Saute sausage in olive oil until no longer pink. Add potatoes, onion, green pepper and cook, stirring occasionally until potatoes are brown and onion and green pepper are limp. Add tomatoes and cook 1 minute. Lightly beat eggs, cream, salt and pepper together. Pour into frypan with sausage and vegetable mixture. Cook, stirring until eggs are set but still moist. Serve on thick slices of toasted Italian bread. Sprinkle with oregano and grated Romano cheese.

French Toast Casserole

Serves 6

1 (10 ounce) loaf French or
Italian bread
8 large eggs
3 cups milk
4 teaspoons sugar

¾ teaspoon salt
1 tablespoon vanilla
2 tablespoons butter, cut in
small pieces

Grease a 13×9 pan. Cut bread into 1-inch thick pieces and arrange
in one layer on bottom of pan. Beat eggs with remaining
ingredients, except butter, and pour over bread in pan. Cover with
foil and refrigerate 4-36 hours. Bake, uncovered, at 350° for 45-50
minutes, or until puffy and lightly browned. Let stand 5 minutes
before serving. Top with hot maple syrup and serve with bacon or
sausage.

Egg and Sausage Casserole

Serves 8 to 10

1½ pounds lightly seasoned
bulk sausage
9 eggs
3 cups milk
1½ teaspoons salt
1½ teaspoons dry mustard

Pepper to taste
12 slices bread, cubed, crusts
removed
1½ cups grated sharp Cheddar
cheese

Brown and drain sausage. Let cool. Meanwhile beat egg with milk.
Add mustard, salt and pepper. Mix in cubed bread and cheese. Add
cooled sausage. Pour into 13×9 baking dish. Refrigerate, covered,
overnight. Remove from refrigerator ½ hour before baking. Sprinkle
with paprika. Bake at 350° for 45 minutes. Let stand 10-15 minutes
before cutting.

Crabmeat Quiche

Serves 6 to 8

½ cup mayonnaise
2 teaspoons flour
2 eggs, beaten
⅓ cup chopped onion
½ cup milk

1 (8 ounce) package frozen
   crabmeat, drained
8 ounces Swiss cheese, grated
9-inch pie crust

Combine mayonnaise, flour, eggs, onion and milk. Stir in crabmeat and cheese. Pour into crust. Bake at 350° for 40-45 minutes. For 10-inch pie, double recipe with the exception of onion. Pie can be made day before. Reheat for 25-30 minutes.

Florentine Rice Quiche

Serves 6 to 8

4 eggs
2 cups cooked rice
⅔ cup grated Swiss cheese
1 (10 ounce) package frozen
   chopped spinach
2 tablespoons butter or
   margarine

½ teaspoon salt
½ pint cottage cheese
¼ cup grated Parmesan cheese
6 tablespoons heavy cream or
   evaporated milk
3 drops hot pepper sauce
¼ teaspoon nutmeg

Grease a 9-inch pie pan. In medium bowl beat one egg. Add rice and Swiss cheese. Stir well. Spread rice mixture evenly in prepared pie pan, making a crust. Refrigerate until ready to fill and bake. Cook spinach as directed on package. Pour into strainer and press out all liquid. Add butter to drained spinach. Set aside. In medium bowl beat remaining 3 eggs, stir in salt, cottage cheese, Parmesan cheese, heavy cream, hot pepper sauce and nutmeg. When well blended stir in spinach. Pour filling into prepared pie crust. Bake at 350° for 30-35 minutes or until firm. To serve, cut into wedges. Crust and filling can be made separately a day ahead. Pour filling into crust about 35 minutes before serving time and bake.

Salmon Quiche

Serves 6

1 cup whole wheat flour
⅔ cup shredded sharp Cheddar
  cheese
¼ cup chopped almonds
½ teaspoon salt
¼ teaspoon paprika
6 tablespoons cooking oil
1 (15½ ounce) can salmon

3 eggs, beaten
1 cup sour cream
¼ cup mayonnaise
½ cup shredded sharp Cheddar
  cheese
1 tablespoon grated onion
¼ teaspoon dried dillweed
3 drops bottled hot pepper sauce

For crust, combine flour, ⅔ cup cheese, almonds, salt and paprika in bowl. Stir in oil. Set aside ½ cup of crust mixture. Press remaining mixture into bottom and up the sides of a 9-inch pie plate. Bake crust at 400° for 10 minutes. Remove from oven. Reduce oven temperature to 325°. Meanwhile, for filling, drain salmon, reserving liquid. Add water to reserved liquid to make ½ cup. Flake salmon, removing bones and skin, set aside. In a bowl, blend together eggs, sour cream, mayonnaise or salad dressing and reserved salmon liquid. Stir in salmon, remaining cheese, onion, dillweed and hot pepper sauce. Spoon filling into crust. Sprinkle with reserved crust mixture. Bake at 325° for 45 minutes or until firm in center.

Mark Twain built two homes in Connecticut. Stormfield in Redding, burned in 1925. Nook Farm, beautifully preserved, in Hartford is open to visitors.

Spinach-Cheese-Mushroom Quiche

Serves 6

Custard:
3 eggs
½ pint heavy cream
¾ cup milk

¼ teaspoon salt
Pinch cayenne, pepper and
　nutmeg

Combine all ingredients.

Filling:
9-inch deep dish pie shell
1 (10 ounce) package frozen
　chopped spinach, cooked,
　well drained
¼ teaspoon salt
⅛ teaspoon pepper

1 teaspoon horseradish
4 tablespoons sour cream
3 tablespoons grated Parmesan
　cheese
½ cup chopped Swiss cheese
6 thinly sliced mushrooms

Partially bake pie shell for 7-10 minutes. Add cooked spinach, salt,
pepper, horseradish and sour cream. Spread mixture in pie shell.
Sprinkle with cheeses and place mushrooms on top. Cover with
custard filling. Bake at 375° about 40 minutes or until set, puffed
and golden brown. Best when baked several hours ahead and
reheated.

*On February 8, 1794, the oldest printed American insurance policy was drawn up by
the firm of Sanford and Wadsworth of Hartford.*

Three Cheese Ham Puff

Serves 6

6 eggs
¾ cup prepared biscuit mix
1 cup milk
8 ounces creamed cottage
   cheese
8 ounces Monterey Jack cheese,
   cut into ¼-inch cubes

1 (3 ounce) package cream
   cheese, cut into cubes
1 slice baked Virginia ham,
   ½-inch thick, cubed
¼ teaspoon salt

Heat oven to 350°. Lightly grease a 2-quart casserole. Beat eggs.
Add biscuit mix and milk; beat until smooth. Stir in remaining
ingredients, pour into casserole. Bake at 350° for 50-55 minutes or
until knife inserted in center comes out clean. Let stand 10 minutes
before serving. Mushrooms are delicious when added to this recipe.
You may also omit ham for a vegetable such as broccoli.

Luncheon-In-One-Dish

Serves 4 to 6
Good for ladies bridge luncheon

2 cups instant rice
1½ cups milk
½ teaspoon salt
¼ teaspoon pepper
1¼ cups grated Swiss cheese

¼ cup grated Parmesan cheese
1 (10½ ounce) can asparagus
   spears, drained
½ to 1 pound cooked ham, cut
   in strips

Combine rice, milk, salt and pepper and bring to a boil. Add ½ cup
Swiss cheese and the Parmesan cheese. Cook until mixture
thickens. Pour into buttered 9-inch pie plate. Arrange asparagus on
top, with tips pointing toward center. Place strips of ham between.
Sprinkle with remaining Swiss cheese. Cover and bake at 350° for
15 minutes. Remove cover and bake until brown, an additional 15
minutes.

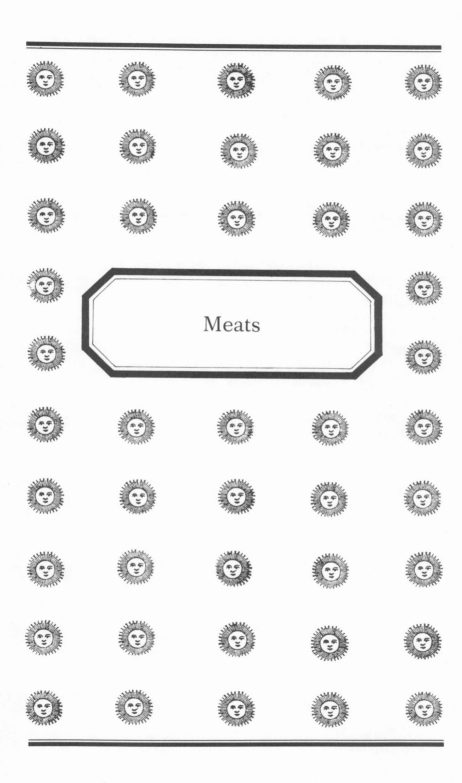

Meats

Fillet of Beef with Foie Gras

Serves 6

1 (4 pound) whole fillet of beef, fat removed	1 (3 ounce) can foie gras

Roast fillet at 450° for 25 minutes for medium rare. Remove from oven and slice almost through until you have eight slices. Spread a liberal amount of foie gras between the slices; press them back together and place under broiler for a few minutes until top of meat is browned and bubbly. Serve with Béarnaise sauce.

Bearnaise Sause

Makes ⅓ Cup

1½ teaspoons tarragon vinegar	¼ teaspoon salt
1½ teaspoons water	Dash paprika
3 thin onions, sliced	2 tablespoons butter, melted
2 egg yolks	

In small saucepan heat vinegar, water and onion to boiling. Remove onion. In double boiler with wire whisk beat egg yolks, salt and paprika. Rapidly beat in vinegar mixture. Cook over hot water, beating constantly until mixture thickens slightly. Add butter gradually, beating until mixture is thick.

Sesame Steak

Serves 8
Prepare early in the day

⅓ cup sesame seed
½ cup salad oil
4 medium onions, thinly sliced
½ cup soy sauce
¼ cup lemon juice
1 tablespoon sugar

¼ teaspoon cracked pepper
2 garlic cloves, crushed
1 (2-3 pounds) boneless beef top
   sirloin steak, cut 1½ inches
   thick
Parsley sprigs for garnish

For marinade: Cook sesame seed in hot oil until golden, stirring
frequently. In 13×9 baking dish, mix sesame seed-oil mixture,
onions, soy sauce, lemon juice, sugar, pepper and garlic. Trim
excess fat from steak; place in marinade, turning to coat both sides.
Cover and refrigerate at least 4 hours, turning steak occasionally.
Preheat broiler. Broil 20-25 minutes for rare. Brush steak often with
marinade; turn steak once; stir onion to prevent burning. To serve,
arrange steak and onions on large heated platter. Garnish with
parsley sprigs.

Beef in Red Wine

Serves 6 to 8

2 pounds beef, cut into cubes
¼ cup flour
1½ teaspoons salt
Pinch pepper
Pinch ground cloves
2 tablespoons oil
2 garlic cloves
½ pound small white onions
2 carrots, cut in chunks

1 pound potatoes, cut up
½ pound turnips, cut in chunks
2 cups dry red wine
Beef broth to cover
1 bay leaf
½ teaspoon thyme
Chopped parsley
½ pound mushrooms
½ pound green beans

Shake beef in seasoned floured bag and brown in oil. Add garlic,
onions and carrots until glazed. Add remaining ingredients except
mushrooms and beans and bake at 350° for 1½ hours. Saute
mushrooms and add to mixture, along with green beans. Bake
additional 30 minutes until meat is tender.

Steak Pizzaiola

Serves 4

¼ cup olive oil
1½ cups canned plum tomatoes, mashed
2 pounds London Broil, cut in ¾ inch strips
2 teaspoons salt

½ teaspoon pepper
½ teaspoon parsley
½ teaspoon onion flakes
⅛ teaspoon garlic powder
½ teaspoon oregano
Grated Parmesan cheese

Place ingredients in large saucepan; bring to boiling. Lower heat and simmer, covered 1½ to 2 hours, stirring occasionally until meat is tender. Serve with spaghetti and Italian bread.

"How About Some Chinese Tonight"

Serves 4
It's quick, easy different

1 pound chuck steak, steak ends, flank steak or whatever
4 tablespoons oil (or ladle of chicken soup)
1 tablespoon garlic powder (or half garlic clove)
1 teaspoon salt
½ teaspoon pepper
½ teaspoon sugar

1 can bean sprouts (or enough to satisfy)
1 large green pepper
2 medium onions
Soy sauce, to taste
3 tablespoons corn starch
¼ cup cold water
Rice

If it's a busy day, in the morning slice steak, cut up onions and pepper into polyethylene bag; pop into refrigerator. When ready to cook, put steak, onions, pepper with cooking oil (or soup) into hot wok (or deep frying pan). Add garlic, salt, pepper, sugar, sprouts and soy sauce. Cook until it looks and smells good (sneak some tastees). You can cook the whole recipe at once or divide into portions and cook individually (if somebodies gonna be late). In small bottle shake cornstarch and water together. Add to main portion and cook until sauce thickens. Serve piping hot over boiled rice.

Win Elliot, Sports Commentator

Teriyaki Steak

Serves 4
A tangy change for summer barbecues

1 can beef consomme
⅓ cup soy sauce
1½ teaspoons seasoning salt
½ teaspoon shredded green
   onion

1 tablespoon Worcestershire
   sauce
1 teaspoon garlic salt
3 tablespoons lime juice
3 tablespoons light brown sugar
1 medium sized flank steak

One to two days before serving, marinate steak in mixture of the above ingredients. Keep steak covered in refrigerator, turning it once or twice each day. Grill over hot charcoal or broil in oven. Baste with remaining marinade.

Beef Birds

Serves 6

8-9 slices round steak, ¼-inch
   thick, 4-5 inches in size
5 slices soft bread, grated fine
2 stalks celery, chopped
1 small onion, chopped
½ teaspoon dried thyme

½ cup cold water, as needed to
   moisten bread
¼ teaspoon salt
Dash of pepper
¾ cup red wine
2 teaspoons bouillon powder
3 tablespoons corn oil

Pound meat to tenderize. Combine bread, celery and onion. Add thyme, salt, pepper and water, using only enough water to moisten mixture well. Place a large spoonful of mixture on each piece of meat and roll meat jelly roll fashion. Secure with wooden pick. In dutch oven, brown the rolled "birds" in oil on all sides. Add wine. Simmer 10 minutes over medium heat. Add bouillon. Reduce to low heat. Simmer 45 minutes to 1 hour. Check every 15 minutes. If the wine sauce cooks down, add a little hot water (about ⅓ cup). Birds can be made with veal or pork. Use white wine for these meats.

Rudy J. Favretti, Author
"For Every House A Garden"

Beef Rollauden

Serves 10 to 12
Can be prepared 1-2 days ahead

12 (¼-inch thick) top or bottom
   round beef slices
Salt and pepper, to taste
Prepared mustard
2 large onions, chopped
2 tablespoons chopped fresh
   parsley

¾ pound raw bacon, chopped
1 cup chopped bread and butter
   pickles
1 carrot, cut in chunks
1 medium onion, chopped
3 tablespoons flour

Pound each slice of beef to tenderize. Add salt and pepper. Spread
each slice of beef with prepared mustard, covering entire slice. Put
1-2 tablespoons onion, parsley and bacon mixture on each slice of
beef. Roll slice in jelly roll fashion and tie with cord. Brown beef
quickly in butter over medium heat. Add carrot and onion to pan.
Sprinkle 2-3 tablespoons flour over the roll-ups and add enough
water to cover the meat. Cover pan and let simmer 1 to 1½ hours.
Remove carrot from pan. Add 1 tablespoon flour to thicken gravy in
pan. Stir well over low heat until desired consistency. Serve with
whole noodles.

Boeuf Eau de Vie

Serves 8

¼ cup flour
1 teaspoon salt
1 teaspoon garlic salt
½ teaspoon freshly ground
   pepper
1 (5 pound) chuck roast

4 tablespoons butter
¼ cup brandy
1 large Bermuda onion, sliced
1 (10½ ounce) can beef broth
1 large bay leaf

Blend flour, salts and pepper; dredge beef with mixture, rubbing in
well. Melt butter in casserole; add meat and brown well on all sides.
Remove from heat. Pour warm brandy over roast and ignite. When
flames die out, spread onion over meat, pour beef broth over all and
add bay leaf. Bake, covered at 250° for 4 hours or until very tender.

German Pot Roast

Serves 8
Good "top of the stove" dinner

1 (5 pound) beef pot roast
2 tablespoons shortening
5 large onions, chopped
3 large molasses cookies,
    crumbled

2 tablespoons sugar
4 tablespoons vinegar
1 bay leaf
2 tablespoons salt

In large skillet, sear roast on all sides in hot fat. Add onions. Cook for 15 minutes. Mix in cookies and remaining ingredients with enough water to cover half the roast. Cover and simmer 4 hours. May add carrots and potatoes if desired.

Tritini

Serves 20
Great for a party - do ahead or freeze

4 pounds ground beef
1 cup minced onion
4 (6 ounce) cans tomato paste
4 (8 ounce) cans tomato sauce
4 teaspoons dried basil
4 teaspoons dried parsley
Salt and pepper, to taste
2 teaspoons oregano
Dash of garlic powder

4 packages frozen chopped
    spinach, thawed and well
    drained
2 pounds cottage cheese
4 (3 ounce) cans sliced
    mushrooms, drained
Dash of lemon juice
½ to 1 pound Mozzarella
    cheese, grated

Saute beef and onion in large skillet. Add next 7 ingredients to meat and simmer 10 minutes or until thick. Combine drained spinach with cottage cheese and mushrooms. Divide each mixture into five equal portions. In 13×9 baking dish arrange 3 lengthwise strips of spinach with 2 strips of meat in between. Sprinkle ½ the Mozzarella over all. Then for the second layer, reverse strips, putting 3 meat strips over the spinach strips and vice-versa. Sprinkle remaining cheese over all. Bake at 375° for 30-40 minutes uncovered.

James L. Buckley,
U.S. State Department Counselor

Sweet and Sour Tongue

Serves 6

1 beef tongue, cooked and sliced
4 ginger snaps
½ cup brown sugar
⅓ cup vinegar
1 teaspoon grated onion

1 cup hot water or tongue broth
1 lemon, thinly sliced
½ cup sliced almonds, blanched
¼ cup raisins

Crumble ginger snaps in medium sized pan. Add brown sugar, vinegar, onion and water or broth. Cook over moderate heat until smooth, stirring occasionally. Add sliced lemon, almonds and raisins with sliced tongue and simmer about 10 minutes or until thoroughly heated.

Hamburger Ring

Serves 6

1½ pounds ground beef
½ cup bread crumbs
2 eggs, beaten
⅓ cup shredded American
   cheese

3 tablespoons milk
1 tablespoon butter
Salt and pepper
Onion powder

Mix all ingredients well and set aside. Butter a ring mold. Pack in hamburger mixture and bake at 375° for 35 minutes. Let cool for ½ hour before unmolding onto serving platter. Serve with wine sauce on the side. Fluffy rice, salad, French bread and of course wine completes this easy meal.

Wine Sauce:
1 cup Hopkins Vineyard Barn
   Red or Burgundy type wine

¼ cup ketchup
1 teaspoon cornstarch

Mix all ingredients in saucepan until boiling, stirring constantly until thickened, about 3 minutes.

Judith W. Hopkins
"Hopkins Vineyard"—New Preston

Grandmother's Stew

Serves 4 to 5
Perfect when the thermometer outside begins to plunge

2 pounds stew beef, trimmed of
fat
1 (1 pound) can tomatoes
4 large carrots, cut in 1-inch
pieces
2 medium onions, quartered
2 large potatoes, cut in 1-inch
pieces

2 teaspoons salt
3 teaspoons tapioca
1 teaspoon sugar
¼ teaspoon pepper
¼ teaspoon basil
2 tablespoons chopped parsley
½ cup red wine

Place all ingredients in covered casserole. Bake at 275° for 5-6
hours. Stir 2 or 3 times while baking. Remove cover last ½ hour.

Sauerbraten

Serves 6
Serve with potatoes and sweet & sour cabbage

1 cup red wine vinegar
½ cider vinegar
½ cup burgundy
2 onions, sliced
1 carrot, sliced
1 stalk celery, chopped
Fresh parsley sprigs
1 bay leaf
2 whole allspice
4 whole cloves

1 teaspoon salt
1 teaspoon pepper
4 pounds chuck or bottom round
pot roast
⅓ cup oil
½ cup cold water
6 tablespoons flour
1 tablespoon sugar
½ cup crushed ginger snaps

Combine first 12 ingredients in covered dish. Marinate roast in
mixture, turning occasionally for 3 full days. Remove meat and
brown in oil on all sides. Add sauce mixture to roast and simmer on
stove 2½ to 3 hours. In small bowl make a paste of water, flour and
sugar. Add paste to strained broth and add crushed ginger snaps.
Simmer 20 minutes more.

Sweet and Sour Beef

Serves 8 to 10

5 pounds beef chuck, cut in 2
  inch cubes
½ cup flour
2 teaspoons salt
Pepper to taste
2 cups sliced onion
¾ cup ketchup

2 tablespoons vinegar
2 tablespoons Worcestershire
  sauce
4 tablespoons soy sauce
½ cup sugar
¾ cup water

Shake beef in mixture of flour, salt and pepper. Arrange in heavy roasting pan and cover with sliced onions. Combine rest of ingredients and pour over beef and onions. Cover tightly and bake at 325° for 3 hours. Serve with rice or noodles.

Deluxe Meat Loaf

Serves 8 to 10
Very pretty sliced—hot or cold

2 pounds lean ground beef
1 pound ground pork
1 cup seasoned bread crumbs
1 onion, chopped
½ cup Parmesan cheese
1 cup grated Swiss, Cheddar or
  Mozzarella
1 package dry onion soup mix

3 eggs, beaten
½ teaspoon oregano
½ cup chopped parsley
¼ teaspoon garlic powder
½ teaspoon pepper
½ cup 7-Up or milk
4 eggs, hard-cooked

Thoroughly mix all ingredients except hard-cooked eggs. Use more liquid if necessary to moisten. Take ½ of meat mixture and form bottom half of loaf in baking dish. Place peeled, whole eggs down the center of loaf, place remaining half of meat mixture on top and form into loaf. Bake, covered at 350° for 45 minutes. Remove cover and continue baking 45 minutes longer.

Bonia

Serves 6
Children's favorite

1 pound lean ground beef
1 pound Italian sausage, sweet
  or hot
1 frying chicken, cut up, or
  desired pieces

2 cups ketchup
½ cup chopped celery
1 medium onion, chopped
1 (6 ounce) can sliced
  mushrooms with liquid

Form ground beef into 1½ inch balls. Thoroughly brown meatballs and sausage. Drain. Place chicken in single layer in 15×10 pan. Tuck meatballs and sausage around chicken. Combine remaining ingredients, mixing well. Pour evenly over meat and chicken. Bake, covered at 350° for 1½ hours. Serve over spaghetti or noodles.

Juarez Chili

Serves 12

1 pound Chili or pinto beans
2 pounds ground beef
4 tablespoons oil
2 medium potatoes, diced
3 onions, chopped
⅓ cup rice
2 stalks celery, chopped
2 (1 pound 12 ounce) cans
  tomatoes

3 garlic cloves, chopped
2 tablespoons salt
1 teaspoon pepper
⅓ teaspoon red or cayenne
  pepper
2 tablespoons Chili powder
2 tablespoons flour
⅓ vinegar

Cook beans 2 hours. Brown meat in oil. Add potatoes, onions, rice, celery, tomatoes and garlic and cook for 1 hour. Add undrained beans, salt and pepper. Simmer one hour. Make paste of chili powder and flour. Add to meat mixture and simmer 1 hour, stirring often. Add vinegar ½ hour before serving.

Moussaka

Serves 4

1 pound ground beef
3 medium onions, chopped
1 tablespoon minced parsley
⅓ cup beer
1 tablespoon tomato paste
2 teaspoons salt

Pepper
2 medium eggplants
2 egg whites, well beaten
½ cup bread crumbs
1 cup white sauce
½ cup grated Parmesan cheese

White Sauce:
2 tablespoons flour
2 tablespoons butter

1 cup milk
Salt and pepper

Brown beef lightly in skillet. Add onion, parsley, beer, tomato paste, salt and pepper. Simmer over low heat 25 minutes, stirring occasionally. Meanwhile cut eggplant in ¼ inch slices; saute in oil. Add egg whites and bread crumbs to meat mixture and blend well. In casserole place half of eggplant slices on bottom and spread meat mixture on top. Cover with remaining eggplant. Pour cream sauce over top. Sprinkle with Parmesan cheese. Bake at 350° for 30 minutes or until well browned.

Boeuf Bourguignonne

Serves 6 to 8

8 slices bacon
2 pounds lean beef, cut into
    1-inch pieces
Flour for dredging
1 can beef broth
2 cups Burgundy wine

⅓ cup cognac
1 garlic clove, minced
1 package fresh carrots, cut into
    bite-sized pieces
1 pound mushrooms, sliced
2 onions, chopped

Fry bacon until crisp. Remove from pan and drain. In bacon drippings brown beef which has been cut and dipped in flour. Place in baking dish. In sauce pan combine beef broth, wine, cognac and garlic. Bring to a boil and pour over browned meat. Crumble bacon on top. Bake, covered, at 325° for 2½ hours. Add carrots, mushrooms and onions. Add additional broth if necessary. Bake for another hour. Serve over cooked noodles.

Stuffed Cabbage

Serves 10

1 large head cabbage
2 pounds ground beef
2 eggs, lightly beaten
½ teaspoon garlic powder
½ teaspoon onion flakes

¼ cup bread crumbs
Seasoned salt, to taste
¼ cup raw rice
1¼ pounds grape jelly
1 large bottle ketchup

Parboil cabbage and separate leaves. Mix meat and rice with eggs and seasoning. In center of each cabbage leaf, place portion of meat mixture. Fold 2 sides of leaf toward center; from narrow edge of leaf, roll up jelly-roll fashion. Dissolve jelly and ketchup in large pot. Add a little water. Add rolled cabbage leaves, seam side down and cook for 2 hours.

Sopa de Fideo

Serves 6 to 8

2 tablespoons shortening
½ pound vermicelli, broken into ¼ inch pieces
1 pound ground beef
3 garlic cloves, minced
2 medium onions, chopped
1 (2½ pound) can whole tomatoes with juice, chopped
½ cup boiling water

1 green pepper, chopped
4 celery stalks, chopped
1 cup whole kernel corn, drained
1 tablespoon salt
1 tablespoon chili powder
1 teaspoon pepper
½ sharp Cheddar cheese, sliced

In heavy skillet brown vermicelli in melted shortening. Add meat and cook, stirring occasionally. Add remaining ingredients except cheese. Add enough hot water to just cover ingredients. Reduce heat; cover and simmer 20 minutes. Place layer of cheese on top of meat mixture. Cover and cook 5 minutes until cheese melts.

Square Meal Snack

Serves 4

2 large green peppers, thinly
  sliced
½ cup thinly sliced onion
½ cup sliced mushrooms
1 tablespoon butter
1 tablespoon olive oil
½ teaspoon ground cumin
Salt and pepper
2 teaspoons mustard

2 tablespoons mayonnaise
½ teaspoon horseradish
4 thick slices toasted whole
  wheat
1 pound cold sliced roast beef or
  baked ham
4 tomato slices
1 cup grated cheese of your
  choice

Saute peppers, onions and mushrooms in melted butter and olive
oil. Add cumin and salt and pepper to taste. Combine mustard,
mayonnaise and horseradish and spread on toasted bread. Place
bread in baking dish and spread with pepper mixture. Add meat and
tomato slice. Top with grated cheese. Place under broiler until
bubbly, brown and melted.

Veal Vermouth

Serves 4
Can be made ahead of time

1½ pounds veal cut into 1-inch
  pieces
Salt and pepper, to taste
Parmesan cheese
Butter or margarine
2 large onions, chopped

4-5 carrots, sliced not too thin
1 cup sliced mushrooms
3 chicken bouillon cubes
1½ cups boiling water
½ cup vermouth or white wine

Combine salt, pepper and Parmesan cheese in plastic bag. Add
several pieces of veal and shake to coat. Repeat until all veal is
coated. Brown veal in butter in heavy skillet and place in 3-quart
casserole. Saute onion, carrots and mushrooms in skillet. Add more
butter if necessary. Meanwhile, dissolve bouillon cubes in water.
Add wine and pour over semi-cooked vegetables. The pour mixture
over veal. Refrigerate casserole until ready to bake. Bake at 325° for
one hour. Juice is excellent over noodles, rice or mashed potatoes.

Veal Scaloppine Française

Serves 6

2 pounds veal, pounded very
   thin
4 ounces flour
Salt and pepper
3 eggs, beaten, diluted with 1-2
   tablespoons water

1 cup butter
¼ cup white wine
Juice of 1 lemon
2 tablespoons chopped parsley
Sliced lemon and chopped
   parsley for garnish

Dredge veal in mixture of flour, salt and pepper. Coat with beaten egg. Place in large heated skillet with ¾ cup of butter. Saute until golden brown on both sides over medium heat. Transfer veal to serving platter. Raise heat under skillet and add wine. Bring to boiling; reduce liquid by ¼. Add lemon juice, parsley and remaining butter. Simmer one minute. Strain over veal. Garnish with lemon and parsley.

Veal Birds Marguerite (Swiss)

Serves 4

¼ pound mushrooms, finely
   chopped
1 small onion, finely chopped
6 tablespoons butter
Salt and pepper, to taste
4 tablespoons bread crumbs
¼ pound sliced ham

1 pound veal cutlets, thinly
   sliced
Flour
1 cup veal or chicken stock
¼ cup dry sherry
2 tablespoons unsalted butter
2 tablespoons chopped parsley

Saute mushrooms and onions in 2 tablespoons butter for 5 minutes. Add salt, pepper and bread crumbs. Place ham over veal and spread mushroom mixture over each piece of ham. Roll and tie with a piece of heavy thread. Brush the "birds" lightly with flour. Lightly brown "birds" in butter. Transfer to covered casserole. Pour stock and sherry over "birds". Bake at 375° for 45-60 minutes. Transfer "birds" to warm serving platter. Reduce pan juices by half. Swirl in 2 tablespoons butter. Strain over veal. Sprinkle with parsley.

Veal Haight Chardonnay

Serves 3 to 4

1½ pounds veal steak, cut ½
   inch thick, into 2-inch pieces
½ pound mushrooms, thinly
   sliced
Snipped parsley

2 cups Haight Chardonnay
Salt and pepper
Flour
¼ cup butter
1 tablespoon lemon juice

Marinate veal, mushrooms and parsley in Chardonnay for one hour.
Remove veal. Pat dry and sprinkle with salt, pepper and flour.
Reserve marinade. Saute veal in hot butter in skillet over very hot
flame until golden brown on both sides. Do not overcook. Add
marinade and lemon juice and simmer until veal is tender. Remove
veal. Reduce marinade by 70 percent, just enough to use over veal.
Serve piping hot.

Sherman P. Haight, Jr.
"Haight Vineyard," Litchfield

Veal and Peppers

Serves 4
Ideal for the diet-conscious

4 medium green peppers
2 tablespoons vegetable oil
1 medium onion, sliced
1 pound veal, cut into 1-inch
   pieces

2 cups canned tomatoes
1 teaspoon salt
Few grains pepper
⅓ cup white wine

Wash, stem and seed green peppers. Cut each into six sections.
Heat 1 tablespoon oil in skillet. Add onion and green pepper and
cook over low heat until tender, stirring occasionally. Remove and
set aside. Add remaining oil to skillet. Add veal and cook until
lightly browned, stirring occasionally. Add tomatoes, salt and pepper
and cook over low heat for 30 minutes. Add green pepper, onion
and wine. Cover and cook 30 minutes. Serve with rice.

Veal Marsala

Serves 8
Delicious with Fettucini Alfredo

2 pounds veal cutlets, pounded
  thin, lightly dredged in flour
¼ cup butter
⅓ cup chicken broth
⅓ cup Marsala wine

1 (4 ounce) can sliced
  mushrooms
1 teaspoon lemon juice
Flour

 Saute cutlets in butter over medium-high heat 2-3 minutes per
side. Remove to platter and keep warm. After all cutlets are cooked
add chicken broth and wine to pan juices. Add mushrooms, lemon
juice and just enough flour to thicken. Bring to boiling for 1
minute. Pour sauce over cutlets and serve. Turkey cutlets may be
substituted. They're less expensive and delicious.

Osso Buco

Serves 4

2 whole veal shanks
3 tablespoons butter
3 tablespoons olive oil
¼ cup chopped celery
1 medium carrot, chopped

1 medium onion, chopped
1 teaspoon chopped parsley
2 tablespoons tomato paste
1 cup dry sherry
Salt and pepper

Have veal shanks sawed into 3 inch pieces. Melt butter and add oil
in deep saucepan. Brown veal well on all sides (about ten minutes).
Add chopped vegetables. Cover and simmer until carrots are soft,
about 15 minutes. Gradually add sherry into which tomato paste has
been well blended; season. Cover and simmer over low heat about
40 minutes. Stir occasionally to prevent burning or sticking, adding
small amount of water if necessary. Serve with rice.

Cheese Filled Veal Cutlets

Serves 4

8 thin veal cutlets
¼ teaspoon salt
5 tablespoons flour
3 tablespoons butter or
 margarine
1 (8 ounce) package Mozzarella
 cheese, thinly sliced

½ pound fresh mushrooms,
 thinly sliced
⅛ teaspoon pepper
½ cup water
½ cup milk
¼ cup dry white wine
1 beef bouillon cube
Parsley for garnish

Pound veal to approximately ⅛-inch between two pieces of wax
paper. Mix salt with flour. Coat cutlets with flour mixture. In
12-inch skillet over medium heat melt butter. Add cutlets, a few at a
time, and cook until lightly browned on both sides. Remove veal
from skillet. Arrange cheese slices on top of 4 cutlets. Top with
remaining cutlets. Secure with toothpicks and set aside. In
remaining pan drippings melt 2 more tablespoons of butter. Add
mushrooms and cook until tender, stirring occasionally. To
mushroom mixture stir in pepper and 1 tablespoon flour until well
blended. Gradually stir in water, milk, wine and bouillon. Heat to
boiling, stirring to loosen brown bits from bottom of skillet. Return
cutlets to skillet. Heat to boiling. Reduce heat to low. Cover and
simmer 5 minutes or until cheese is melted. Remove toothpicks.
Place cutlets and sauce on large platter. Garnish with parsley.

Real Easy Pork Chops

Serves 6 to 8

6-8 pork chops, 1½-inch thick
6-8 slices Swiss or Provolone
 cheese

1 cup sour cream
Salt and pepper, to taste
Pinch chopped parsley

Grease 13×13 baking dish. Place pork chops in bottom of dish. On
each pork chop place a piece of cheese. Spoon 2 tablespoons of sour
cream on top of each slice of cheese. Sprinkle with salt, pepper and
parsley. Cover with foil and bake ½ hour at 350°. Uncover and bake
at 325° for 1 hour until cheese and sour cream brown and meat is
fork tender.

Roast Pork with Roasted Potatoes

The Governor's Favorite

Center cut pork roast, boned and rolled. Cover roast with pepper and sage. The last 45 minutes of cooking spread applesauce over roast. This gives it a nice, crusty coating.

Governor and Mrs. William A. O'Neill

Corn Dressing for Roast Pork

Serves 6

3 cups bread crumbs, cubed
2 eggs
¾ cup diced green pepper
¾ cup diced onion

Salt and pepper, to taste
Poultry seasoning, to taste
½ cup chopped celery
1 (1 pound) can creamed corn

Mix all ingredients except creamed corn in large bowl. Corn is added just before placing casserole in oven. Pour 2 tablespoons of pork drippings into bottom of 2-quart casserole. Add creamed corn to dressing mix and place in casserole. Add 2-3 more tablespoons of pork drippings over dressing. Bake at 350° for 30-35 minutes or until golden brown and crispy on top. Serve with roast.

Dijon Pork Chops

Serves 2

2 tablespoons butter
2 thick pork chops
1 onion, thinly sliced
1 stalk celery, thinly sliced

½ cup white wine
½ cup water
2 tablespoons Dijon mustard

Melt butter in skillet and brown pork chops. Transfer to braising pan. In skillet, saute onion and celery. Add wine and water, bring to a boil. Pour over chops. Season with salt. Cover pan and braise at 300° for 1½ hours. Remove chops to a warm platter. Add mustard to sauce in pan; simmer a few minutes and pour over chops.

Gourmet Pork Chops

Serves 4

4 slices Swiss cheese, diced
¼ cup chopped fresh parsley
½ cup chopped fresh
   mushrooms
4 thick loin pork chops

3 tablespoons shortening
1 egg, slightly beaten
½ cup bread crumbs
½ cup Chablis

Combine cheese, parsley and mushrooms. Slit each pork chop for a pocket. Fill with cheese mixture. Melt shortening in skillet. Dip pork chops into egg and then into bread crumbs. Brown chops in melted shortening. Add Chablis. Reduce heat to simmer. Cover and cook 45 minutes or until chops are tender. Remove to hot platter. Season sauce with salt to taste. Pour over chops. Garnish with parsley sprigs.

Glazed Ham Loaf

Serves 6

1 pound ground cooked ham
1 pound ground fresh pork
½ cup crushed corn flakes
1 egg, beaten
2 tablespoons chili sauce
2 tablespoons evaporated milk
½ teaspoon prepared mustard
2 tablespoons chopped green
   pepper

¼ cup chopped celery
¼ cup onion
2 tablespoons vegetable oil
½ cup firmly packed brown
   sugar
2 teaspoons prepared mustard
¼ teaspoon ground cloves
Pineapple slices (optional)
Maraschino cherries (optional)

Combine meat, corn flakes, egg, chili sauce, milk and mustard. Mix well. Saute pepper, celery and onion in oil until tender. Stir into meat mixture. Combine sugar, mustard and cloves; mix well. Spread sugar mixture in a greased 9×5 loaf pan; top with pineapple and cherries, if desired. Pack meat mixture into loaf pan. Bake at 350° for 1½ hours. Remove from pan before slicing.

Pork Chops Luxembourg

Serves 6

½ pound bacon
1 (15 ounce) jar applesauce
2 pounds sauerkraut, drained
1 tablespoon brown sugar
½ teaspoon mustard
4 ounces dry white wine

½ teaspoon black pepper
Pinch thyme
Pinch oregano
6 loin pork chops, 1-inch thick
¼ teaspoon paprika
1 ounce cognac

Cut bacon into small pieces and fry until crisp. Mix with applesauce, sauerkraut, sugar, mustard, wine, pepper, thyme and oregano. Place in shallow 12×24 inch casserole dish. Saute chops until light brown on both sides. Place on top of mixture in casserole and sprinkle with paprika. Cover and bake at 300° for 90 minutes. Add cognac and simmer another 5 minutes.

Ham and Egg Bake

Serves 4 to 5
A perfect way to use leftovers

¼ cup chopped onion
¼ cup chopped green pepper
2 tablespoons butter
3 tablespoons flour
1 (10½ ounce) can chicken and
   rice soup

1 cup milk
2 hard-cooked eggs, sliced
2 cups cubed, cooked ham
1 package refrigerated biscuits

Cook onion and pepper in butter until tender. Stir in flour; add soup and milk. Cook and stir until thickened and bubbly. Set aside a few egg slices for garnish; mix remaining egg and ham into soup mixture. Bring to boiling. Pour into a 10×6 baking dish, arrange biscuit halves around outer edge of casserole on top of mixture and top center with reserved egg slices. Bake at 450° for 10-12 minutes or until biscuits are golden.

Basque Skillet Dinner

Serves 6
Retains flavor for reheating

2 pounds Italian sweet sausage
1 cup chopped onion
1 cup chopped green pepper
4 medium potatoes, diced
2 (1 pound) cans tomatoes

1¼ cups water
2 teaspoons lemon juice
1 or 2 beef bouillon cubes
½ teaspoon thyme
Salt and pepper

Cut sausage into bite-sized pieces and brown in skillet. Add onions and peppers and cook until tender. Add remaining ingredients. Cover and simmer 30-45 minutes.

Italian Sausage and Mushrooms

Serves 6
Dish most requested by UConn Basketball players

2 tablespoons olive oil
2 pounds Italian sweet sausage
1 pound fresh mushrooms,
   sliced

1 (6 ounce) can tomato paste
¼ cup water

Place olive oil in heavy pan. Remove sausage from casings; break into small pieces and add to oil. Simmer over medium-low heat until sausage is well done. Remove sausage from pan using a slotted spoon. Add mushrooms to the remaining liquid in pan and simmer until tender. Return sausage to pan and mix well with mushrooms. Combine tomato paste with water and add to mixture, stirring until well blended. Simmer 10 minutes and serve with Italian bread. (Note: 4 small sliced frying peppers may be added, cooked along with sausage).

Butterflied Leg of Lamb with Zinfandel Sauce

Serves 8
A change of pace from the usual grilled meat

1 leg of lamb, butterflied

Marinade:
½ cup soy sauce   1 tablespoon thyme
½ cup olive oil   1 teaspoon rosemary
½ cup sesame oil   1 teaspoon dry mustard
½ cup parsley leaves   ½ teaspoon mace
2 garlic cloves, mashed   ½ teaspoon oregano

Combine ingredients in blender and use as marinade. Reserve ½
cup for Zinfandel sauce.

Zinfandel Sauce:

Add 1 cup Zinfandel wine to sauce. Simmer gently. Pass as sauce
with lamb.
Grill lamb on charcoal or gas grill to desired doneness.

Lamb Paprikash

Serves 6

2 pounds lean lamb, cut into 1   1 cup chopped onion
  inch pieces   2 teaspoons salt
1 garlic clove, minced   1-2 teaspoons paprika
2 tablespoons oil   3 tablespoons flour
1 (16 ounce) can tomatoes,   ½ cup cold water
  chopped   1 cup sour cream

Brown lamb and garlic in oil. Stir in tomatoes, onion, salt and
paprika. Cover and bring to boiling. Reduce heat and simmer for 1
to 1½ hours or until meat is tender. Combine flour and cold water;
stir into stew. Cook and stir until mixture thickens and bubbles. Stir
½ cup of the hot gravy into sour cream. Return to stew. Heat
through but do not boil. Serve over hot, cooked noodles. Sprinkle
with parsley.

Connecticut Lamb Stew

Serves 4

½ cup diced slab bacon
3 pounds of lamb, cut into cubes
¼ cup flour
1 tablespoon sugar
1 teaspoon salt
¼ teaspoon pepper
¼ cup chopped shallots or green onions
2 garlic cloves, minced
1 (28 ounce) can whole tomatoes
2 cans condensed beef broth

1 teaspoon rosemary, crumbled
½ teaspoon thyme, crumbled
2 tablespoons butter
12 small white onions
4 medium turnips, pared and quartered
3 medium potatoes, pared and sliced
4 large carrots, chopped
1 (10 ounce) package frozen peas

Brown bacon and set aside. Combine lamb with flour, sugar, salt and pepper in large bowl; toss to coat. Brown lamb in bacon drippings. Remove pieces as they brown to Dutch oven. Pour off all but 1 tablespoon of drippings. Add shallots and garlic. Saute until tender, stir in tomatoes, beef broth, rosemary and thyme. Bring to a boil, stirring constantly. Add to lamb along with bacon. Cover and bake at 350° for 1 hour. While lamb is baking, saute onions, turnips and potatoes in butter for about 10 minutes. Add glazed vegetables and carrots to lamb, pushing them under the liquid. Cover and bake an additional 30 minutes. Stir in peas. Garnish with chopped parsley.

Braised Lamb Chops with Zucchini

Serves 4

4 shoulder lamb chops
½ teaspoon rosemary or thyme
Salt and pepper

2 cups hot water
¾ cup rice
2 medium zucchini, sliced thick

Brown chops lightly. Season with rosemary, salt and pepper. Push chops to one side in skillet. Add water; stir in rice. Cover and simmer 10 minutes. Push rice aside. Add zucchini; season with salt and pepper. Cover and simmer until zucchini is tender, about 10 minutes. Add more water to rice if needed.

Leg of Lamb with White Beans

Serves 10

1 pound dried navy beans	3 teaspoons salt
6 cups cold water	¼ teaspoon pepper
¼ cup butter	2 (1 pound) cans Italian plum
3 garlic cloves	tomatoes, drained
2 pounds onion, thinly sliced	1 (7 pound) leg of lamb
1 teaspoon dried rosemary leaves	Chopped parsley
1 teaspoon dried thyme leaves	

Wash and drain beans. In Dutch oven combine beans with cold water; bring to boiling. Reduce heat and simmer 2 minutes. Cover; remove from heat, let stand 1 hour. Drain beans, reserving liquid. Add water to make 2 quarts. Return beans and liquid to Dutch oven; bring to boiling. Reduce heat and simmer gently, covered, for 1 hour or until beans are tender but not mushy. Drain beans in colander. In hot butter in large skillet saute 1 crushed garlic clove and onion until golden. In shallow roasting pan combine beans, onion mixture, ½ teaspoon rosemary and thyme, 2 teaspoons salt, pepper and tomatoes. Mix well. Trim fat off lamb. Make 6 small slits in meat and insert slivers of 2 garlic cloves. Sprinkle lamb with remaining rosemary, thyme and salt. Place lamb on top of bean mixture. Roast, uncovered, 3 to 3½ hours. Let roast stand 20 minutes before carving. Serve sliced lamb with beans, sprinkled with parsley.

In Hartford, Sam Colt engineered "the gun that tamed the West."

Sweet-Sour Ragout of Lamb with Figs

Serves 4

2½ pounds boneless lamb,
   trimmed and cut into 1-inch
   cubes
2 garlic cloves, minced
¼ cup cider vinegar
¼ teaspoon ground cinnamon
¼ teaspoon ground ginger
⅛ teaspoon ground red pepper
3 tablespoons vegetable oil
3 medium onions, sliced

½ cup slivered almonds
½ cup chicken stock
½ cup beef stock
Salt and pepper
10 dried figs, cut into eighths
1 tablespoon dark brown sugar
½ cup raisins
Pulp of 2 large lemons, seeded
   and chopped

Combine lamb, garlic, vinegar, cinnamon, ginger and red pepper in bowl. Cover and let marinate in refrigerator 8-24 hours. Transfer lamb to colander using slotted spoon. Drain well. Heat oil in heavy skillet over high heat. Add onion and cook, stirring frequently until deep golden brown. Push onion to side of pan. Add lamb and almonds, tossing until lamb is seared. Reduce heat to low. Add chicken stock, beef stock and any remaining marinade. Season with salt and pepper. Cover and simmer until lamb is almost tender, about 1¼ hours. Add figs and sugar. Cover and cook until lamb is tender, 15-30 minutes. Increase heat to high. Uncover. Stir in raisins and lemon pulp. Boil until sauce is carmelized and lamb is glazed, about 12 minutes. Adjust seasoning, adding more vinegar if desired.

The Mystic Seaport is a forty acre site devoted to the celebration of Connecticut's Seafaring legacy. Coopers and sailmakers practice their crafts in period buildings and vessels such as the Charles W. Morgan; one of the last of the great American wooden whalers.

Crown Roast of Lamb

Serves 6 to 8

1 (4-6 pound) crown roast of   Pepper
    lamb (12-16 ribs)

Place roast, rib ends up in large, shallow baking dish (no need for rack). Rub ribs with pepper. Fill crown with 2 cups of stuffing. Roast, uncovered, 20-22 minutes per pound for medium rare, 25-30 minutes for well-done. Transfer to warm platter and let sit for 15-20 minutes. Put paper frills on rib ends or pitted green olives or preserved kumquats.

Pecan Bulgur Wheat Stuffing

Makes 4 Cups

1 yellow onion, peeled and
    minced
½ cup minced celery
½ pound mushrooms, minced
½ cup butter
1 cup bulgur wheat

1¾ cups chicken broth
1 teaspoon salt
1 teaspoon thyme
¼ teaspoon pepper
½ cup minced pecans

Saute onion, celery and mushrooms in butter until pale golden. Add bulgur wheat and stir fry 2-3 minutes. Add remaining ingredients except pecans, cover and simmer ½ hour or until liquid is absorbed. Mix in pecans; add salt to taste. Can be baked separately in a well-greased casserole. Bake at 350° for 20 minutes.

Poultry

Gratin Italienne

1 pound chicken, minced
2 tablespoons butter
1 medium onion, finely chopped
1 tablespoon flour
3 tablespoons sherry

½ pint chicken stock
Salt and pepper
2 pounds spinach
½ pound noodles

Melt butter. Add onion and cook until soft. Increase heat. Add chicken and stir well with wooden spoon until meat begins to brown. Blend in flour, sherry and stock. Bring to a boil. Season with salt and pepper and simmer gently for 1½ hours until tender. Blanch the spinach for 3 minutes. Drain, refresh and press between two plates to remove all excess moisture. Poach noodles until al dente. Drain and tip into large mixing bowl. Cover with lukewarm water.

Bechamel Sauce:
3 tablespoons butter
3 tablespoons flour
1½ cups milk
Salt and pepper

3 tablespoons butter
2 ounces grated cheese
   (Cheddar and Parmesan)

Prepare bechamel sauce and cover with buttered wax paper to prevent skin from forming.

Tomato Coulis:
1 (16 ounce) can Italian
   tomatoes
1 can tomato puree
1 medium onion, thinly sliced
1 tablespoon butter

1 bay leaf
½ teaspoon chopped basil
1 teaspoon arrowroot mixed with
   1 tablespoon water

Cook onion slowly in butter until soft. Add tomatoes (break up well), herbs and season with salt and pepper. Cover and simmer till pulpy and rich looking. Take off heat. Remove bay leaf and add arrowroot and water. Bring back to boiling.

(continued)

Heat 1½ tablespoons butter to brown. Add spinach and heat gently until any remaining moisture evaporates, but don't let it dry. Place half the spinach at bottom of deep, buttered gratin dish and cover with half the bechamel sauce. Drain noodles. Place in large pan with butter and toss over heat until well coated with butter and any water has evaporated. Season with pepper and turn into gratin dish. Cover with tomato coulis, then spoon in chicken mixture. Put remaining spinach over meat and cover with layer of bechamel sauce and scatter cheese over top. Bake at 350° for 30-35 minutes.

Joanne Woodward
Academy Award Winning Actress

Baked Chicken Souffle

Serves 16
Serve with hot fruit for brunch

10 slices white bread, crusts removed
8 cups diced cooked chicken
1 pound fresh mushrooms, sliced
1 cup butter
1 (8 ounce) can water chestnuts, drained and sliced
¾ cup mayonnaise
5 eggs, well beaten

2½ cups milk
1 teaspoon salt
2 cans cream of mushroom soup
2 cans cream of celery soup
12 slices processed sharp cheese
1 (2 ounce) jar pimiento, chopped
2 cups buttered coarse bread crumbs

Line large 17×11½ oblong buttered casserole dish with bread on bottom and sides. Top with diced chicken. Saute mushrooms in butter for 5 minutes. Add to water chestnuts and spoon over chicken. Dot with mayonnaise. Top with cheese slices. Combine eggs with milk and salt. Pour over chicken. Mix soups with pimiento and pour over all. Cover with foil. Store in refrigerator overnight. Bake at 350° for 1½ hours. Sprinkle on buttered bread crumbs the last 15 minutes.

Baked Chicken Croquettes

Serves 4

3 tablespoons butter
3 tablespoons flour
1 (6 ounce) can mushrooms,
   minced
Chicken broth
¼ teaspoon onion powder
Dash pepper
1 teaspoon Worcestershire sauce

½ teaspoon curry powder,
   optional
1 tablespoon parsley flakes
Salt to taste
2 cups chicken, diced
2 eggs
Crushed butter crackers

Melt butter in skillet. Blend in flour. Measure chicken broth and liquid from mushrooms to make 1 cup. Add to butter mixture. Cook, stirring occasionally until smooth and thickened. Stir in onion powder, pepper, Worcestershire sauce, curry and parsley. Salt to taste. Bring to boiling. Add mushrooms and chicken to skillet. Bring to boiling. Reduce heat and beat in eggs, one at a time. Cook, stirring for 1 minute. Spread in shallow baking dish. Chill until firm enough to handle. Shape croquettes. Coat with mixture of crushed crackers. Place on greased baking sheet. Bake at 350° for 20-30 minutes or until golden brown. Serve with chicken gravy.

Breast of Chicken Saute

Serves 12

1 cup flour
Salt and pepper
12 boneless chicken breasts, cut
   in half
1 cup butter
¾ finely chopped onion

2 cups dry white wine
4 cups chopped fresh
   mushrooms
2 cups seedless grapes
3 cups light cream
Chopped parsley

Season flour with salt and pepper. Dredge chicken in seasoned flour and saute in butter until lightly browned. Add onions and cook until tender, but not browned. Add wine and mushrooms. Cover and cook gently about 25-30 minutes or until done. Add grapes and cook 3-5 minutes longer. Remove chicken to platter. Stir cream into mushrooms mixture and reheat. Pour sauce over breasts. Sprinkle with parsley.

Bihon Guisado

Serves 6 to 8
A recipe from the Philippines

5-10 garlic cloves
½ cup vegetable oil
1 medium onion, sliced
¼ pound cabbage
1 medium carrot, sliced
1 celery stalk, sliced
2 cups diced, cooked white
    chicken meat

1 pound fresh shrimp
2 cups chicken broth
4 tablespoons soy sauce
2 teaspoons salt
3 (8 ounce) packages rice
    noodles (pre-soaked)

Saute garlic in oil until golden; add vegetables, chicken and shrimp.
Simmer 2 minutes. Add chicken broth, soy sauce and salt. Boil 5
minutes over medium high heat; add noodles, mixing with a
wooden spoon so as not to break noodles. Serve immediately.

Walnut Chicken

Serves 12
Good for cold buffet

6 chicken breasts

Chicken broth enriched with
    carrots, celery and onion

Cook chicken in broth for about 15 minutes. Let cool in broth.
Remove meat from bones and slice in finger-shaped pieces.

Walnut Mayonnaise:
1 egg
Juice of 1 lemon
1 teaspoon dry mustard
1 teaspoon salt
Pepper

¼ cup walnut oil
1¼ cup vegetable oil
¾ cup walnuts
⅓ cup chicken stock

Using steel blade, put egg, lemon juice, mustard, salt and pepper in
bowl of food processor. Combine oils and pour into running
processor until mixture emulsifies. Add walnuts and process until
finely chopped. Add chicken broth to thin to desired consistency.
Coat chicken with walnut mayonnaise and serve.

Chicken Baked in Beer and Tomatoes

Serves 8
Tastes even better if made the day ahead

2 (2½ pound) fryers	⅓ cup bacon drippings
⅓ cup flour	1 garlic clove
2 teaspoons salt	¾ cup chopped onion
Pepper	¾ cup chopped green peppers
½ teaspoon paprika	4 medium tomatoes

Dip chicken in flour seasoned with salt, pepper and paprika. Brown in bacon drippings with garlic. Transfer chicken to large greased casserole. Discard garlic. Saute onion and green pepper until tender. Sprinkle over chicken. Peel and quarter tomatoes. Arrange over chicken.

Sauce:

2 cups beer	½ teaspoon thyme
¼ cup tomato paste	1 teaspoon salt

Blend all ingredients and pour over chicken. Baked at 350° for 1½ hours. This recipe can be prepared up to the baking stage the day before, then cooked when company arrives. Good over rice.

Sweet and Sour Chicken

Serves 4 to 6

1 (8 ounce) bottle Russian dressing	1 (10 ounce) jar apricot preserves
1 envelope dry onion soup mix	4 whole chicken breasts, cut in half

Combine first 3 ingredients. Place chicken in well buttered shallow dish. Pour sauce over chicken and bake, uncovered at 350° for 1¼ hours, basting twice. Delicious served over rice or chow mein noodles. Perfect on chicken wings, or small chicken legs and serve as an appetizer.

Chicken Breasts with Lemon and Brandy

Serves 6
Impress your guests!

6 whole chicken breasts, boned
  and skinned
½ cup flour
1 teaspoon oregano
Salt and pepper

2 tablespoons lemon juice
2 tablespoons brandy
2 tablespoons parsley, finely
  chopped for garnish

Combine flour, oregano, salt and pepper in paper bag. Split breasts
and dredge in seasoned flour. Saute chicken in hot butter for 12
minutes or until white and tender. Do not overcook. Increase heat
and add lemon juice and brandy. Ignite brandy. When flames have
died, garnish with parsley and serve.

Walnut Stuffed Chicken Breasts

Serves 12

12 whole chicken breasts,
  halved, skinned and boned
4 cups Cheddar cheese
1 cup chopped walnuts
1 cup fresh bread crumbs
4 tablespoons minced onion
½ teaspoon salt
¼ teaspoon pepper

1 cup flour
6 tablespoons butter or
  margarine
2 (10½ ounce) cans cream of
  chicken soup
1 cup white wine
4 tablespoons chopped parsley

Place chicken breasts between 2 pieces of waxed paper and pound
until ¼-inch thick. In small bowl combine 2 cups shredded cheese,
walnuts, bread crumbs, onion, salt and pepper. Spoon 1½
tablespoons of filling into center of each breast. From narrow end,
roll each breast, jelly-roll style. Roll chicken in flour. Let stand 10
minutes. Melt butter in large skillet. Add chicken and saute until
lightly browned on all sides. Mix soup and wine together and pour
over chicken. Cover and cook over low heat for 15 minutes. May be
prepared in advance to this point. Cover and refrigerate up to 24
hours. Remove cover from chicken and sprinkle 2 cups grated
cheese and parsley over all. Bake at 350° for 15-20 minutes or until
bubbly.

Chicken Elizabeth

Serves 4

4 chicken breasts, cut in half
2 tablespoons butter
1 medium white onion, chopped
⅓ green pepper, chopped
3 ounces dry vermouth
1 pint sour cream

¼ cup bleu cheese
1 tablespoon lemon juice
1 teaspoon salt
Dash pepper, tarragon and
   paprika

In large skillet saute chicken in butter, turning until lightly brown. Place chicken in 1½ quart casserole skin side up. Retain juices in pan. Combine remaining ingredients with pan juices. Pour over chicken and bake, covered, at 350° for 1 hour.

Chicken Waikiki Beach

Serves 2-4

2 whole chicken breasts
½ cup flour
⅓ cup salad oil

1 teaspoon salt
¼ teaspoon pepper

Wash chicken and pat dry. Coat with flour. Heat oil in large skillet. Brown chicken on all sides. Remove to shallow roasting pan, skin side up. Sprinkle with salt and pepper.

Sauce:

1 (1 pound, 4 ounce) can sliced
   pineapple
2 tablespoons cornstarch
1 tablespoon soy sauce
1 chicken bouillon cube

1 cup sugar
¾ cup cider vinegar
¼ teaspoon ginger
1 large green pepper, cut in
   circles

Drain pineapple, pouring syrup into 2-cup measure. Add water to make 1¼ cups. In medium saucepan combine remaining ingredients except pepper. Bring to boiling, stirring constantly. Boil 2 minutes. Pour over chicken. Bake at 350° for 30 minutes. Add green pepper and pineapple. Cook 30 minutes longer.

Chicken Peruvian

Serves 4 to 6

8-12 pieces chicken
3 tablespoons butter
1 small onion, minced
4 whole cloves
½ bay leaf
½ teaspoon cumin seed
1 cup consomme
1 cup white wine

½ cup white raisins
½ cup almonds, blanched and
  shredded
½ cup heavy cream
2 egg yolks
¼ cup white wine
Salt and pepper, to taste

Brown chicken in butter. Add onion, cloves, bay leaf, cumin and consomme. Cover and simmer gently. When partially cooked, add wine, raisins and almonds. Simmer until tender. In separate bowl, blend cream, yolks and ¼ cup wine. Stir small amount of the consomme sauce into cream sauce and return to skillet. Stir until thickened. Do not boil. Add salt and pepper if necessary.

Smoked Chicken Breasts

Special Goshen quick and easy dinner for unexpected guests:

I always keep several of Ron Nodine's smoked chicken breasts on hand in case I need something elegant for a special occasion. For 4 to 6 people: cook 1 cup rice, flush with cold water, and mix with salad dressing: 1 part lemon juice to 3 or 4 parts oil, salt and freshly ground pepper to taste, 1 large garlic clove finely chopped, pinch of dry mustard, pinch of tarragon. Place in baking dish around sides. Cut up 2 or 3 chicken breasts, depending on size, and put in nest of rice. For hot weather, mix lemon juice and curry powder to taste in Hellman's mayonnaise, and cover. For cold weather, make Hollandaise to cover after dish comes out of oven. I make Hollandaise the easy way. In saucepan, melt 1 stick butter; add three scant tablespoons lemon juice, salt and white pepper to taste. Keep on low heat. Add three whole eggs and stir till thickened. This dish, served hot or cold, always gets enthusiastic comments and requests for the recipe.

Madeleine L'Engle (Mrs. Hugh Franklin)
Author "The Summer of the Great Grandmother"

Chicken Englaise

Serves 6

6 chicken breasts, skinned and boned
1 cup olive oil
½ cup sherry
1 garlic clove, crushed
1 teaspoon freshly ground pepper
Juice of 1 lemon
8 teaspoons mustard
2 tablespoons butter

Flatten chicken and marinate in oil, ¼ cup of the sherry, garlic, pepper and ½ of the lemon juice for at least 2 hours or overnight. Turn once or twice. Remove from marinade and place on baking dish. Spread mustard on both sides of chicken. Broil 8 minutes on one side, 5 minutes on the other. Remove from pan and pour off excess oil. Add remainder of sherry, juice and butter to drippings. Heat and stir 1-2 minutes. Pour over chicken. Serve with rice. May also be broiled directly on grill.

Lemon Roast Chicken

Serves 6

1 (4 pound) roasting chicken
1 tablespoon butter
1 teaspoon dried tarragon
Salt and pepper
¼ cup butter
3 tablespoons fresh lemon juice
Potatoes, peeled and halved

Wash and dry chicken. Melt butter and tarragon and put inside chicken. Season inside and out with salt and pepper. Place chicken on rack in roasting pan, breast side down. Melt butter and mix with lemon juice. Brush chicken all over with mixture. Roast at 350° for 1 hour, basting every 15 minutes. Turn chicken breast side up and continue roasting for another hour, basting chicken as before using pan juices. Potatoes can be roasted in pan with chicken.

Chicken Ratatouille

Serves 4

3 cups cooked chicken, cut up
¼ cup vegetable oil
2 small zucchini squash,
  unpared and thinly sliced
1 small eggplant, peeled and cut
  into 1-inch cubes
1 large onion, thinly sliced

1 medium green pepper, seeded
  and cut into 1-inch pieces
1 (16 ounce) can tomato wedges
1 teaspoon salt
1 teaspoon Italian herb
  seasoning

Heat oil in skillet. Add zucchini, eggplant, onion and green pepper.
Cook, stirring occasionally, about 15 minutes. Add chicken,
tomatoes, salt and seasoning. Heat through and serve.

Chicken Simon & Garfunkel

Serves 6

3 chicken breasts, boned,
  skinned and halved
½ cup butter
Salt and pepper
6 slices Mozzarella cheese
Flour
1 egg, beaten

Fresh bread crumbs
2 tablespoons parsley
¼ teaspoon sage
¼ teaspoon rosemary
¼ teaspoon thyme
½ cup dry white wine

Flatten chicken between wax paper. Spread with ½ of the butter.
Season with salt and pepper. Place 1 slice of cheese on each
chicken breast. Roll up and fasten ends with toothpicks. Coat lightly
with flour. Dip in egg and roll in bread crumbs. Arrange in baking
dish. Melt remaining butter with seasonings. Bake at 350° for 30
minutes with butter mixture, basting occasionally. Pour wine over
chicken and bake additional 20 minutes, continue basting. Serve
over rice.

Chicken Thigh Casserole

Serves 6 to 8

8-10 chicken thighs
Salt and pepper, to taste
2 tablespoons butter
½ cup dry sherry
½ cup chicken bouillon
1 package beef or
   beef/onion/mushroom dry
   soup mix

1 (8 ounce) can tomatoes,
   mashed
2 tablespoons lemon juice
½ teaspoon garlic powder
¼ teaspoon oregano
1 (4 ounce) jar mushrooms,
   sliced

Season chicken thighs with salt and pepper and saute in butter until brown. Transfer thighs to casserole dish. In saucepan mix sherry, bouillon, beef soup mix, tomatoes, lemon juice, garlic powder, oregano and mushrooms. Simmer until cooked and thickened. Pour over chicken and bake at 350° for 1 hour. Serve over rice.

Jade Chicken

Serves 6
Different and delicious

6 chicken breasts, boned,
   skinned and cubed
2 tablespoons oil
10 tablespoons brown sugar
5 tablespoons soy sauce
Garlic salt, optional

Pepper to taste
1 cup walnuts
1 tablespoon cornstarch,
   dissolved in water
1 bunch seedless grapes

In skillet brown chicken slightly in hot oil. Sprinkle with brown sugar and simmer 5 minutes. Add soy sauce, garlic salt, pepper and walnuts. Cook 5 minutes more. Remove chicken. Thicken gravy with cornstarch and water. Combine chicken and gravy. Freeze for future use or bake, covered at 325° for 1 hour. Stir a few times during baking to distribute sauce and prevent sticking. Add water if necessary. Add grapes for the last 5 minutes of baking. Serve with wild rice.

Lemon Chicken—Texas Style

Serves 4

1 (2½ pound) chicken, cut into serving pieces
2 teaspoons finely minced garlic
1 tablespoon vegetable oil
1 tablespoon finely grated lemon rind
3 tablespoons lemon juice

3 tablespoons unsalted chicken broth, or water
1 teaspoon oregano
½ teaspoon dried thyme
Freshly chopped parsley, for garnish

Rub chicken pieces with garlic. Rub oil over the inside of a baking dish large enough to hold chicken pieces in one layer. Add the chicken, skin side down. Sprinkle with lemon rind. Pour lemon juice and broth over all. Sprinkle with oregano and thyme. Bake at 400° for 20 minutes. Turn chicken pieces and continue baking another 20 minutes or till done. Sprinkle with parsley and serve.

Pot Au Feu

Serves 4 to 5
Renoir's wife served this dish which was a favorite of her husbands friends.

1 chicken, cut into pieces
3 tablespoons olive oil
2 tablespoons butter
½ cup finely chopped onion
1 (28 ounce) can tomatoes, whole or crushed
1 tablespoon fresh parsley

1 teaspoon thyme
1 bay leaf
1 garlic clove
Salt and pepper, to taste
⅓ cup sliced mushrooms
⅓ cup black olives
Jigger of brandy or wine

Brown chicken in olive oil in heavy skillet. Remove from pan. Discard oil. Put chicken back in pan with butter, onions, tomatoes and seasonings. Simmer over low heat 1 to 1½ hours. One half hour before serving add mushrooms, black olives, and brandy or wine. Delicious with crusty French bread and a salad. Serve in bowls as the broth is the best part.

Oven Fried Chicken Supreme

Serves 6

2 frying chickens, split	⅓ teaspoon pepper
½ cup flour	⅔ cup mayonnaise
2 teaspoons salt	⅓ cup tomato ketchup

Combine flour, salt and pepper in a paper bag. Add chicken and shake. Place chicken, skin side down on lightly greased sheet. Mix mayonnaise and ketchup. Pour ½ of mixture over chicken evenly. Bake at 375° for 30 minutes. Remove from oven. Turn and cover the skin side with remaining mayonnaise mixture. Return to oven for 45 additional minutes.

Stir Fry Chicken

Serves 4

1 tablespoon sherry	12 green onions or scallions
2 tablespoons cornstarch	¼ teaspoon crushed red pepper
1 pound boneless chicken breasts, cut in ½-inch pieces	½ cup roasted, unsalted peanuts
⅓ cup soy sauce	1 can sliced water chestnuts (optional)
½ cup water	1 can bamboo shoots (optional)
4 tablespoons vegetable oil	½ pound sliced fresh mushrooms (optional)
2 (⅛ inch) pieces ginger root	
2 green peppers, cut into ¾-inch slices	

In medium bowl mix sherry and 1 tablespoon cornstarch. Add chicken. Stir to coat and refrigerate 20 minutes or longer. Mix soy sauce, water and remaining cornstarch. In wok or large skillet heat 2 tablespoons oil on high heat. Add ginger root. Cook 15 seconds, stirring constantly. Add green peppers and onions. Chestnuts, bamboo shoots and mushrooms can be added at this time. Stir fry 2 minutes. Transfer to bowl. Add remaining 2 tablespoons oil to wok. When hot, add chicken and red pepper. Stir fry 2 minutes until chicken loses pink color and turns white. Add peanuts, cooked vegetables and soy sauce mixture. Bring to full boil, stirring constantly until thickened and all ingredients are coated. Discard ginger root. Serve immediately with rice.

Skillet Luau

Serves 4 to 6

1 small green pepper, cut into
  thin strips
1 large garlic clove, minced
2 teaspoons curry powder
2 tablespoons butter
1 (10½ ounce) can cream of
  chicken soup

⅓ to ½ cup water
1½ cups chicken, cooked and
  cubed
1 cup drained pineapple chunks
Cooked rice
Toasted slivered almonds

In saucepan cook green pepper, garlic and curry in butter until pepper is tender. Stir in soup, water, chicken meat and pineapple. Heat, stirring occasionally. Cook rice for 6. Pack into ring mold. Unmold on platter. Fill center with chicken mixture, garnish with slivered almonds. If chicken is cooked ahead, this recipe takes very little time.

Turkey Superior

Serves 6

1 tablespoon butter
¼ cup chopped onion
¼ cup chopped green pepper
1 (1 pound, 12 ounce) can
  tomatoes
1 cup water or broth
¼ cup cooking oil
1 teaspoon salt
1 teaspoon garlic powder

Dash of cayenne
1 cup long grain rice
1 (6 ounce) jar marinated
  artichoke hearts, lightly
  drained
2 cups diced cooked turkey
½ cup walnuts, diced
¼ cup stuffed green olives,
  sliced

Melt butter in small skillet. Add onion and green pepper. Cook slowly until soft. In large saucepan combine the above with tomatoes, water, oil and seasonings. Stir in rice and artichoke hearts. Cover and bring to boiling. Reduce heat and simmer, covered, 25 minutes, or until rice is cooked, stirring occasionally. Add turkey, walnuts and olives. Heat well and serve.

Chicken Livers in Tomato-Wine Sauce

Serves 4

1 pound chicken livers
⅓ cup flour
1 teaspoon salt
¼ teaspoon pepper
⅓ cup vegetable oil
1 cup chopped onion

1 garlic clove, minced
1 (8 ounce) can tomato sauce
⅓ cup white or red wine
1 bay leaf
1 tablespoon chopped parsley

Wash chicken livers. Combine flour, salt and pepper. Roll livers in flour mixture. Heat oil in skillet and add livers. Brown, turning often for 5 minutes. Remove livers to warming platter. Add chopped onion and garlic to remaining oil in skillet. Saute over medium heat. Drain excess oil and discard. Add tomato sauce, wine, bay leaf and parsley to cooked onion and simmer until thick. Pour sauce into chafing dish and place cooked chicken livers on top of sauce. Serve immediately. Can be served as an hors d'oeuvre. Cut livers in bite-sized pieces and dipped in sauce using toothpicks.

Chicken Liver Stroganoff

Serves 6
Easy, hearty, delicious and such a reasonable dish!

½ pound mushrooms, sliced
4 tablespoons butter
1 onion, chopped
1 pound chicken livers
½ cup chicken broth

½ teaspoon salt
½ teaspoon pepper
1 tablespoon flour
1 cup sour cream

Cook the mushrooms in 2 tablespoons butter. Set aside. Cook the onion in 2 tablespoons butter. Return mushrooms and add the chicken livers which have been drained, cut in half, and any fat removed. Add the broth and the salt and pepper. Cover and simmer for 8 to 10 minutes stirring occasionally. Add the flour to the sour cream and stir into the cooked mixture. Heat thoroughly without bringing to a boil. May be reheated in double boiler.

Chicken Livers with Rice

Serves 4

1⅓ cup water
½ cup rice
½ teaspoon salt
½ teaspoon butter
1 chicken bouillon cube
4 slices bacon
1 medium onion, diced

6-8 mushrooms, coarsely
  chopped
1 medium green pepper, diced
1 stalk celery, diced
1 tablespoon olive oil
6-8 chicken livers

Cook rice with salt, butter and bouillon. Saute bacon, onion, mushrooms, green pepper and celery in olive oil. When tender add chicken livers. When livers are tender, add rice and cook until warmed through. Season with salt, garlic salt and pepper.

Rock Cornish Hens

Serves 6

6 rock cornish pullets
½ cup butter
1¼ cups water
Salt and pepper, to taste
1 tablespoon water (or more to
  make paste)

3 teaspoons flour
½ cup light cream
Sauce coloring
½ teaspoon sugar

Rub insides of pullets with salt and pepper. Sear in butter in a Dutch oven until golden brown, ten to twelve minutes. ("If a clock is not available, play the 'Minute Waltz' ten to twelve times"). Add water and let simmer, covered, until tender, approximately thirty-five minutes. Remove birds. Prepare sauce. Stir like crazy into drippings a paste of cold water and three teaspoons flour. Stir in cream, salt, tasteless coloring and sugar. Pour sauce over pullets and serve.

Victor Borge
Musician-Comedian

Petti De Pollo Alla Bolognese

Serves 4

2 chicken breasts, skinned and
  boned
Salt and pepper
Flour
3 tablespoons butter
2 tablespoons oil

4 thin slices Prosciutto
4 thin slices Fontina, Mozzarella
  or Swiss cheese
2 teaspoons grated Parmesan
  cheese
2 tablespoons chicken stock

Carefully slice each chicken breast to make 4 thin slices. Place in
between two sheets of wax paper and pound to flatten. Dip in
seasoned flour and shake off excess. In heavy skillet brown chicken
in butter and oil. Transfer chicken to shallow, buttered baking dish.
Place a slice of Prosciutto and then a slice of cheese on each piece
of chicken. Sprinkle with grated cheese and dribble chicken stock
over top. Bake at 350° for 10 minutes or until cheese is melted.
Serve at once.

Chicken With Herbs

Serves 4
Easy gourmet meal

1 fryer, cut up
16 sage leaves
½ cup flour
1 teaspoon rosemary
¼ teaspoon salt

¼ teaspoon black pepper
4 tablespoons butter
1 garlic clove
4 tablespoons olive oil
¼ cup cognac

Cut a pocket in each chicken piece and stuff with two sage leaves.
Secure with toothpick. Thoroughly mix flour, rosemary, salt and
pepper. Spread on a piece of wax paper. Melt butter in skillet. Peel
garlic and cut into four pieces. Put into skillet with butter; add oil.
When garlic is brown, dredge chicken in flour mixture and fry in
butter-oil mixture until well browned, about 20 minutes. Remove
from skillet and set on paper towels. Pour cognac into pan and
deglaze. Allow to thicken slightly. Place chicken on dishes and
cover with pan juices. Serve immediately.

Chicken With Lobster Sauce

Serves 6 to 8
Company fare

4 chicken breasts, split, skinned
    and boned
¼ cup butter
2 tablespoons sherry
1 (12 ounce) box fresh
    mushrooms, sliced

2 tablespoons flour
1½ cups chicken stock
1 tablespoon tomato paste
Salt and pepper to taste
2 (10 ounce) packages frozen
    lobster tails

Season chicken with salt and pepper. Heat butter in large skillet.
Add chicken and brown until golden. Spoon sherry over chicken.
Remove chicken and place in a shallow baking dish. Cover and
bake at 300° 1 hour or until tender. Add mushrooms to skillet and
saute until tender. You may have to add a little more butter. Blend
in flour and chicken stock. Simmer, stirring until thickened. Season
with tomato paste, salt and pepper. Simmer 15 minutes. Meanwhile,
prepare lobster tails by removing shells and cutting into bite-sized
pieces. Add lobster meat to sauce and simmer until just heated
through. Serve chicken on large platter topped with sauce,
arranging lobster attractively on top.

*The tiny rural village of Sharon was once considered to be the Mousetrap Capital of
the World. Its traps were "not merely better . . . they were the very best."*

Chicken Brissette

Serves 4
Quick n' easy—tasty too!

4 boneless chicken breasts
1 can cream of mushroom soup
8 ounces sour cream

1 (8 ounce) package thinly
  sliced ham
4 slices bacon
Salt and pepper, to taste

Combine soup and sour cream in a bowl. Mix thoroughly. Grease
baking dish with butter. Cover bottom of dish with sliced ham.
Place chicken on top of ham. Place one strip of uncooked bacon on
top of each piece of chicken. Pour combined soup mixture over
chicken, spreading as evenly as possible. Bake at 325° for 45
minutes. Garnish with parsley or paprika. Serve with rice or
noodles.

Linda Blair
Actress

White Peking Duck With Orange Sauce

Serves 2
A special dinner for two

1 (4-5 pound) duck, split
6 ounces orange juice
1 cup sugar
1 teaspoon orange marmalade

1 teaspoon cornstarch
Pinch of salt
1 cup Grand Marnier
1 orange, sliced thin for garnish

Bake duck on rack at 325° for 2 hours. Meanwhile combine
remaining ingredients except garnish and simmer for 1 hour. When
duck has baked for 2 hours, baste frequently with sauce every 15
minutes for 1 hour. Place on warm serving platter. Cover with
remaining sauce. Garnish with sliced orange and fresh parsley.

Ducklings A L'Orange

Serves 8

2 (5 pound) ready to cook ducklings, quartered	Orange sauce
½ cup Burgundy	1 cup orange marmalade
	Orange peel

Remove giblets and necks, set livers aside for orange sauce. Wash ducklings well under running water, drain and dry. Place duckling pieces, skin side up, on rack in large, shallow roasting pan. Pour Burgundy over ducklings. Roast, uncovered at 425° for 30 minutes. Reduce temperature to 375° and roast 1½ hours, removing fat from roasting pan with a baster every half hour. Meanwhile, make orange sauce. Spread duckling with marmalade. Roast 10 minutes longer. Remove to heated platter. Spoon some of the sauce over top. Garnish with parsley and orange peel cut in thin strips.

Orange Sauce

Makes 2 Cups

5 large oranges	2 teaspoons meat-extract paste (not liquid)
⅓ cup butter	
Livers from ducklings	Dash of pepper
⅓ cup brandy	2 cups condensed chicken broth, undiluted
½ tablespoon minced garlic	
¼ cup flour	¾ cup Burgundy
1½ tablespoons ketchup	½ cup orange marmalade

Grate peel from 2 oranges to measure 4 tablespoons. Holding oranges over bowl to catch juice, peel and remove sections, set aside. Squeeze and reserve 1 cup orange juice; also reserve peel from 1 orange for garnish. In 3 tablespoons hot butter in medium skillet, brown livers well. Remove pan from heat. In small saucepan heat brandy slightly. Ignite; slowly pour over livers. When flames subside, remove livers; set aside. Add remaining butter, 4 tablespoons grated peel and the garlic to skillet; saute 3 minutes. Remove from heat; stir in flour, ketchup, meat-extract paste and pepper until well blended. Gradually stir in broth, Burgundy, marmalade and reserved orange juice. Bring to boiling, stirring constantly. Reduce heat and simmer 15 minutes, stirring occasionally. Meanwhile, chop livers. Add to sauce, along with orange sections. Heat gently.

Mushroom Stuffing

For 12-15 Pound Bird

1 cup chopped onion
1 cup diced celery
¼ cup butter
1½ pounds mushrooms,
   chopped

1 teaspoon salt
Dash of pepper
1 (8 ounce) package stuffing
   mix
½ cup chopped parsley

Saute onion and celery in butter, 3-4 minutes. Add mushrooms, salt and pepper. Cook 5 minutes, stirring occasionally. Prepare stuffing mix according to package directions. Add sauteed vegetables and parsley. Mix thoroughly. Stuff turkey lightly.

Turkey Stuffing

For 14-16 Pound Turkey

12 ounces sausage meat
8 cups seasoned bread crumbs
2 cups diced celery
1 egg
1 onion, chopped
2 teaspoons grated orange rind

Salt and pepper, to taste
1 teaspoon thyme
½ teaspoon sage
½ teaspoon marjoram
¼ teaspoon parsley
¼ cup orange juice

Cook sausage until brown. Transfer to large bowl, reserving fat in pan. Mix meat with bread crumbs, celery and egg. Cook onion in sausage fat until tender. Add onion, seasonings and orange juice to bread mixture. Stuff turkey and bake according to turkey size.

Oyster Stuffing

For 10-12 Pound Bird

½ cup chopped celery
½ cup chopped onion
1 bay leaf
¼ cup butter
6 cups dry bread crumbs
1 tablespoon chopped parsley

3 cups chopped raw oysters
1 teaspoon poultry seasoning
Salt and pepper
2 eggs, beaten
1¾ cups oyster liquid and milk

Cook celery, onion and bay leaf in butter until tender but not brown. Discard bay leaf. Add bread crumbs and parsley to butter mixture; mix thoroughly. Add oysters, seasonings and eggs. Add enough liquid mixture to moisten.

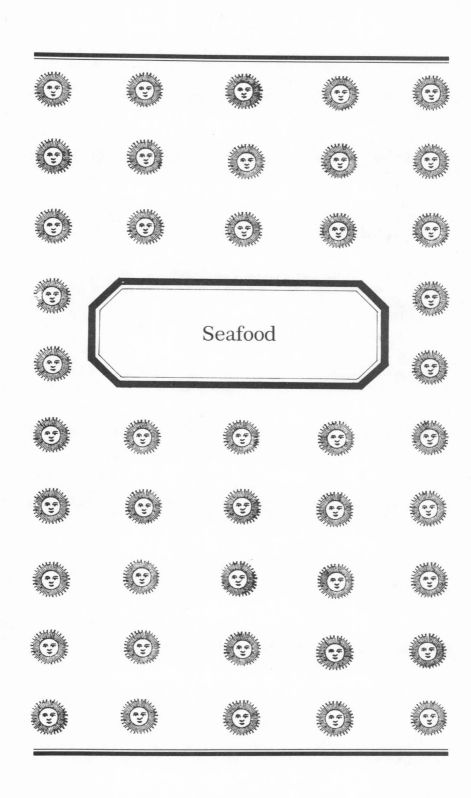

Seafood

Stuffed Sole Newburg

Serves 8
Great company dish

3 slices white bread, crusts removed
2 tablespoons dry sherry
1 tablespoon grated Cheddar cheese
⅛ teaspoon salt

1 cup lobster meat, cooked and cubed
2 pounds fillet of sole
2 tablespoons butter or margarine, melted
½ cup milk
Salt

Coarsely crumble bread. Combine with sherry, cheese, salt and lobster. Spoon some of mixture along one end of each fillet. Roll up and fasten with toothpick. Arrange in flat baking dish. Pour butter and milk over fillets and sprinkle lightly with salt. Bake at 350° uncovered, for 25 minutes. Meanwhile prepare sauce.

Newburg Sauce:
4 tablespoons butter
2 tablespoons flour
1 cup milk
1 cup heavy cream
1 teaspoon salt

⅛ teaspoon paprika
1 cup lobster meat, cooked and cubed
2 tablespoon dry sherry

Melt 2 tablespoons butter in saucepan. Remove from heat and blend in flour. Gradually stir in combined milk and cream. Bring to boiling, stirring constantly, until smooth and thickened. Add salt and paprika. Melt remaining 2 tablespoons butter in skillet. Add lobster and sherry. Cook slowly for 5 minutes until liquid is absorbed. Served rolled fillets topped with sauce.

A covered bridge in West Cornwall has been in continuous service since 1837.

Fish with Sweet-Sour Sauce

Serves 4
Will satisfy even a non-fish lover!

1 pound fish fillets, flounder or haddock	1 egg
	½ cup water
1 tablespoon cooking sherry	½ teaspoon salt
1 tablespoon vinegar	1 quart cooking oil
¾ cup flour	

Cut fish into 1½ inch pieces. Marinate in sherry and vinegar for 2 hours. Make a batter of flour, egg, water and salt. Drain fish and dip pieces into batter. Deep fry in hot oil until golden brown.

Sweet-Sour Sauce:	1 tablespoon soy sauce
3 stalks green onions, chopped	4-5 tablespoons brown sugar
½ cup chopped green pepper	1 cup water
2 tablespoons corn oil	1½ tablespoons cornstarch
3 thin slices fresh ginger root or ⅛ teaspoon ground ginger	2 tablespoons vinegar

Saute onions and green pepper in oil. Add ginger, soy sauce, sugar and water. Boil for 1-2 minutes. Dissolve cornstarch in small amount of cold water and use to thicken sauce. Add vinegar. Pour sauce over hot deep-fried fish or serve separately. Sauce is also good served with rice.

Fish Casserole

Serves 6
Easy, delicious

1 pound haddock	1 (10¾ ounce) can cream of shrimp soup
1 pound scallops	
1 (4½ ounce) can shrimp	50 butter crackers, crushed
	½ cup butter or margarine

Cut haddock into bite-sized pieces. Place in a 10-inch casserole dish. Wash shrimp and scallops and spread over haddock. Add undiluted soup. Stir, combining soup and fish. In skillet melt butter. Add crushed crackers. Mix well. Spread crackers over fish mixture and pat gently. Bake at 350° for 30-35 minutes, uncovered.

Stuffed Flounder with Mushroom Caper Sauce

Serves 6

6 strips bacon
1 (8 ounce) package herb
   stuffing mix
Butter or margarine, melted

2 tablespoons minced parsley
¼ cup minced onion
6 thin flounder fillets, or any
   white fish

Fry bacon crisply. Drain and measure drippings. Crumble bacon.
Prepare stuffing mix according to package directions, adding
enough melted butter to bacon drippings to equal amount of fat
called for. Stir in bacon, parsley and onion. Mix well. Spread equal
amount of stuffing on each fillet. Roll up and secure with toothpick.
Place each roll upright in well greased muffin cup. Brush with
additional melted butter. Bake at 375° for 30 minutes. If necessary,
brush again with butter. Brown under broiler. Serve with mushroom
caper sauce.

Mushroom Caper Sauce:
1 (3 ounce) can broiled sliced
   mushrooms
Milk or cream

1 (10¾ ounce) can cream of
   mushroom soup
2 tablespoons capers

Drain mushrooms. Measure broth and add enough milk or cream to
measure ⅓ cup. Blend with soup. Add mushrooms and capers.
Heat. Pour over flounder roll-ups. Pass additional sauce.

Salmon and Broccoli

Serves 4
A favorite Japanese fish dish

2 tablespoons oil
1 onion, cut in 1 inch chunks
¾ pound broccoli, cut ¾ inch
   thick

1 pound boned, skinned salmon
   steak, cut into 1½ inch
   chunks
3 tablespoons Japanese sake
2 tablespoons soy sauce

Heat oil in wok over high heat; fry onion until limp. Add broccoli
and stir-fry for 3 minutes. Stir in salmon, sprinkle in sake; cover
and steam over low heat until broccoli is tender but crispy. Sprinkle
soy sauce just before removing from heat.

Barbecued Salmon

Serves 4

1 large garlic clove, peeled	2 cups dry sherry
1 teaspoon Dijon mustard	4 large salmon steaks
3 tablespoons soy sauce	Lemon wedges

Place garlic, mustard and soy sauce in food processor and process to paste. Add ½ cup sherry; blend well. Pour into glass bowl adding rest of sherry. Add salmon, turning so they are well coated with marinade. Marinate 1 hour, turning occasionally. Grill salmon steaks approximately 2 minutes on each side over very hot charcoal.

Spanish Swordfish

A dazzler for the outdoor grill

This is a rather simple dish that I learned from an old Spanish fisherman who cooked it on the beach at Torremolinas, back when the beach was primitive and not overrun with high rises and Scandanavian package tours. You start with a steak of *fresh* swordfish which must be cut in a uniform two-inches in thickness. If the steak slopes in thickness, it cannot cook properly. The swordfish is steeped in a marinade of lime juice and thyme for several hours and before cooking it over a hot charcoal fire that has reached the point where the charcoal has attained a gray consistency. After the fish has been placed on the grill, it should be saturated with fresh lemon juice and liberally covered with small chunks of margarine and sprinkled with fresh thyme. It should be cooked for ten minutes on each side, turning it only once, and putting lemon juice, thyme and margarine on the turned side.

The cook should have at hand a freshly-cut pine bough. The swordfish is removed from the grill, the pine bough is placed on the fire, and the fish is put on top of it. The pine needles will first give off a white smoke and then ignite, the pine-scented flame searing the swordfish, which should be removed as soon as the flame of the pine needles dies down. The result is a moist, succulent fish that tastes of the delicate blend of thyme, charcoal and pine.

A. E. Hotchner, Author
"The Man Who Lived at the Ritz"

Curry Marinated Swordfish Steaks

Serves 4

2 teaspoons curry powder
⅓ cup corn oil
1 tablespoon lemon juice
1 tablespoon cider vinegar

1 teaspoon salt
2 pounds swordfish steaks, cut
   into serving-size pieces

Combine curry powder, corn oil, lemon juice, vinegar and salt. Pour over swordfish in shallow baking dish. Marinate overnight. Remove fish from marinade. Drain and broil until lightly brown, 10-15 minutes, depending on thickness of fish. Allow ten minutes per inch of thickness of fish. Baste frequently with marinade. Do not overcook.

Seafood Au Gratin

Serves 8

3 tablespoons flour
3 tablespoons butter
1 cup milk
½ cup light cream
½ cup chicken broth
¾ cup shredded Cheddar cheese
6-8 ounces mushrooms, cooked
2 tablespoons chopped onion
1 teaspoon salt

¼ teaspoon paprika
2 tablespoons sherry
8 ounces broad noodles, cooked
1 (7½ ounce) package Alaskan
   king crab meat
1 (12 ounce) package
   langostinos
1 pound medium shrimp, cooked
Buttered bread crumbs

Make white sauce with flour, butter and milk. Add cream and chicken broth. Cook until thick. Add cheese, mushrooms, onion, salt, paprika and sherry. Add noodles and seafood. Mix well. Sprinkle with bread crumbs. Bake at 350° for 30 minutes or until bubbly. Can also top with slivered almonds before baking.

Broiled Swordfish with Mustard

Serves 2

1¼ pound swordfish steak
Freshly ground black pepper, to
  taste
2 tablespoons butter or
  margarine

2 teaspoons mustard
1 teaspoon mustard seeds
Lemon wedges
Melted butter or margarine

Sprinkle swordfish with black pepper. Heat butter in a baking dish
large enough to hold swordfish. Brush steak on both sides with
mustard and sprinkle with mustard seeds. Place 4-5 inches from
broiler and broil 3-4 minutes. Turn fish and broil on other side 4-5
minutes. Do not overcook. Serve with lemon wedges and melted
butter.

Langostino Casserole

Serves 8

6 slices bread, trim crust, cut
  into cubes
½ pound sharp cheese, cut in
  small cubes
2 (8 ounce) packages
  langostinos

¼ cup butter or
  margarine, melted
5 whole eggs
1 pint milk
½ teaspoon dry mustard,
  optional
Salt and pepper to taste

Butter 2-quart casserole. Put in bread and cheese cubes. Add
langostinos and mix evenly. Pour melted butter over mixture. Beat
eggs, milk, mustard, salt and pepper. Pour over langostinos.
Refrigerate covered until ready to serve, at least 2 hours or
overnight. Bake at 350° for 1 hour in covered casserole. Looks like a
beautiful souffle. Serve immediately.

Baked Spanish Style Fish

Serves 6
The seasonings provide a different flavor

6 slices white fish fillets
¼ teaspoon salt
¼ teaspoon black pepper
¼ teaspoon mace or nutmeg
1 large onion, thinly sliced
2 tablespoons diced pimiento

6 thick slices tomato
3 tablespoons chopped green
  onion
1 cup mushrooms, thinly sliced
½ cup dry sherry or white wine
1 cup bread crumbs, toasted

Wipe fish with a damp cloth. Sprinkle with salt, pepper and mace.
Arrange onion slices and pimiento in bottom of 12×8 baking dish.
Top with seasoned fish slices, arranged side by side. Cover each
piece of fish with a tomato slice. Sprinkle with green onions. Scatter
mushrooms over all. Add wine and top with bread crumbs. Bake,
uncovered at 350° for 35-40 minutes or until fish flakes easily.

Crab or Shrimp Delight

Serves 8
Great for bridge group!

8 slices white firm bread
Butter
2 cups crab, shrimp or tuna
1 (3 ounce) can mushrooms
½ pound grated sharp Cheddar
  cheese
Onion (optional)

Green pepper (optional)
Pimiento (optional)
3 eggs
½ teaspoon salt
½ teaspoon dried mustard
Pepper
2 cups whole milk

Trim off crusts of bread and save to make dried bread crumbs.
Butter bread lightly. Use 1½-inch deep casserole. Put 4 slices of
bread in bottom. Add desired fish. Spread it out over bread in
casserole. Sprinkle mushrooms, Cheddar cheese and remaining 4
slices of bread over fish. Sprinkle more grated cheese on top.
Chopped onions, green peppers or pimiento may be used if desired.
Beat eggs. Add salt, pepper, mustard and milk. Beat well. Pour over
bread and fish mixture. Store covered in refrigerator overnight. Bake
at 350° for 45 minutes. This makes a custard-like dish and is
excellent in flavor.

Broccoli-Sole Au Gratin

Serves 4

¼ cup butter or margarine
¼ cup flour
¾ teaspoon salt
1½ cups milk
4 ounces Swiss cheese
1 pound fish fillets

1 tablespoon lemon juice
½ teaspoon garlic salt
¼ teaspoon pepper
Paprika
2 cups frozen cut broccoli,
    thawed

In saucepan over medium heat, melt butter. With wire whisk blend in flour and salt. Cook until bubbly. Gradually add milk. Cook, stirring constantly until sauce thickens and boils for 1 minute. Reduce heat. Stir in cheese and cook until cheese is melted and smooth. Set aside. Cut fish crosswise into 4 pieces. Place in center of 12×8 baking dish. Sprinkle with lemon juice, garlic salt and pepper. Spoon half the sauce over fish and sprinkle with paprika. Fold broccoli into remaining sauce and arrange around fish. Bake at 375° uncovered, for 35-40 minutes or until fish flakes easily.

New Orleans Oyster Loaf

Serves 6

1 large loaf French bread or 6
    individual crusty rolls
1 garlic clove
¼ cup butter or
    margarine, melted

3 dozen oysters and liquid
Salt and pepper, to taste
Dash hot pepper sauce

Split bread lengthwise but not completely through. Scoop out soft center, leaving crusty shell 1-inch thick. Tear soft bread in coarse crumbs with fork and set aside. Rub inside of shell with garlic and brush inside and out with 2 tablespoons butter. Drain oysters and reserve liquid. Saute oysters with remaining butter just until edges curl, about 5 minutes. Fill loaf with oysters. Combine ½ crumbs with ½ cup liquid and use to complete filling. Sprinkle with salt, pepper and hot sauce. Wrap loaf in cheese cloth moistened with milk, twisting ends tightly and folding under bread. Bake on sheet in preheated oven at 350° for 30 minutes. Unwrap, slice and serve.

Vegetable-Stuffed Striped Bass

Serves 3 to 4

1 whole striped bass (about 2¼ pounds)
1 medium onion, thinly sliced
1 small green pepper, thinly sliced
1 small tomato, thinly sliced
¼ cup minced parsley
Salt and freshly ground pepper
1 teaspoon tarragon
2 tablespoons butter, melted
1 cup dry red wine

Clean fish. With sharp knife, slit bass, remove backbone carefully. Layer onion, green pepper, tomato and parsley in cavity; sprinkle with salt, pepper and tarragon. Dot with butter. Sew up cavity. Flour fish lightly, brush with melted butter and season with salt and pepper. Place in large roasting pan. Pour on wine. Bake at 425° until fish flakes easily, about 30 minutes, basting frequently with wine.

Seafood Casserole

1 large onion, chopped
2 tablespoons vegetable oil
1 (10 ounce) package frozen spinach
1 (3 ounce) package cream cheese
1 cup cottage cheese
2 teaspoons Italian seasoning
1 egg, beaten
1 can cream of celery soup
⅓ cup milk
1 (8 ounce) package frozen shrimp or crab
½ package shell noodles
1 pound fish fillets, cubed
3 tablespoons Parmesan cheese
Paprika

Cook onion in oil. In separate pan cook frozen spinach and drain. Add to onion along with cream cheese, cottage cheese and seasonings. Add remaining ingredients. Mix well. Grease 13×9 baking dish. Cook noodles according to directions. Put layer of shelled noodles on bottom. Cover with fish and cheese mixture. Put remaining noodles on top. Sprinkle with Parmesan cheese and paprika. Bake at 350° for 45 minutes.

Stuffed Sea Trout

Serves 8
Delightfully simple

1 (7 pound) sea trout
1½ pounds Alaska King crab
  legs, picked and shredded

1 cup butter
Italian bread crumbs
Salt and white pepper to taste

Remove head from trout. Clean and debone without cutting through it from front to back. Melt 6 ounces of butter in skillet. Saute crab meat lightly. Remove from heat. Add sufficient bread crumbs to absorb butter. Let cool. Stuff fish with crab mixture. Fold fish over, using metal skewers, placed one inch apart in fish and lace with kitchen twine. Line a jelly-roll pan with aluminum foil. Coat foil and outside of fish with remaining butter. Bake at 350° for 10 minutes for each ½-inch thickness of fish, about 30-40 minutes. Cool and slice in 1½ inch pieces. Pour pan drippings over fish when serving.

Calcutta Shrimp Curry

Serves 4

2 onions, chopped
1 stalk celery, chopped
1 carrot, chopped
1 cup butter
1 green pepper, chopped
2 bay leaves
4 whole cloves
1 tablespoon flour
3 tablespoons curry powder

2 (10 ounce) cans chicken broth
½ cup heavy cream
1 tablespoon Worcestershire
  sauce
2 pounds shrimp, cooked and
  cleaned
2 cups hot steamed rice
½ cup seedless raisins
Toasted coconut

In heavy saucepan simmer onion, celery and carrot in butter for 1 hour. Do not brown. Add green pepper, bay leaves and cloves, and cook 15 minutes. Remove bay leaves and cloves, add flour combined with curry powder and mixed with broth and cream. Add Worcestershire sauce and shrimp. Bring to boiling. Serve immediately on dry fluffy rice on large platter, piled high around edges. Sprinkle with parsley and paprika. In separate bowls, serve raisins, toasted coconut, slivered almonds and at least one kind of chutney.

Crab Cakes

Serves 4

1 pound fresh crab meat, in chunks
2 slices white bread, crumbled
1 egg, beaten
1 tablespoon chopped parsley
Salt and pepper, to taste
½ teaspoon celery salt

⅛ teaspoon dry mustard
Small amount of mayonnaise, just enough to hold cakes together
Shortening
Butter

Mix all ingredients together in bowl. Form into 2-inch patties. Fry in hot shortening mixture (½ shortening, ½ butter) until golden brown.

Crab Curry

Serves 6 to 8

1 garlic clove, minced
1 large onion, minced
¾ cup butter
1 large apple, minced
3 tablespoons flour
1½ cups water

3 chicken bouillon cubes
1 cup evaporated milk
Dash of Worcestershire sauce
Dash of tabasco
1 tablespoon curry powder
1 pound lump crabmeat

Saute garlic and onion in butter. Add apple. Do not brown. Add flour to thicken. Add rest of ingredients except crabmeat. Simmer for 1 hour. This long, slow cooking eliminates any raw taste of curry powder. Add crabmeat and heat. Serve on rice with accompaniments of crisp bacon, grated hard boiled eggs, chutney and minced green onion.

Lobster with Black Beans

From Kalihi

Cooking oil
1 large lobster tail (in shell)
½ teaspoon cornstarch
2 teaspoons Chinese black beans
2 garlic cloves
¾ cup chicken broth

White pepper
¼ teaspoon monosodium
  glutamate (optional)
1 egg
Green onions
Chinese parsley

Place oil in skillet for deep frying. Cut off tip of tail and chop into about 8 pieces. Sprinkle with cornstarch and mix thoroughly. Set aside. Wash beans and chop finely together with garlic. Place lobster in deep fat and stir about 30 seconds and remove from oil. In another heated skillet place 1 tablespoon oil and move pan about to coat bottom. Add beans and garlic and stir. Follow with broth, pepper and monosodium glutamate. Mix in cornstarch mixture to thicken gravy. Beat egg and add to mixture. Turn off heat as soon as egg appears cooked. Garnish with green onion and parsley.

Lobster Coquilles

Serves 4

1 pound lobster meat
½ pound mushrooms, thinly
  sliced
½ cup sliced scallions
4 tablespoons butter or
  margarine

1 (10 ounce) can cream of
  shrimp soup
⅓ cup grated Swiss cheese
¼ cup dry white wine
⅔ cup bread crumbs

Cut cooked lobster meat into bite-sized pieces. Saute mushrooms and scallions in 2 tablespoons butter in skillet until soft. Reserve. Empty soup into saucepan. Cook over low heat until thawed. Stir in cheese until melted. Stir in wine, lobster, mushrooms and scallions. Spoon mixture into four scallop shells or casseroles. Melt remaining butter and add bread crumbs. Sprinkle over seafood. Bake at 350° for 15 minutes or until bubbly.

Baked Scallops

Serves 6

60 bay scallops
2 tablespoons butter
1 onion, minced
½ pound mushrooms
Parsley

1½ tablespoons flour
1 cup white wine
1 egg yolk
Bread crumbs

Put scallops in boiling water with salt for 3 minutes. Strain and reserve water. In saucepan melt butter. Add onion, mushrooms and parsley. Simmer 5-10 minutes on low heat. Add flour and stir. Pour in 1 cup of water from scallops, and wine. Stir 5 minutes. Add egg yolk and scallops. Place in scallop shells and sprinkle with bread crumbs. Dot with butter. Bake at 350° for 20 minutes.

Scallops Parisienne

Serves 4

1 pound fresh scallops
1 (4 ounce) can sliced
    mushrooms
2 tablespoons chopped onion
2 tablespoons butter
1 can condensed Cheddar
    cheese soup

2 teaspoons lemon juice
Dash pepper
Dash crushed thyme leaves
Dash marjoram
2 tablespoons bread crumbs
Paprika

Quickly brown scallops in small amount of butter until cooked. Brown mushrooms and onion until tender. Add soup, lemon juice and seasonings. Mix with scallops. Put into casserole. Top with buttered bread crumbs. Sprinkle with paprika. Bake at 350° for 30 minutes or until hot.

Stuffed Fillets

Serves 4

4 fish fillets
2 cups bread crumbs
1 teaspoon capers
10 black olives, chopped
Salt and pepper, to taste

1 egg
1 teaspoon parsley
1 (1 pound) can plum tomatoes
Oregano

Pat fish fillets dry. Mix bread crumbs, capers and black olives. Add salt and pepper. Mix in egg and parsley. Fill each fillet and roll, jelly-roll style. Secure with toothpick. Pour plum tomatoes on top and a little oregano. Bake at 350° for 45 minutes or until fish flakes easily.

New Orleans Shrimp Pie

Serves 8

3 pounds shrimp, cooked and
  cleaned
2 slices stale bread, cubed
½ cup dry white wine
½ teaspoon salt
¼ teaspoon pepper

¼ teaspoon mace
¼ teaspoon thyme
¼ teaspoon nutmeg
2 tablespoons chopped parsley
2 tablespoons butter

Moisten bread in wine. Add seasonings. Add all but 2 cups of shrimp (to be reserved for sauce). Put shrimp and bread mixture in casserole dish. Sprinkle with bread crumbs and dot with 2 tablespoons of the butter. Bake at 375° for 25 minutes.

Sauce:
2 tablespoons butter
1 (29 ounce) can tomatoes
2 tablespoons chopped celery

1 bay leaf
1 cup clam juice
Few drops of lime juice

Chop 2 cups of shrimp and saute in 2 tablespoons butter 4-5 minutes. Add remaining ingredients and simmer for 3-4 minutes. Pour hot sauce over baked casserole and serve at once.

Baked Stuffed Shrimp

Serves 4

12-16 jumbo raw shrimp
1 small can minced clams
3 tablespoons butter, melted
1 teaspoon grated onion
3 drops hot sauce
1 teaspoon each, finely chopped
  celery, parsley and green
  pepper

Melted butter
Dash garlic powder
Dash salt and pepper
⅛ teaspoon lemon juice
¼ cup fine, dry bread crumbs

Wash, shell and devein shrimp. Arrange shrimp in single layer on lightly greased baking sheet. Combine rest of ingredients. Spread about 1 teaspoon of mixture on each shrimp. Pour a little melted butter over each shrimp with stuffing. Bake at 450° for 10-15 minutes only. Serve with side dish of melted butter.

Shrimp Creole

Serves 4

1 pound shrimp, cooked and
  cleaned
2 tablespoons vinegar
2 large onions, chopped
½ cup butter
1 pound mushrooms, sliced

2 large green peppers, chopped
4 tablespoons flour
1 teaspoon salt
1 pint milk
1 cup tomato sauce
1 tablespoon sugar

Marinate shrimp in vinegar. Saute onion in butter. Add mushrooms and green pepper and saute. Add flour, salt, tomato sauce and sugar. Drain shrimp and add to mixture. Bring to a boil. Serve on toast.

Shrimp with Macadamia Nuts

Serves 4

1 cup water
½ pound shrimp
½ teaspoon salt
⅛ teaspoon pepper
½ cup coarsely chopped salted
    macadamia nuts

⅓ cup butter
6 tablespoons flour
1 tablespoon chili sauce
1½ cups milk

Bring water to boiling. Add shrimp, salt and pepper. Bring to a boil
and cook 3 minutes. Drain, reserving liquid. Cook nuts in butter
until lightly browned. Blend in flour. Add shrimp liquid, chili sauce
and milk. Cook, stirring until thick. Add shrimp and serve with rice
or noodles. Filbert or almond may be substituted for macadamia
nuts.

Old Fashioned Charleston Shrimp Casserole

Serves 6

8 slices firm white bread, crusts
    trimmed and torn into crumbs
1 cup dry white wine
1 cup medium sherry
¼ cup butter, softened

1 teaspoon salt
¼ teaspoon nutmeg
¼ teaspoon pepper
2 pounds cooked shrimp, shelled
    and deveined

Soak bread in wine and sherry in a deep bowl. Mash butter in bread
with a fork to make a paste. Beat in salt, nutmeg and pepper. Add
shrimp and mix well. Turn into a buttered 1½ quart casserole.
Bake, uncovered at 350° for 40 minutes or until top is crusty and
golden. Serve with broiled tomatoes and hot cornbread. In the
tidewater country this dish is also made with oysters or crabmeat.

Seafood Chardonnay

Serves 6

2 tablespoons butter
3 shallots, minced, or ¼ cup
   minced onion
2 garlic cloves, minced
1 tablespoon chopped chives
2 tablespoons fresh bread
   crumbs
Salt and pepper

¼ pound sliced, cooked, cleaned
   shrimp
3 large fish fillets, about 2
   pounds (Turbot is delicious
   and especially recommended)
1½ cups Haight Chardonnay
1 tablespoon lemon juice

In 2 tablespoons hot butter in a small skillet, saute shallots and garlic 2 minutes. Add chives, bread crumbs, salt and pepper and continue to cook, shaking, 2 more minutes. Add shrimp and cook 1 additional minute, stirring. Remove skillet from stove. Sprinkle fillets lightly with salt and pepper. Spread with shrimp mixture, roll up and place in a shallow baking dish. Mix 1 cup of wine and lemon juice and pour over fish. Bake at 400° for ½ hour or until easily flaked with a fork. While fish is baking, prepare sauce.

Sauce:
2 tablespoons butter
1 tablespoon flour
1 cup milk
½ cup Haight Chardonnay

1 tablespoon soy sauce
3 egg yolks, beaten
Grated Parmesan cheese

Melt 2 tablespoons butter in double boiler. Stir in flour, then add milk slowly, stirring until smooth and thickened. Add ½ cup wine, soy sauce, ½ teaspoon salt, dash of pepper and cook 2 minutes. Stir in egg yolks and continue cooking until smooth and thick. Lift fish rolls onto platter and spoon on sauce. Sprinkle with Parmesan cheese.

Sherman P. Haight, Jr.
"Haight Vineyard," Litchfield

Neapolitan Clams

Serves 4

48 littleneck or cherrystone
  clams, well scrubbed and
  purged
½ cup olive oil
1 tablespoon finely minced garlic
1 teaspoon crushed red pepper
  flakes

1 tablespoon dried oregano
¼ cup chopped parsley
½ cup dry white wine
3 cups coarsely chopped fresh,
  skinned tomatoes

Scrub clams and drain. Heat oil in large skillet and saute garlic, pepper, oregano and parsley. Add wine and cook, reducing liquid by ½. Add tomatoes; cover and simmer 15 minutes. Transfer sauce to large pot. When ready to serve add clams. Cover and cook until clams open, 5-10 minutes depending on size.

Sauces, Preserves, & Relishes

Beggars Marinade

Makes 1 Quart

¾ cup oil
¾ cup soy sauce
1 teaspoon oregano

2½ cups Burgundy wine
1¼ tablespoons garlic powder

Mix all ingredients together. Marinate meat for 1 hour or longer.
Heat sauce and serve over meat.

Bourbon Marinade

Makes 3 Cups
Cheers!

¼ cup bourbon
¼ cup brown sugar
¼ cup Worcestershire sauce

1 small bottle soy sauce
1¼ cups water

Combine all ingredients and use to marinate beef in refrigerator
overnight.

Mom's Bar-B-Que Sauce

Makes 1 Pint
Excellent for chicken and London Broil

1 (14 ounce) bottle ketchup
½ cup vinegar
¼ cup sugar
½ teaspoon dry mustard
2 teaspoons dried minced onion
½ teaspoon oregano
½ teaspoon garlic salt

½ teaspoon salt
½ teaspoon pepper
½ teaspoon parsley flakes
¼ teaspoon paprika
¼ teaspoon curry powder
½ teaspoon celery salt

Combine all ingredients in saucepan and simmer for 10 minutes. A
pinch of red pepper may be added for a hot sauce. More or less
sugar and vinegar may be added to suit taste. Refrigerate. Keeps
well.

Chili Sauce

Makes 8 Pints
Grandmother's recipe

12 pounds skinned and cored
    ripe tomatoes
5 sweet peppers, seeded and
    chopped
5 hot peppers, seeded and
    chopped
6 onions, chopped

2 tablespoons salt
1¼ cups vinegar
2 cups sugar
1 tablespoon cinnamon
1 teaspoon cloves
1 teaspoon allspice
1 teaspoon ginger

Combine chopped tomatoes, peppers and onions in large kettle. Add remaining ingredients and simmer about 3 hours or until thick, stirring occasionally. Pour into hot clean jars leaving ½ inch head space and process in boiling water bath for 10 minutes. Remove from heat. Cool naturally.

Sweet and Sour Sauce

Makes 1 Quart

3 tablespoons cornstarch
1 cup vinegar
1 cup sugar
Few dashes tabasco
1 tablespoon Worcestershire
    sauce

1 tablespoon prepared mustard
2 green peppers
1 red pepper
1 (16 ounce) can pineapple
    chunks

Mix cornstarch in vinegar and cook with sugar until clear. Add tabasco, Worcestershire sauce, mustard, green and red peppers, cut in large pieces. Add pineapple chunks and juice. Pour over browned meat, fish or poultry. Bake or serve as directed.

Buttermilk Curry Sauce

Makes 1 Quart

½ cup butter
1 tablespoon curry powder

1 cup flour
1 quart buttermilk

In top of double boiler melt butter; add curry powder. Remove from heat and slowly stir in flour to make a smooth paste. Gradually add buttermilk, stirring constantly with wire whisk. Return to heat and cook over hot, but not boiling water. This is delicious when you add shrimp, deep fried breaded chicken, cooked lamb and/or batter deep fried vegetables. Serve with rice.

Ham Sauce

Makes 2 Cups
Ham never tasted so good

½ cup butter
2 teaspoons flour
1 cup sugar
1 cup vinegar

1 cup prepared mustard
1 cup beef bouillon
1 cup dark seedless raisins

Melt butter. Stir in flour until smooth. Add remaining ingredients and cook in top of double boiler until thick. Serve hot or at room temperature.

Raisin Sauce

Makes 2½ Cups

1 cup raisins
1 cup water
1 cup orange juice
½ cup orange marmalade

4 tablespoons sugar
2 tablespoons cornstarch
½ teaspoon salt
Dash of cloves

Bring first four ingredients to a boil. Set aside. Mix remaining ingredients. Add to hot mixture. Cook over medium heat until thick. Marvelous with ham.

Failproof Hollandaise

Makes 1 Cup

½ cup butter
⅓ cup boiling water
4 egg yolks

Salt to taste
2 tablespoons lemon juice

Melt butter in top of double boiler. Stir in boiling water and egg yolks. Using wire whisk over simmering water, stir constantly until thick. Remove from heat. Add salt and lemon juice. This sauce may be reheated over warm water. Taste for seasoning. You may prefer more lemon.

Ground Cherry Marmalade

Makes 2 Pints

4 cups "ground cherries" or
  "husk tomatoes"
⅓ cup lemon juice

Grated lemon or orange rind
8 cups sugar
1 (6 ounce) bottle liquid pectin

Crush cherries, heat over low flame. Bring to a boil and simmer for 10 minutes, making sure the cherries do not stick or burn. Measure 4 cups of liquid, to which you add rind, lemon juice and sugar. Reboil this mixture at a rolling boil for 2 minutes. Remove and add liquid pectin. Stir several minutes. Pour into sterilized jars.

Perusing a spring seed catalog several years ago, I found a picture of a large, lovely green plant bearing small Japanese lantern shaped flowers. Reminding me of my Iowa homestead and my mother's garden, we ordered and planted the seeds for these "ground cherries," (also called "husk tomatoes.") The seeds germinated easily despite Northwestern Connecticut's unpredictable weather, the plants flourished and hundreds of small green turning to yellow lanterns appeared. When ripe, the lanterns dry and reveal a marble-sized yellow fruit, almost like melon in flavor. The marmalade recipe is my daughter's attempt to simulate what I recall my mother making in Iowa many, many years ago.
                    Chris Hughes in "As The World Turns"

Basic Tomato Sauce

Exact measurements of sugar and salt are the secret

1 large onion, chopped
1 garlic clove, minced
¼ cup oil
1 (28 ounce) can tomatoes
2 (6 ounce) cans tomato paste
1 cup water

1 tablespoon sugar
1½ teaspoons salt
½ teaspoon pepper
1 bay leaf
1 to 1½ teaspoons oregano

Saute onion and garlic in oil. Add tomatoes (which have been put through blender for a few seconds) and remaining ingredients. Simmer, uncovered for about an hour. Remove bay leaf. If desired, add browned pork, browned meatballs and simmer gently for an hour more.

Crab Sauce

Makes 4 Cups

¼ cup oil
2 garlic cloves, chopped
¾ cup finely chopped onion
½ cup chopped fresh parsley
1 (6 ounce) can tomato paste
1 cup water
1 (1 pound, 3 ounce) can tomatoes, mashed

1½ teaspoons salt
¼ teaspoon pepper
1½ teaspoons dried oregano
2 (6½ ounce) cans king crabmeat, drained
⅓ cup sherry
Parmesan cheese

Saute garlic, onion and parsley in hot oil gently. Combine paste with water, a little at a time, until smooth; add to pan. Add tomatoes, salt, pepper and oregano. Bring to boil. Reduce heat and simmer, uncovered for about an hour, stirring occasionally. Remove any cartilage from crab. Add crab and sherry, simmering for 15 more minutes. Serve with favorite pasta. Sprinkle generously with freshly grated Parmesan cheese and more chopped parsley.

Note: There are as many crab sauces as there are crabs. This is not the traditional, fresh crab sauce. It is totally different but every bit as delicious. For people who don't like to handle the real, live thing.

Family Evening Spaghetti Sauce

Brown one pound ground beef with three or four large onions, cut up. Add 1 can Italian tomatoes, 1 can tomato paste. Add 3 tablespoons chili powder, ⅓ cup oregano, lots of garlic. Optional: ½ cup red wine; 1 can anchovies instead of salt. Simmer for at least 3 hours, preferably all day. Cook thin spaghetti 10 to 12 minutes. Test by throwing strand against wall or kitchen cupboard door. If it sticks, the spaghetti is done. Do not overcook the pasta! This allows infinite variations. We often add green peppers when they are available. Sliced mushrooms added at the last minute give a touch of elegance. Serve with a big green salad. And, if nobody is worried about weight, with a long loaf of French or Italian bread with garlic butter—and use lots of butter and lots of garlic. For those who do not like garlic, herb butter may be substituted: to the butter or oleo add a handful of bouquet garni or fine herbs.

Hugh Franklin,
Dr. Charles Tyler, in "All My Children"

White Clam Sauce and Pasta

Serves 4

¼ cup olive oil
¼ cup butter or margarine
6 garlic cloves, minced
1 pound mushrooms, sliced

1 large onion, diced
2 cans minced clams with liquid
1 cup chopped parsley
¼ cup dry vermouth

Saute garlic, mushrooms and onion in oil and butter until tender. Add clams and parsley. Stir. Add vermouth. Simmer 5 minutes. Serve over spaghetti or noodles.

Clam and Anchovy Sauce with Hard Cooked Eggs

Makes 4 Cups

5 good sized garlic cloves,
  crushed
1 large onion, minced
¼ cup oil
1 (2 ounce) can anchovy fillets
1 (28 ounce) can tomatoes

1 (6 ounce) can tomato paste
¼ cup chopped fresh parsley
3 (7½ ounce) cans minced
  clams, reserve juice
6 hard cooked eggs

Saute garlic and onion in oil. Drain and chop anchovy fillets. Add and simmer until fillets are reduced to a paste form, stirring constantly. Add mashed tomatoes, paste, parsley and clam juice. Simmer sauce 1 hour, stirring occasionally. Chop eggs in large pieces and add with reserved clams to sauce before serving over your favorite noodles or pasta. Serve with Parmesan cheese.

Note: This is alot of fun to make. The eggs may seem all wrong, but you must try it to appreciate the subtle flavors in this memorable sauce. An excellent cook, thought they were mushrooms! This culinary private-eye was also surprised she was eating anchovies!

At Bunker Hill, Israel Putnam of Pomfret gave the order "Don't fire until you see the whites of their eyes."

Praline Ice Cream Sauce

Makes 1½ Cups

1 cup firmly packed light brown
   sugar
¼ cup light corn syrup
½ cup half & half

2 tablespoons vanilla
⅛ teaspoon salt
1 cup pecans, coarsely chopped

Combine all ingredients in a saucepan. Cook over medium heat,
stirring constantly, for 10 minutes or until sauce is thick and
smooth. Cool slightly. Serve over vanilla ice cream.

Chocolate Sauce

Makes 1 Quart
When poured over ice cream this gets chewy!

4 squares unsweetened
   chocolate
2 tablespoons butter
1 cup boiling water

3 cups granulated sugar
6 tablespoons light corn syrup
Pinch of salt
1 teaspoon vanilla

Melt chocolate and butter together in top of double boiler. When
melted, slowly add one cup boiling water. Stir until smooth. Slowly
add sugar and syrup, blending well. Add salt. Boil slowly for 12-15
minutes. Remove from heat. Let cool slightly and add vanilla.
             Mrs. Malcolm Baldrige, wife of Secretary of Commerce

Melba Sauce

Makes 1⅓ Cups

2 cups fresh raspberries or
   2 (10 ounce) packages frozen,
   thawed and drained

½ cup red current jelly
¼ cup sugar
2 tablespoons kirsch

Place raspberries in saucepan. Add jelly and sugar. Bring mixture to
a boil, crushing raspberries, stirring for 5 minutes until thick. Put
sauce through a fine sieve. Add kirsch. Serve chilled sauce over
peach halves and vanilla ice cream.

Rum-Raisin Sauce

Makes 1½ Cups
Heavenly on ice cream

½ cup raisins
½ cup dark rum
1 cup sugar

¼ cup water
½ cup heavy cream

Marinate raisins in ¼ cup rum for a few hours or until they are plump. In a saucepan, combine sugar and water and bring to a boil over moderate heat. Cook until it is golden caramel, swirling the pan. Remove from heat and pour in cream and ¼ cup rum, stirring constantly. Add raisins and serve warm sauce over vanilla ice cream.

Peach Marmalade

Makes 6 Jars

4 pounds peaches, chopped
2½ cups sugar
Juice of 3 oranges

1 (10 ounce) bottle maraschino
    cherries, chopped
6 peach pits

Combine all ingredients. Cook two hours. Remove peach pits. Pour into sterilized jelly jars when cool. Cover with melted paraffin to seal.

Pickled Chinese Beets

3 (1 pound) cans beets
1 cup sugar
2 tablespoons cornstarch
24 whole cloves
3 tablespoons ketchup

3 tablespoons cooking oil
Dash of salt
1 teaspoon vanilla
1½ cups beet juice

Mix all ingredients in pan and cook for 3 minutes or until mixture thickens over medium heat. When cool store in refrigerator.

Hot Pepper Jelly

Makes 6-7 Half Pints
Great to give as Christmas gifts

¾ cup ground hot peppers
1¼ cups ground green peppers
1½ cups white vinegar
6½ cups sugar

Juice of 1 lemon
1 (6 ounce) bottle pectin
Red or green food coloring

Remove seeds and veins from peppers and grind or put through
food processor. Mix in all ingredients except pectin and food
coloring. Simmer 45 minutes. Bring to a rolling boil for 1 minute.
Remove from heat and let stand 5 minutes. Add pectin and food
coloring. Stir well. Seal in sterilized jars. Serve with pork or lamb.
May spread on cream cheese and serve with crackers.

Spiced Pineapple

Makes 3 Cups

1 (1 pound, 4 ounce) can
    pineapple chunks, with juice
¼ cup vinegar
12 whole cloves

¼ cup sugar
Grated peel of 1 lemon
3 (3 inch) sticks cinnamon

Combine all ingredients in bowl. Cover and refrigerate for 1 week
before serving.

Strawberry Rhubarb Jam

Makes 7-8 Cups

5 cups rhubarb cut in 1-inch
    slices
1 cup sliced strawberries

3 cups sugar
1 (6 ounce) package
    strawberry-flavored gelatin

In large pan combine rhubarb, strawberries and sugar. Let stand ½
hour. Bring to a boil and simmer 12 minutes. Remove from heat
and add gelatin. Mix well until gelatin is dissolved. Pour into
sterilized jars and seal. Excellent on hot biscuits.

Fruit Crock

A welcome gift at holiday time

Start this gift in May and complete in December. As each fruit comes into season, peel, seed and slice and measure. Put in a porous earthenware crock or clay pot. Berries of all kinds may be used. (Bananas make the mixture cloudy and citrus fruits give off too much acidity). As each fruit is added, an equivalent amount of sugar and vodka is poured into the crock. Vodka is used because it is tasteless and will not distort the pure fruit flavor. You may add a little flavored brandy if you wish.

Don't be alarmed when fruit begins to froth and ferment. This is supposed to happen. It will also turn a deep dark brown color as the season progresses. Continue adding fruit, sugar and vodka until the end of the fall; then leave it undisturbed for 2-3 months.

The heady juices are for pouring over ice cream and other creamy desserts, for poaching other fruits such as winter pears, for spooning over waffles and pancakes, for flavoring drinks and punches and for making fruit vinegar.

Share your crock among your friends, putting a little of the fruit and syrupy juice in beautiful earthenware or glass containers and enclose a note explaining its use.

Freezer Pickles

Makes 2 Quarts
Much easier than canning

4 cups sliced, unpeeled cucumbers	4 tablespoons water
2 cups sliced onions	1 cup sugar
4 teaspoons salt	½ cup cider vinegar
	1 teaspoon dill weed

In large bowl mix cucumbers, onions, salt and water. Stir and let stand 2 hours. Drain, do not rinse. Mix sugar, vinegar and dill weed; add to cucumbers. Stir. Put pickles in quart or pint containers and freeze. Pickles will be ready to eat after a couple of days in freezer and throughout the rest of the year.

Cranberry Catsup

Makes 4 Cups
Excellent hot or cold

1 pound fresh cranberries
1½ cups cider vinegar
2 cups cold water
2½ cups light brown sugar
2½ cups sugar

1 teaspoon salt
2 teaspoons cinnamon
½ teaspoon cloves
½ teaspoon allspice

In 4-quart pan cook cranberries, vinegar and water until skins pop.
Press mixture through strainer and combine with remaining
ingredients. Cook, uncovered over moderate heat for 20-30 minutes
until mixture becomes slightly thick. Pour into sterilized jars and
seal. This also makes an excellent basting sauce.

Refrigerator Pickles

For a spicy addition

2 cups sugar
1 cup vinegar
1 tablespoon salt

6 cups sliced cucumbers,
  unpeeled
1 cup sliced red onion
1 cup sliced green pepper

Combine sugar, vinegar and salt. Pour mixture over sliced
vegetables and mix. This may be served a couple of hours after
mixing. Keeps well in refrigerator in covered container.

Winchester Relish Sauce

Very tasty

36 medium tomatoes
8 onions
Bunch of celery
6 sweet red peppers

5 tablespoons salt
4 cups sugar
1 quart cider vinegar

Chop vegetables and add remaining ingredients; cook until thick.
Put in jars and refrigerate when cool. Delicious with meat. Recipe
may be cut in half.

Tomato-Apple Chutney

Makes 8 Pints

10 cups diced ripe tomatoes
   (about 5 pounds)
6 cups diced tart apples
2 large onions, chopped
1 (15 ounce) package seedless
   raisins
2 garlic cloves, minced
1 pound dark sugar

1 tablespoon salt
2 teaspoons crushed dried hot
   red pepper
1 tablespoon ground cinnamon
1 teaspoon ground allspice
½ teaspoon ground ginger
½ teaspoon ground cloves
2 cups cider vinegar

Combine all ingredients in a large kettle. Heat, stirring constantly, to boiling; cover. Simmer 10 minutes, uncover. Simmer, stirring often, 30 minutes longer or until thick. Ladle into hot sterilized jars; seal, following manufacturer's directions. Cool jars, label and date. This is a delicious condiment to serve with beef or pork. However, it is great in combination with other foods. Two of our favorites follow.

For sweet and sour meatballs: prepare your favorite meatball recipe; shape into 1 inch balls. Do *not* brown. Bring to a boil a sauce made of a pint of the tomato-apple chutney, a small jar of jelly (such as grape or currant), and about a cup of water. Drop meatballs into sauce and simmer slowly about an hour. Can be served immediately, but we think they taste best if kept in the refrigerator for several days to "ripen."

Combine a pint of the chutney with the following:

A can of whole kernal corn, drained
A can of chick peas
A can of kidney beans (red)
A can of black beans
A jar of pickled onions (or onion relish)

This will keep beautifully for weeks in refrigerator. Highly nutritious for snacking. (Ignore any calories you happen to spot.)

Summer Squash Pickles

Makes 4 Pints
Tasty, different pickle

⅔ cup salt
¾ cup cold water
8 cups sliced small zucchini
 squash or yellow squash
2½ cups sugar
2 cups white vinegar

2 teaspoons mustard seed
1 teaspoon celery seed
2 green peppers
2 medium sized onions, sliced
1 jar pimientos, cut in small
 pieces

In large bowl stir salt in cold water. Add sliced squash and weigh down with cover. Let stand 3 hours in refrigerator; drain. Combine sugar, vinegar, mustard and celery seed in kettle. Bring to a boil. Add green pepper, squash, onions and pimiento. Return to boiling and ladle into sterile jars with tight lid. When cool, refrigerate. Will be ready to eat in 1-2 days.

Jane's Hot Dog Relish

Makes 6 Pints

4 cups chopped onions
4 cups chopped cabbage
4 cups chopped green tomatoes
4-6 sweet red peppers, chopped
½ cup salt
4 cups cider vinegar

2 cups water
6 cups sugar
1 tablespoon celery seed
2 tablespoons mustard seed
1½ teaspoons turmeric powder

Mix chopped vegetables with salt. Let stand overnight; rinse and drain. Combine remaining ingredients with vegetables. Mix well; heat to boiling and simmer 20 minutes, stirring often. Seal in sterilized jars. Keeps well.

Rhubarb Relish

Makes 2 Quarts
Delicious with poultry or meat

1 quart finely chopped rhubarb	1 teaspoon salt
1 quart chopped onions	1 teaspoon cinnamon
3 cups sugar	1 teaspoon cloves
2 cups cider vinegar	1 teaspoon allspice

Combine all ingredients in large kettle. Bring to a boil. Reduce heat and simmer, uncovered for 1½ hours until thick. Stir occasionally to prevent burning. Pour into sterile jars and seal with paraffin. Can be frozen.

Zucchini Relish

Makes 6 Pints

10 cups ground zucchini	1 tablespoon nutmeg
4 cups ground onion	1 tablespoon turmeric
1 ground green pepper	2 tablespoons celery seed
1 ground red pepper	4 cups sugar
5 tablespoons salt	2½ cups white vinegar
1 tablespoon cornstarch	

Grind vegetables in meat grinder. Mix together with salt and let stand overnight. Wash and drain well. Mix with remaining ingredients in kettle. Simmer 30 minutes. Pour into sterile jars while hot and seal.

Fruit Leather

Quick way to preserve excess fruits or over-ripe berries

1 tablespoon honey
2 cups puree of any of the
  following:

apples, apricots, bananas,
  berries, grapes, peaches,
  pears, pineapple,

Wash core and cut fruit into chunks (leave skins on). Place small amount of fruit in blender and start processing. Apples may need a small amount of water to get started. Keep adding fruit until you have 2 cups of puree. Add 1 tablespoon honey to each 2 cups puree if desired. If it tastes good as a sauce, it will taste good dried. Cover cookie sheets with plastic wrap, masking taped occasionally so it won't curl. Spread puree about ¼ inch thick, place in dehydrator or lowest setting of oven and dry (4-6 hours or overnight). When it is firm and chewy, roll up the leather, store in airtight container and label. (Experiment by combining fruits, spiced with cinnamon, coriander or nutmeg)

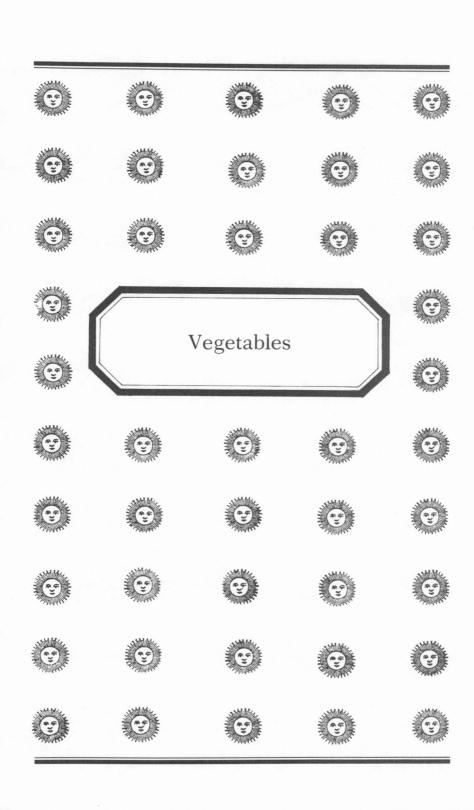

Vegetables

Baked Asparagus with Cheese Sauce

Serves 4 to 6

1½ pounds asparagus
1½ teaspoons butter
1½ teaspoons flour
2 cups grated Swiss or Cheddar
   cheese
¼ teaspoon salt

¼ teaspoon prepared mustard
1½ cups milk
4-5 hard cooked eggs, peeled
   and sliced
Paprika

Steam asparagus five minutes and drain. Melt butter in saucepan;
add flour, and cook, stirring for several minutes. Add remaining
ingredients, except eggs; stir until thick. In buttered shallow baking
dish layer asparagus, eggs and sauce. Sprinkle with paprika. Bake at
350° for 10-20 minutes.

Lima-Sausage Casserole

Great for buffet

3 (10 ounce) packages Fordhook
   lima beans, partially cooked
1 pound Italian hot sausage
½ cup chopped green pepper
1 cup chopped onion

½ cup chopped celery
1½ cups tomato juice
1½ teaspoon salt, optional
2 tablespoons brown sugar

Place drained lima beans in a 2 quart casserole. Remove sausage
from casings; cut into bite-sized pieces. In skillet brown sausage
and remove from pan. Pour off most of the fat. In remaining fat,
saute onion, green pepper and celery. Mix all remaining ingredients
together and pour over lima beans. Bake at 350° in covered
casserole for 45-60 minutes.

Asparagus-Mushroom Casserole

Serves 8 to 10

4 cups fresh mushrooms, halved
1 cup chopped onion
4 tablespoons butter
2 tablespoons flour
1 teaspoon chicken bouillon
   granules
½ teaspoon salt
Dash of pepper
½ teaspoon ground nutmeg

1 cup milk
2 (10 ounce) packages frozen
   cut asparagus, cooked and
   drained
¼ cup chopped pimiento
½ cup sliced water chestnuts
1½ teaspoons lemon juice
¾ cup soft bread crumbs
1 teaspoon butter, melted

Cook mushrooms and onion in butter until tender, about 10 minutes. Remove vegetables; set aside, leaving butter in skillet. Blend in flour, chicken granules, salt, pepper and nutmeg. Add milk. Cook and stir until bubbly. Stir in mushrooms and onion, cooked asparagus, pimiento, chestnuts and lemon juice. Place in 1½ quart casserole. Sprinkle with bread crumbs and butter and bake at 350° for 35 minutes.

Chinese String Beans

Serves 3 to 4

4 tablespoons oil
1 teaspoon salt
Dash pepper
1 pound lean chopped beef
¼ cup finely chopped onion
2 garlic cloves, minced

1 cup beef bouillon
1 pound string beans, cut in
   bite-sized pieces
2 tablespoons cornstarch
¼ cup cold water
Soy sauce

Heat oil, salt and pepper in large frying pan. Add beef, onion and garlic and cook until beef is well done. Add bouillon and string beans. Cover and cook over moderate heat until beans are barely tender. Blend together cornstarch and cold water. Add to meat, stirring constantly until juice thickens. Add soy sauce to taste. Serve with rice and toasted almonds.

Artichoke Bottoms with Oysters and Spinach

Serves 4 to 8

8 large artichoke bottoms
2 tablespoons butter
1 cup finely chopped scallions
2 packages fresh spinach leaves,
  cleaned
Salt to taste

Freshly ground pepper
½ cup heavy cream
8 oysters
¼ cup freshly grated Gruyere or
  Parmesan cheese

Arrange artichokes, bottom side down, on baking dish. Heat butter
in saucepan and add scallions. Cook, stirring briefly. Add spinach
and cook, stirring until wilted. Add salt and pepper. Divide spinach
mixture in half. Use half to stuff artichoke shells. Return remaining
spinach mixture to stove and add cream. Bring to a boil and cook
two minutes. Add oysters and cook briefly just until edges curl,
30-40 seconds. Do not over cook. Arrange one oyster on top of each
spinach-filled artichoke shell. Spoon spinach in cream over all.
Sprinkle each portion with cheese. Bake at 450° for 30 minutes.

Broccoli, Cauliflower Supreme

Serves 4 to 6
A real change of pace

1 bunch fresh broccoli
1 head cauliflower
2 scallions
6 fresh mushrooms
2-3 tablespoons peanut oil

2 tablespoons tamari (soy
  substitute)
2 slices Muenster cheese, cut
  into strips

Clean broccoli and cauliflower and break into flowerets. Chop
scallions. clean and slice mushrooms. Heat wok or large skillet on
medium-high heat. Drip peanut oil around the sides, it will pool in
bottom of wok. Add scallions and stir. Add broccoli and cauliflower,
stir frying until crisp-cooked. Add mushrooms and stir. Add tamari
and stir. Place cheese strips over all and cover until cheese melts.
Serve immediately.

Dixie Pineapple Beans

Serves 6

¼ cup light molasses
¼ teaspoon ground cinnamon
¼ teaspoon ground ginger
⅛ teaspoon ground nutmeg
½ teaspoon salt
2 (16 ounce) cans vegetarian
    beans

1 small can pineapple chunks
2 tablespoons pineapple juice
½ teaspoon lemon juice
½ cup chopped pecans
1 tablespoon light molasses
1 tablespoon butter, melted

Combine ¼ cup molasses, cinnamon, ginger, nutmeg and salt in
1½ quart casserole. Add beans, pineapple, pineapple juice, lemon
juice and ¼ cup of the pecans. Mix well. In cup, combine
remaining pecans, 1 tablespoon molasses and butter. Spoon around
edge of beans. Bake at 350° for 40-45 minutes, or until beans are
bubbly.

Stuffed Eggplant

Serves 4

2 small eggplants
½ pound ground beef
1 large onion, finely chopped
1 medium tomato, chopped
3 garlic cloves, pressed
3 tablespoons vegetable oil
¼ cup chopped parsley

1 teaspoon garlic salt
½ teaspoon pepper
½ teaspoon dried oregano
1 cup water
¼ pound Cheddar cheese cut
    into 8 strips

Wash eggplant; cut in half lengthwise. Remove pulp, leaving ¼
inch shells; set aside. Cut pulp into cubes and saute with ground
beef, onion, tomato and garlic in oil until beef is browned and onion
tender. Stir in parsley, salt, pepper and oregano. Stuff shells with
eggplant mixture and place in a 13×9 baking dish; pour water into
dish. Cover with foil and bake at 350° for 30 minutes. Top each
eggplant half with 2 strips of cheese and bake, uncovered an
additional 5 minutes or until cheese melts. Garnish with chopped
parsley.

Baked Beans

Serves 6 to 8
Easy and very good

1 pound white navy beans
1 medium onion, finely chopped
½ pound salt pork
1 cup molasses
½ cup brown sugar
1 cup ketchup

1 teaspoon salt
½ teaspoon dry mustard
½ teaspoon garlic powder
   (optional)
2½ cups water

Soak beans overnight. Bring to a boil for 1 hour or till tender; drain. Saute onion slowly and remove. Brown salt pork slices. Blend together remaining ingredients and put into a bean pot and stir. Add salt pork. Bake at 325° for 2 hours.

Sesame Beans and Celery

Serves 4

3 cups fresh green beans
1 cup sliced celery
½ onion, chopped
2 tablespoons whole wheat flour
2 teaspoons brown sugar
1 teaspoon salt
1 cup yogurt
⅛ teaspoon pepper

½ teaspoon oregano
Dash garlic powder
½ cup low-fat cottage cheese
¼ cup toasted, ground sesame
   seeds
½ cup bread crumbs
1 tablespoon butter or margarine

Cut beans into ¾-inch lengths. Cook beans, celery and onion in small amount of water for 10 minutes. Drain. Stir in flour, brown sugar and salt. Add yogurt. Pour into deep baking dish. Mix seasonings with cottage cheese and spread over vegetables. Sprinkle with sesame meal and bread crumbs. Dot with butter and bake at 350° for 30 minutes.

Connecticut Baked Beans

Serves 10 to 12

4 cups dried beans (2 pounds)
1-2 pounds salt pork, diced
1 teaspoon salt
¾ cup maple syrup or ½ cup
   brown sugar
½ teaspoon ginger
½ teaspoon cinnamon

¼ teaspoon nutmeg
½ teaspoon mace
1 tablespoon dry mustard
2 medium onions, chopped
1 cup molasses
1 garlic clove, chopped
1 (20 ounce) can tomato juice

Soak beans overnight. Keep water level above beans. Next day, simmer beans for 2-3 hours until tender. Drain and reserve liquid. Add remaining ingredients with beans. Add enough bean liquid to cover. Cover and bake slowly at 250° for 6-8 hours. Add boiling water as needed to cover beans while baking. Uncover during last ½ hour of baking to brown top.

Beets in Orange and Lemon Sauce

Serves 4 to 6

2 pounds beets
½ cup orange juice
½ cup lemon juice
2 tablespoons cider vinegar
1½ tablespoons cornstarch

2 tablespoons sugar
1 teaspoon salt
¼ cup butter
1 teaspoon grated orange peel
1 teaspoon grated lemon peel

Gently wash beets, leaving skins intact; remove leaves. Place beets in large saucepan, cover with cold water, bring to boiling. Reduce heat, simmer, covered, 45 minutes or until tender. Drain and cool. Peel and cut into ¼ inch slices. In same saucepan combine orange and lemon juices, vinegar and cornstarch; stir until smooth. Bring to boiling, stirring, mixture will be thickened and translucent. Add sugar, salt and beets, cook gently uncovered 10 minutes or until heated through. Stir in butter and orange and lemon peels.

Brussels Sprouts with Yogurt

Serves 4 to 6

2 pounds small Brussels sprouts
1 tablespoon butter
2 small tomatoes, chopped
2 teaspooons chopped chives
½ teaspoon nutmeg

Salt and pepper
1 cup plain yogurt
¼ cup Parmesan cheese
¼ cup toasted almond slivers

Cook cleaned Brussels sprouts in boiling salted water or steam for 5 minutes until tender. Remove and drain thoroughly. Place sprouts in a buttered casserole dish. Cover with tomatoes and chives. Season with nutmeg, salt and pepper. Pour yogurt over top. Then sprinkle with cheese and almonds. Bake at 350° for 15 minutes or until top is nicely browned. Serve hot.

Broccoli Souffle

Serves 10 to 12
A good side dish with meat or chicken

1 pound medium noodles
½ cup butter, melted
2 cups milk

2 (10 ounce) packages frozen,
  chopped broccoli
2 packages onion soup mix
6 eggs, well beaten

Cook noodles until not quite done. Combine with melted butter. Add milk and slightly cooked and drained broccoli. Add combined onion soup mix and beat eggs. Pour into 13×9 greased baking dish. Bake, covered, at 350° for ½ hour. Uncover and bake ½ hour longer. (Spinach may be substituted for broccoli).

Rice and Broccoli Casserole

Serves 6
Marvelous with steak

1 (1 pound) bag frozen, chopped
   broccoli
1 large onion, chopped
1 cup cooked rice (⅓ cup raw
   rice)
¼-½ teaspoon salt

1 (10½ ounce) can undiluted,
   condensed cream of
   mushroom soup
¾ cup grated Cheddar cheese
½ cup milk
¼ cup butter or margarine
Buttered bread crumbs

In large saucepan cook broccoli and onion in butter until onion is limp and broccoli no longer frozen. Add remaining ingredients and mix until well blended. Place in a greased 2½ quart casserole. Top with buttered bread crumbs and bake at 350° for 30 minutes.

Cheese-Vegetable Medley

Serves 10 to 12
Great as a vegetable dish or main course

1 tablespoon oil
1 large onion, coarsely chopped
2 large peppers, cut in chunks
3 summer squash, cut in
   chunks
3 zucchini, cut in chunks
½ pound small mushrooms

2 large tomatoes, chopped
1 teaspoon salt
⅛ teaspoon pepper
¾ teaspoon thyme
1½ cups herb stuffing mix
2 cups shredded Swiss cheese

Heat oil in large skillet. Add onion and peppers; saute 3 minutes. Add squash, zucchini and mushrooms and saute 3 minutes. Add tomatoes and seasonings; cook 1 minute. Spread stuffing mix over bottom of buttered casserole. Layer half of vegetables over stuffing. Top with 1 cup cheese and remaining vegetables. Cover with remaining cheese. Cover casserole and bake at 350° for ½ hour. Voila!

Carrot and Cauliflower Pie

Makes 9-Inch Pie

2 cups finely crushed stuffing
  mix
¼ cup butter, melted
1 cup chopped onion
1 garlic clove, minced
2 tablespoons butter
4 cups cooked cauliflower

½ cup sliced, cooked carrots
½ teaspoon oregano
1 tablespoon parsley
Salt and pepper, to taste
1½ cups shredded Cheddar
  cheese
Buttered bread crumbs

Combine stuffing mix and butter. Press into a 9-inch pie plate. Bake at 375° for 8-10 minutes. Saute onion and garlic in butter. Add onion mixture to cauliflower, carrots, oregano, parsley, salt and pepper. Sprinkle ¾ cup cheese over bottom of crust. Spoon vegetables on top. Add remaining cheese on top and sprinkle with buttered bread crumbs. Bake at 375° for 30 minutes.

Heavenly Carrots

Serves 6 to 8
A nice addition to any meal

4 cups sliced, parboiled carrots
1½ cups plain croutons
1 cup grated Cheddar cheese
2 eggs, beaten
¼ cup milk

¼ cup butter, melted
1½ teaspoons Worcestershire
  sauce
1 teaspoon salt

Mix carrots, croutons and cheese. Put in 1½ quart buttered casserole. Mix remaining ingredients. Pour over carrot mixture. Bake, uncovered at 400° for 20 minutes.

Corn Pudding

Serves 6
Tastes like corn fritters but much simpler

2-3 tablespoons oil
2 (16 ounce) cans creamed corn
1 cup flour

1 heaping teaspoon baking
  powder
4 large eggs
Salt and pepper, to taste

Put oil in 13×9 baking dish and heat for a few minutes in oven at 350°. Mix remaining ingredients together and pour in dish. Bake for 1 hour.

Breaded Cauliflower

Serves 4

1 medium cauliflower, broken
  into flowerets
½ cup white wine vinegar
Salt and pepper, to taste

1 egg
½ cup milk
1 cup bread crumbs
Butter

Cook cauliflower in water to cover with dash of salt and vinegar. Cook until crisp-tender. Drain. Separate egg and whip egg white and yolk separately. Combine yolk and milk. Roll flowerets in egg-milk mixture, then in egg whites and finally in bread crumbs. Sprinkle with salt and pepper and fry quickly in butter.

Broiled Baked Potato Skins

Baked potatoes
Sweet butter, softened

Salt and pepper
Grated cheese, optional

Bake potatoes, cool and scrape the insides thoroughly, reserving potato pulp for other use. Cut skins carefully into long strips about 1 to 1½ inches wide. Butter them generously with softened butter. Sprinkle with salt, pepper and cheese. Broil until brown and crisp, about 6-7 inches from broiler, making sure they don't burn. Can also be used as an appetizer.

Italian Style Mushrooms

Serves 6

1 (8 ounce) can tomato sauce
1 pound mushrooms, sliced
2 tablespoons chopped onion
1 garlic clove, crushed
½ teaspoon salt

⅛ teaspoon pepper
¼ teaspoon oregano
2 tablespoons butter or
    margarine
1 teaspoon sugar

Blend all ingredients in medium saucepan. Simmer over medium heat until mushrooms are tender and sauce has thickened, about 20 minutes. Serve.

Mushrooms Florentine

Serves 6 to 8
Especially nice with roast beef

1 pound fresh mushrooms
2 (10 ounce) packages frozen,
    chopped spinach, cooked and
    drained
1 teaspoon salt

¼ cup chopped onion
¼ cup butter, melted
1 cup grated Cheddar cheese
Garlic salt

Wash and dry mushrooms. Slice off stems. Saute stems and caps until brown. Line shallow 10-inch casserole with spinach which has been seasoned with salt, onion and melted butter. Sprinkle with ½ cup cheese. Arrange mushrooms over the spinach. Season with garlic salt. Cover with remaining cheese. Bake at 350° for 20 minutes or until cheese is melted and brown.

Far East Celery Casserole

Serves 8

4 cups diagonally sliced celery
    (1 inch)
1 (10½ ounce) can undiluted,
    condensed cream of celery
    soup
1 (5 ounce) can water
    chestnuts, drained and thinly
    sliced

¼ cup diced pimiento
¾ cup soft bread crumbs
¼ cup slivered almonds, lightly
    sauteed
2 tablespoons butter, melted

Cook celery in small amount of salted water until crisp-tender. Mix
celery, soup, water chestnuts and pimiento; pour into 1-quart
casserole. Top with bread crumbs blended with almonds and melted
butter. Bake, uncovered, at 350° for 35 minutes. (Casserole may be
made early in the day, ready for baking at serving time).

Red Cabbage with Apples and Wine

Serves 4

1 medium head red cabbage
4 strips bacon, diced
1 onion, chopped
2 teaspoons vinegar

1 cup red wine
2 green apples, peeled, cored
    and chopped
Salt and pepper, to taste

Core cabbage and remove tough outer leaves. Finely shred cabbage.
Drop into boiling salted water and cook for 10 minutes or until
cabbage is wilted. Drain. In large skillet fry bacon until crisp. Add
onion and saute until golden. Add vinegar slowly, red wine and
cabbage. Cover and simmer for 30 minutes. Add apples and simmer,
covered for 30 minutes. Season to taste with salt and pepper.

Corn-Zucchini Bake

Serves 8

1 pound zucchini
¼ cup chopped onion
1 tablespoon butter
2 eggs, beaten
1 (10 ounce) package frozen
corn, cooked

1 cup shredded processed Swiss
cheese
¼ tablespoon salt
¼ cup fine dry bread crumbs
2 tablespoons grated Parmesan
cheese
1 tablespoon butter, melted

Slice zucchini 1-inch thick. Cook, covered in small amount of salted
water until tender, 15-20 minutes. Drain and mash. Cook onion in 1
tablespoon butter until tender. Combine beaten egg, zucchini,
onion, corn, Swiss cheese and salt. Put in 2 quart casserole.
Combine bread crumbs, Parmesan and melted butter. Sprinkle on
top. Bake at 350° for 40 minutes.

Eggplant Julienne

Serves 4

5 slices bacon
1 onion, chopped
1 eggplant, pared and cut into
¼ inch strips
1 (1 pound) can tomatoes, cut
up

1 teaspoon sugar
¾ teaspoon basil
½ teaspoon salt
Dash pepper
2 tablespoons parsley

In skillet, cook bacon until crisp. Remove bacon and crumble.
Reserve 2 tablespoons drippings. Cook onion in drippings until
tender but not brown. Stir in bacon, eggplant, tomatoes, sugar,
basil, salt and pepper. Cover and simmer 10 minutes. Turn into
serving dish and sprinkle with parsley.

Eggplant (Bhurta)

Serves 4

1 large eggplant
1 small onion, finely chopped
1 tablespoon butter
¼ teaspoon ground cumin

½ teaspoon ground coriander
1 medium tomato, chopped
¼ cup yogurt
Salt and pepper, to taste

Bake unpeeled eggplant at 350° until soft to the touch, about 1 hour. Cool slightly; peel and mash in colander to remove excess juices. Saute onion in butter until brown. Add spices and tomato. Cook until soft. Add eggplant, yogurt, salt and pepper. Mix well. Cook 15 minutes. (May be frozen up to 2 weeks. Thaw and heat long enough to let juices evaporate).

Curried Fruit

Serves 8 to 10
Perfect side dish with ham or pork

1 (29 ounce) can pear halves
1 (29 ounce) can peach or
  apricot halves
1 (29 ounce) can pineapple
  chunks

12 marashino cherries
⅓ cup butter
¾ cup dark brown sugar
4 teaspoons curry powder

On the day before serving, thoroughly drain all fruit and arrange, cut side up, in shallow casserole. Decorate with cherries. Melt butter, add sugar and curry and cook until dissolved. Pour over fruit. Cover casserole and bake at 325° for 1 hour. Cool and refrigerate. Reheat to use and serve hot. For variation: substitute 3 large sliced bananas for pear halves and 2 tablespoons dark brown mustard for curry powder.

Saugatuck Creamed Onions

Serves 8

30-35 small white onions, peeled
1 tablespoon butter
1 tablespoon flour
½ cup milk

1 cup light cream
½ teaspoon salt
Dash of white pepper

Cook onion in boiling, salted water 15-20 minutes. Drain well. Melt butter in saucepan, stir in flour, stirring constantly. Add milk, cream, salt and pepper. Stir with whisk until sauce bubbles. Add onions; bring to boiling. Simmer 2-3 minutes.

Roasted Peppers

4 whole green or red peppers
    (or a combination of both)
½ cup olive oil
¼ cup tarragon vinegar

2 tablespoons capers
1 garlic clove, crushed
1 teaspoon basil
½ teaspoon pepper

Place peppers in a shallow pan. Broil, turning for 12-15 minutes. Let cool. Cut in half, pull off skin, remove seeds and pulp and cut lengthwise into ¼-inch strips. Place in a bowl. In a jar combine remaining ingredients. Shake until blended. Pour over peppers, toss and refrigerate. Warm to room temperature before serving.

"Do-Ahead" Mashed Potatoes

Serves 12

5 pounds potatoes
2 tablespoons butter
1 teaspoon salt
¼ teaspoon pepper

1 cup sour cream
1 (8 ounce) package cream
    cheese
1 teaspoon onion salt

Boil potatoes and mash with remaining ingredients. Place mixture in greased casserole. Dot with butter and cover. Refrigerate. To serve, bake at 350° for 15 minutes. Remove cover and bake an additional 15 minutes.

Potato Pancakes

Serves 8
Delicious with pot roast

1 medium onion	1 tablespoon flour
6 Idaho potatoes	½ teaspoon baking powder
1 egg	Salt and pepper

Peel and grate onion; set aside. Peel and grate potatoes. Combine with onion. Add egg and blend with fork. Add flour, baking powder, salt and pepper. Drop by spoonful and flatten into hot shortening iron frying pan. Cook until golden brown on both sides. Place on paper towels to drain and serve with apple sauce.

Bert Parks
Actor-T.V. Personality

Eli Whitney, whose cotton gin earned him distinction as the "Savior of the South" also pioneered mass production methods at his Hamden gun shop.

Sweet Potato Casserole

Serves 6

2 (17 ounce) cans sweet potatoes, mashed	½ teaspoon salt
	½ teaspoon ginger
2 tablespoons butter, melted	¼ teaspoon cloves
1 cup eggnog	2 tablespoons grated orange rind
¾ cup sugar	½ cup chopped pecans

Mix together first 7 ingredients. Fold in orange rind and nuts. Pour into a 2 quart casserole. Bake at 375° for 40 minutes.

Herbed Tomatoes

Serves 8

⅔ cup parsley
1 tablespoon fresh basil or
  1½ teaspoons dried basil
1 large shallot
¾ cup olive oil

¼ cup red wine vinegar
½ teaspoon sugar
½ teaspoon salt
Freshly ground pepper
8 firm tomatoes

Mince parsley, basil and shallots in processor and blend briefly the remaining ingredients. Slice tomatoes and cover with dressing. Marinate several hours. Drain, reserving dressing for another use.

Baked Tomatoes Stuffed with Barley

Serves 6

6 tomatoes
¼ pound mushrooms, sliced
2 tablespoons butter
1 tablespoon flour
2 cups barley, steamed
1 cup sour cream

1 tablespoon dill, snipped, or
  1 teaspoon dried dill
1 tablespoon pignolia nuts,
  optional
¾ teaspoon salt
Dill for garnish

Cut a ½ inch slice from top of tomatoes, remove pulp, leaving a ¼ inch shell. Remove seeds, chop and reserve pulp. Sprinkle shells with salt, invert and let drain for 20 minutes. Saute mushrooms in butter for 3 minutes. Add flour, stirring for a few minutes then stir in barley, sour cream, reserved tomato pulp, dill, nuts and salt. Fill tomato shells. Place tomatoes in a buttered baking dish. Bake at 375° for 20 minutes. Top each tomato with a sprig of dill when serving.

Mushroom Stuffed Tomatoes

Serves 6

6 medium tomatoes
1 pint fresh mushrooms, chopped
2 tablespoons butter or margarine
½ cup sour cream

2 egg yolks, beaten
¼ cup fine dry, seasoned bread crumbs
Salt and pepper, to taste
Dash thyme

Slice stem end from tomatoes. Scoop out pulp. Turn lightly salted shells upside down to drain. Finely chop the pulp. Measure 1 cup and set aside. Saute mushrooms in butter until tender. Combine sour cream and egg yolks. Add to mushrooms with tomato pulp. Mix well. Stir in bread crumbs and seasonings. Cook, stirring gently, until mixture thickens. Fill tomato shells with mixture. Place in baking dish. Sprinkle with topping. Bake at 375° for 25 minutes or until browned.

Topping:
¼ cup seasoned bread crumbs
2 tablespoons butter, melted

1 tablespoon grated Parmesan cheese

Tomatoes Rockefeller

Serves 12
Delicious with fish

6 large tomatoes
2 (10 ounce) packages frozen chopped spinach, cooked, well drained
2 cups bread crumbs
6 scallions, chopped
6 eggs, beaten

¾ cup butter, melted
½ cup Parmesan cheese
1 tablespoon minced garlic
¼ teaspoon thyme
Salt and pepper, to taste
1 tablespoon seasoned salt

Cut tomatoes in half, hollow out slightly. Mix remaining ingredients in order given. Fill tomatoes with spinach mixture. Place on greased cookie sheet and bake at 350° for 20 minutes. Mixture may be frozen.

Florentine Rice Ring

Serves 8
A pleasing combination

2 (10 ounce) packages frozen,
  chopped spinach
5-6 cups cooked rice
1 teaspoon salt

¼ teaspoon garlic salt
¼ cup butter or margarine
1½ cups grated Parmesan
  cheese

Cook spinach as directed and drain well. Cook rice as directed
adding salt, garlic salt and 2 tablespoons butter. Measure and
reserve 2 tablespoons Parmesan cheese to garnish ring. Combine
rice, spinach, remaining butter and cheese. Mix lightly until
blended. Lightly pack into well oiled 6½ cup ring mold. Let stand 1
minute. Loosen edges and unmold onto heated serving platter.
Sprinkle with reserved cheese.

Rice Pilaff

Serves 6

½ cup fine egg noodles,
  uncooked
¼ cup butter or margarine
1 cup long grain rice

2½ cups chicken broth
Raisins, currants or pignolia
  nuts (optional)
Salt and pepper, to taste

Saute noodles in butter until lightly browned. Add rice and chicken
broth. Cover and bring to a boil. Reduce heat and simmer on low
heat for about 20 minutes. If desired, any one or a combination of
raisins and nuts can be added. Salt and pepper, to taste. Remove
from heat and allow to stand as long as 30 minutes before serving.
Can be made several hours in advance and heated just before
serving so rice will be fluffy and grains separated.

Riscotto Alla Milanese

Serves 10 to 12

Riscotto is a classic dish of the North—the most famous version being riscotto Milanese and, when properly cooked, is one of the delights of Italian cuisine. Riscotto is almost always eaten as a dish by itself and rarely accompanies anything other than osso buco, the equally well-known and robust Veal stew from Milan.

2 tablespoons butter
2 teaspoons olive oil
1 small onion, finely chopped
1 ounce raw beef marrow
2 cups Italian rice
¾ cup dry white wine

4 cups of chicken stock
Pinch of powdered saffron
Salt and pepper, to taste
2 tablespoons butter
4-5 level tablespoons Parmesan
   cheese

Heat butter and oil in large saucepan. Add the onion and gently cook, covered for 5 minutes or until onion is soft but still white. Add beef marrow taken from marrow bone. Add rice and cook gently for 3 minutes, turning all the time until each rice grain is coated with butter and oil. Add the wine and cook over moderate heat until it evaporates. Add chicken stock and when the rice has absorbed all the liquid, stir in a large pinch of powdered saffron, salt and pepper and remaining butter and Parmesan cheese. Stir frequently with a fork and allow to cook for 20-30 minutes. The rice should be creamy but still firm. Pass extra butter and Parmesan cheese when serving.

The late Ella Grasso
Former Governor of Connecticut

From 1860 to 1885, Westport's roads thronged with ox-teams hauling succulent onions to the Saugatuck River; where they were transported to New York markets.

Spinach-Artichoke Casserole

Serves 16
Interesting combination

4 (10 ounce) packages frozen
    spinach, cooked and well
    drained
1 cup chopped onion
¼ cup butter, melted

1 pint sour cream
⅔ cup, minus 3 tablespoons
    Parmesan cheese
1 can artichoke hearts, cut into
    halves

Saute onion in butter. Add sour cream and cheese. Drain artichoke
hearts. Mix spinach with sour cream and onion. Place in large
shallow baking dish. Press artichoke hearts into mixture. Bake at
350° for 30 minutes.

Spinach Hau Pia

Serves 12
The best spinach dish you've ever tasted

3 (10 ounce) packages frozen
    chopped spinach, thawed and
    drained
3 cups dry cottage cheese
3 cups flaked coconut

4 eggs
1½ cups sour cream
⅓ cup flour
⅓ cup soy sauce

Place spinach on paper towels and squeeze out as much liquid as
possible. Combine spinach, cottage cheese and coconut. In blender,
combine eggs, sour cream, flour and soy sauce. Blend until smooth.
Fold into spinach mixture. Spoon into ungreased 2½-quart
casserole. Refrigerate, covered, up to 2 days. Bake, uncovered at
350° for 40-45 minutes. Allow to stand 10 minutes before serving.

Summer Squash and Tomatoes

Serves 6
Special when picked from the garden

4 small yellow squash
4 small tomatoes
2 tablespoons red pimiento
¼ cup finely chopped parsley
1 lemon

3 tablespoons butter
2 tablespoons oil
Salt and pepper, to taste
1 tablespoon sugar

Wash squash, do not peel, cut off ends. Slice in half lengthwise and then lengthwise again and dice. Peel tomatoes and dice. Chop pimiento and parsley. Grate rind, squeeze lemon and keep separate. Melt 2 tablespoons butter in skillet. Add 1 tablespoon oil. When hot, add the squash. Coat each piece with oil and butter. Cook over low heat 3-4 minutes. Add tomatoes, salt and pepper. Cook, covered, 2-3 minutes. Remove lid and add remaining oil and butter. Add lemon juice. Cook 2 minutes more. Test vegetables for tender crisp. Add lemon rind and sugar. Mix thoroughly. Stir in pimiento and parsley.

Summer Squash Casserole

Serves 6

2 pounds yellow summer
  squash, peeled and sliced
¼ cup chopped onion
1 can condensed cream of
  chicken soup

1 cup sour cream
1 cup shredded carrots
1 (8 ounce) package
  herb-seasoned stuffing mix
½ cup butter, melted

In saucepan cook squash and onion in boiling salted water for 5 minutes; drain. Combine soup and sour cream. Stir in carrots. Fold in drained squash and onion. Combine stuffing mix and butter. Spread half of stuffing mixture in bottom of 12×7 baking dish. Spoon vegetable mixture on top. Sprinkle remaining stuffing over vegetables. Bake at 350° for 25-30 minutes.

Apple Yams

Serves 6 to 8

6 medium yams or sweet
   potatoes or
   1 (2½ pound) can drained
   yams
4 peeled, sliced tart apples

¼ cup chopped pecans
Cinnamon
¾ cup firmly packed brown
   sugar
½ cup butter, melted

Bake sweet potatoes, piercing skin and allowing 40-60 minutes at 400°, or cook, covered, in boiling salted water 30-35 minutes, until tender. Drain, cool slightly, and remove skins. Grease a 1½ quart baking dish. Alternate layers of sliced sweet potatoes and apples, sprinkling each layer with nuts, cinnamon, brown sugar and butter. Arrange layer of apples attractively over top. Bake, covered at 350° for 30 minutes. Uncover and bake an additional 45 minutes.

Fritata

Serves 8

¾ cup chopped green pepper
1½ cups sliced mushrooms
1½ cups chopped zucchini
¾ cup chopped onion
1 large garlic clove, minced
3 tablespoons oil
6 eggs, beaten

¼ cup light cream
1 pound cream cheese, diced
1½ cups shredded Cheddar
   cheese
2 cups cubed white bread
1 teaspoon salt
¼ teaspoon pepper

Saute pepper, mushrooms, zucchini, onion and garlic in oil until zucchini is tender. Cool slightly. Beat eggs with cream. Add cream cheese, Cheddar cheese, bread, salt, pepper and sauteed vegetables. Mix well. Pour into greased 10-inch spring-form pan. Bake at 350° for 1 hour or until set in center. Let stand 10 minutes before cutting.

Ratatouille

Serves 6 to 8
A summer favorite

2 teaspoons olive oil
2 teaspoons finely minced garlic
  clove
1 cup coarsely chopped onion
1 large eggplant
3 medium zucchini
1 large green or red pepper
3 cups coarsely chopped
  mushrooms
2 teaspoons dried oregano
2 teaspoons chopped
  parsley
3 tomatoes, peeled, seeded and
  chopped
1 bay leaf
1 teaspoon sugar
1 teaspoon seasoned salt
½ teaspoon freshly ground
  pepper
Alfalfa sprouts for garnish

Heat oil in dutch oven or large saucepan, cook garlic and onion until tender. Add eggplant, zucchini, pepper, mushrooms, oregano and parsley. Stir well. Let simmer about five minutes. Vegetables must remain crisp. Add tomatoes and remaining ingredients except garnish and cook over low heat for 30 minutes or until heated through. Serve hot or cover mixture and refrigerate to serve chilled. To garnish, top with alfalfa sprouts.

Guilford's Henry Whitfield House, built in 1639, is said to be the oldest stone house in the United States.

Stuffed Zucchini

Serves 6

2-3 large zucchini
2 eggs, well beaten
1½ cups shredded sharp
 Cheddar cheese

½ cup small curd cottage
 cheese
2 tablespoons chopped parsley
½ teaspoon salt
Pepper

Wash and cut ends of zucchini. Cook in boiling salted water for
10-12 minutes until tender, but firm; drain. Cut in half lengthwise.
Scoop out centers. Invert to drain on paper towel. Mix remaining
ingredients together. Fill zucchini. Put in greased baking dish.
Bake, uncovered at 350° for 15 minutes. Raise heat to 450° and
cook additional 5 minutes.

Zucchini Pancakes

Serves 4
Nutritious and delicious

3 cups grated zucchini
½ cup flour
1 teaspoon baking powder

½ teaspoon salt
2 tablespoons dried onion
2 eggs

Combine all ingredients. Mix well. Pour batter by ¼ cup fulls onto
hot, well-greased griddle. Mixture will be thick; spread slightly.
Brown lightly, turn. Cheese may be grated directly on finished side.
Cheese will melt while cooking. Brown second side. Add butter each
time batter is placed on the griddle. These make a full meal when
served with a salad.

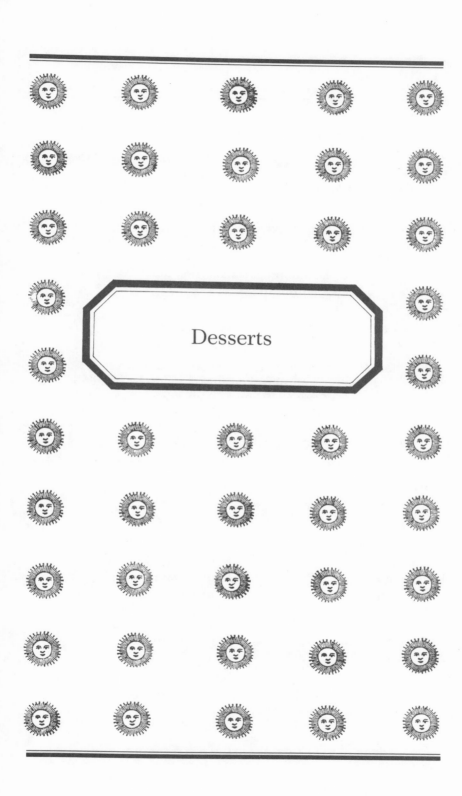

Desserts

Almond Cake

Serves 6 to 8
Served at the Finnish Embassy

2 eggs	1 tablespoon baking powder
½ cup sugar	2 tablespoons cream
Grated rind from ½ orange	½ cup butter, melted
1 cup flour	½ cup slivered almonds

Preheat oven to 350°. Beat eggs and sugar until thick and lemon colored. Add rind. Sift flour and baking powder. Stir into egg mixture. Add cream and melted butter. Turn into greased and floured 9-inch pie plate. Sprinkle almonds on top. Bake for 30-35 minutes until golden brown.

Topping:

2 tablespoons butter	½ cup sugar
1 tablespoon flour	½ tablespoon cream

Melt butter. Add flour, sugar and cream and bring to a boil. Cool. Pour over warm cake and spread evenly. Place under broiler 3-4 seconds. Watch very carefully. Serve in small wedges as this cake is very rich. Can be served warm or cold.

Apple Pie Cake

Serves 6
A Treat in Autumn

½ cup butter	½ teaspoon salt
¾ cup sugar	½ teaspoon nutmeg
1 egg, slightly beaten	⅛ teaspoon cloves
1 cup flour	1 teaspoon vanilla
1 teaspoon baking powder	2 cups chopped apples
1 teaspoon cinnamon	½ cup pecans

Preheat oven to 350°. Melt butter over low heat. Remove from heat and blend with sugar and egg. Add all other ingredients and mix well. Pour into thoroughly greased 9-inch pie pan. Bake for 40-45 minutes. Serve warm with ice cream.

Almond Torte

Serves 8 to 12
Company dessert

8 ounces unblanched almonds
   ground into very fine powder
1 teaspoon baking powder
8 eggs, separated
8 heaping tablespoons sugar

1 tablespoon vanilla
2 tablespoons whiskey
Whipped cream
Unsweetened chocolate
Nuts

Preheat oven to 300°. Add baking powder to almond powder. Mix and set aside. Place egg yolks in large mixing bowl. Add sugar and beat until light and lemon colored. Add liquids. Beat egg whites until stiff. Add nut mixture to egg yolk mixture and stir. Batter will have the consistency of mud. Gradually add beaten egg whites. Handle gently. Batter should be fluffy. Pour into greased 9 inch spring form pan and bake for 1 hour or until cake tester comes out clean. When cool, cut into 2 layers and spread with whipped cream. Sprinkle with grated nuts or bitter chocolate for decoration.

Applesauce Cake

Serves 8 to 10
Old recipe from Grandma

½ cup sugar
½ cup brown sugar
½ cup shortening
1 egg
2 cups flour
½ teaspoon salt
1 teaspoon cinnamon
½ teaspoon ground cloves

½ teaspoon ground nutmeg
1 tablespoon cocoa
1½ cups cold, sweetened
   applesauce
2 teaspoons baking soda
½ cup raisins
½ cup chopped nuts

Preheat oven to 350°. Cream shortening and sugar. Beat in egg. Sift dry ingredients together. Add to mixture and stir well. Add applesauce with baking soda dissolved in it. Beat well. Add raisins and nuts and mix well. Pour into greased 10-inch tube pan or bundt pan and bake for 1 hour until done. Cool on cake rack and frost with favorite frosting or sprinkle with confectioners' sugar.

Apple Walnut Supreme Cake

Serves 10

4 cups chopped tart apples
1¾ cups sugar
2 eggs
½ cup vegetable oil
2 teaspoons vanilla or rum flavor

2 cups flour
2 teaspoons baking soda
1 teaspoons salt
2 teaspoons cinnamon
1 cup chopped walnuts

Preheat oven to 350°. Combine apple and sugar and set aside. In large bowl mix eggs, oil and flavoring. Add dry sifted ingredients alternately with apple mixture; stir in walnuts. Bake in greased and floured 13×9 pan for 45-50 minutes. Do not underbake; test cake with toothpick. If desired, drizzle with Lemon Glaze.

Lemon Glaze:
1 cup confectioners' sugar
1½ tablespoons lemon juice

½ teaspoon vanilla
1 tablespoon corn syrup

Blend all ingredients together until smooth.

Carrot Cake

Serves 12

3 eggs, beaten
2 cups sugar
1⅓ cups oil
2 cups flour
1 teaspoon baking powder
2 teaspoons cinnamon
2 teaspoons baking soda

1 teaspoon salt
1 teaspoon vanilla
2 cups grated carrots
1 cup coarsely chopped walnuts
1 (8 ounce) can crushed
    pineapple and juice
1 cup shredded coconut

Preheat oven to 350°. Combine eggs, sugar, oil and dry ingredients. Stir in carrots, pineapple, nuts and coconut. Bake for 45-50 minutes in 13×9 pan or tube pan.

Frosting:
1 (3 ounce) package cream
    cheese
1½ cups confectioners' sugar

1 teaspoon vanilla and water to
    make proper spreading
    consistency

Mix and spread on cooled cake.

Blueberry Cake with Lemon Sauce

Serves 12 to 15

½ cup butter
1 cup sugar
3 eggs
2 cups flour
1 teaspoon baking powder
1 teaspoon baking soda

½ teaspoon salt
1 cup sour cream
2 teaspoons vanilla
2 cups blueberries
½ cup brown sugar

Preheat oven to 325°. Cream butter and sugar. Add eggs, one at a time. Add sifted dry ingredients alternately with sour cream. Stir in vanilla. Fold in 1 cup berries. Pour ½ of batter into greased and floured 13×9 pan. Cover with remaining berries. Sprinkle with brown sugar. Top with rest of batter. Bake 45-50 minutes. Serve with lemon sauce:

Lemon Sauce
½ cup sugar
1 tablespoon cornstarch
¼ teaspoon salt
¼ cup cold water
½ cup boiling water

3 tablespoons lemon juice
1 teaspoon grated lemon rind
½ teaspoon vanilla
2 tablespoons butter

Combine sugar, cornstarch and salt in saucepan. Gradually stir in cold water, then boiling water. Cook until smooth, clear and slightly thickened. Stir in remaining ingredients.

Hot Water Gingerbread

Serves 9

⅓ cup butter or margarine
⅔ cup boiling water
1 cup molasses
2½ cups flour
½ teaspoon baking soda

½ teaspoon salt
2 teaspoons ginger or
  1 teaspoon ginger with
  1 teaspoon cinnamon and
  ¼ teaspoon cloves

Preheat oven to 350°. Melt butter in hot water. Add molasses and sifted dry ingredients. Beat vigorously. Bake in greased 8×8 pan for 35-40 minutes or greased muffin pans for 25-35 minutes.

Cheesecake

Serves 12

Crust:

2½ cups ground graham
  crackers
½ cup plus 2 tablespoons butter
  or margarine

1 teaspoon cinnamon
1 tablespoon sugar
½ cup finely chopped nuts

Mix thoroughly. Press into spring-form pan.

Filling:

1 pound cottage cheese
1 pound cream cheese
1½ cups sugar
4 eggs, beaten
2 teaspoons vanilla

4 tablespoons cornstarch
3 tablespoons flour
½ cup butter, melted
1 pint sour cream

Preheat oven to 325°. Mix all filling ingredients until smooth. Pour
on crust. Bake for 1 hour. Turn oven off and leave in for 1 more
hour without opening door. Remove and cool. Top with fruit of your
choice.

Chocoholic's Quick-Fix Cheesecake

Serves 8 to 10
May cause addiction

1½ cups chocolate wafers,
  crushed
⅓ cup butter, melted
1 (8 ounce) package cream
  cheese
½ cup sugar

1 teaspoon vanilla
2 eggs, separated
1 (6 ounce) package chocolate
  bits, melted
1 cup heavy cream

Preheat oven to 325°. Mix wafers and butter together. Press into
bottom of spring form pan. Bake for 10 minutes. Mix softened
cream cheese, ¼ cup of sugar and vanilla. Add 2 beaten egg yolks
and melted chocolate bits. Beat egg whites until stiff peaks form.
Gradually add remaining sugar. Add to chocolate mixture. Whip
heavy cream and fold into mixture. Pour over crumb crust and
freeze. Decorate with additional whipped cream if desired.

Individual Cheesecakes

Serves 24

2 (8 ounce) packages cream
   cheese
2 eggs
¾ cup sugar
1 teaspoon vanilla

24 cupcake papers, preferably
   foil
24 vanilla wafers
2 cans pie filling: cherry,
   blueberry, pineapple, etc.

Preheat oven to 375°. Soften cream cheese at room temperature.
Beat with electric mixer. Add eggs, vanilla and sugar. Beat well. Put
vanilla wafers into each cupcake paper. Fill to ¾ full with batter.
Bake for 10 minutes. Cool. Spoon pie filling on top of each.
Refrigerate until ready to serve. Can also be served with whipped
cream on top.

Chocolate Sheet Cake

Serves 16

½ cup butter or margarine
4 tablespoons cocoa
½ cup oil
1 cup water
2 cups flour

2 cups sugar
½ cup buttermilk or sour milk
1 teaspoon baking soda
2 eggs
1 teaspoon vanilla

Preheat oven to 400°. Bring first 4 ingredients to boiling in
saucepan. Sift flour and sugar together. Pour chocolate sauce over
dry ingredients. Mix well. Combine remaining ingredients and mix
well. Place in 15×11 greased and floured pan. Bake for 20 minutes.

Frosting:
½ cup butter or margarine
4 tablespoons cocoa
⅓ cup buttermilk or sour milk
1 pound confectioners' sugar

1 teaspoon salt
1 teaspoon vanilla
1 cup chopped nuts

Bring butter, cocoa and buttermilk to boiling. Add remaining
ingredients and mix until smooth. Add nuts and frost cooled sheet
cake.

Chocolate Swirl Cheesecake

Serves 8
One cheesecake feeds about 3 UConn basketball players

1 cup chocolate cookie crumbs
¼ cup butter, melted
3 tablespoons sugar
3 (8 ounce) packages cream
    cheese
1 cup sour cream
1 cup sugar

2 tablespoons flour
3 eggs, separated
2 tablespoons Kahlua
6 ounces chocolate chips, melted
    and cooled
Whipped cream

Preheat oven to 350°. Combine crumbs, butter and sugar. Press into bottom of spring form pan. Chill. Beat cheese, sour cream, sugar and flour. Add yolks, one at a time, beating well after each. Whip egg whites until stiff and fold into cheese mixture. Add Kahlua and melted chips and gently swirl through cheese mixture with a table knife. Carefully pour into pan. Bake for 60 minutes. Turn off oven and (very important) allow to cool with oven door open.

Coconut Cake

Serves 8 to 10

1 pound puff pastry dough
4 eggs
1½ cups superfine sugar
4½ cups finely grated
    unsweetened coconut (also
    called macaroon coconut)

1 tablespoon butter, melted
1½ teaspoons vanilla
⅔ cup apricot preserves
½ cup whipping cream

Preheat oven to 350°. Lightly grease an 8 inch springform pan. Roll pastry to ¼ inch thickness and line bottom and sides of pan with dough, trim overhanging edges. Beat eggs in large mixing bowl until thoroughly blended and foamy. Add sugar gradually and continue beating until very light, about 2-3 minutes. Blend in coconut, butter and vanilla. Spoon into pastry-lined pan. Place on baking sheet, preferably one with sides, and bake 60-70 minutes, until golden brown. Remove from oven and cool slightly. Release from pan and cool completely. Decorate top of cake with rim of apricot preserves and whipped cream.

Chocolate Crazy Cake

Serves 6 to 8

⅓ cup salad oil or margarine
2 squares unsweetened
  chocolate, melted
1 egg, beaten
1 cup sugar
1¼ cups flour
½ teaspoon salt

½ teaspoon baking soda
½ teaspoon vanilla
¾ cup water
¾ cup chocolate bits, nuts,
  marshmallows (any
  combination)

Preheat oven to 350°. Place oil in 9 inch round baking pan. Add melted chocolate, egg, sugar, flour, salt, baking soda and vanilla. Gently mix for 2 minutes. Fold in the chocolate, nuts and marshmallows. Bake for ½ hour.

Greek Christmas Cake

Serves 24

1 cup butter, softened
2 cups sugar
12 eggs, separated
2 cups finely ground zwieback

2 cups finely ground walnuts
2 teaspoons baking powder
½ teaspoon cinnamon

Syrup
2 cups sugar
1 cup water

2 teaspoons lemon juice

Preheat oven to 325°. In large bowl cream together butter and sugar until light and fluffy. Add egg yolks, one at a time, beating well after each addition. Add zwieback crumbs, walnuts, baking powder and cinnamon. Combine mixture well. Beat egg whites until stiff peaks form; fold ⅓ of whites into mixture, then fold the mixture gently but thoroughly into remaining whites. Turn batter into a buttered and floured 13×9 baking pan and bake for 35-40 minutes. Let cake cool on rack for 5 minutes. In saucepan dissolve sugar and water and boil for 10-15 minutes. Remove from heat and stir in lemon juice. Arrange cake on serving platter and spoon syrup over cake. Chill cake and serve with whipped cream.

Mississippi Mud Cake

Serves 12

4 squares unsweetened chocolate	2 cups flour
2 cups boiling water	1 teaspoon baking powder
2 cups sugar	1 teaspoon baking soda
6 tablespoons butter	1 teaspoon salt
	2 eggs

Preheat oven to 300°. Melt chocolate in boiling water. Simmer 1 minute. Add sugar and butter. Stir and cool. Add flour, baking powder, baking soda, salt and eggs. Beat well. Bake in greased and floured tube pan for 1 hour. Cool and split cake into 2 layers.

Filling:
1 (3 ounce) package chocolate
   pudding

Make pudding according to package directions. Spread between layers of cake.

Topping:

1 pint heavy cream	1 package instant hot chocolate mix

Whip together cream and chocolate mix. Spread over top. Top with chocolate curls if desired.

Rhubarb Cake

Serves 9

2 cups diced rhubarb	2 cups flour
½ cup sugar	1 teaspoon baking soda
½ cup butter or margarine	1 tablespoon cinnamon
1¼ cups sugar	Dash salt
1 egg	1 cup sour milk
1 teaspoon vanilla	

Preheat oven to 350°. Mix rhubarb and sugar. Set aside. Cream butter; add sugar, egg and vanilla. Add all sifted dry ingredients, alternating with milk. Bake in 9-inch square pan for 1 hour. Serve warm, plain or with ice cream or whipped cream.

Thunderbolt Kraut Chocolate Cake

Serves 12
Unusually delicious

⅔ cup butter
1½ cups sugar
3 eggs
1 teaspoon vanilla
2¼ cups sifted whole wheat
   flour
1 teaspoon baking powder

¼ teaspoon salt
½ cup unsweetened cocoa
1 teaspoon baking soda
1 cup water
⅔ cup rinsed, drained and finely
   chopped sauerkraut

Preheat oven to 350°. Cream butter with sugar. Beat in eggs and vanilla. Sift together dry ingredients, add alternately with water to egg mixture. Stir in sauerkraut. Turn into greased and floured 9-inch tube pan. Bake for 40 minutes or until cake tests done. Cool and frost with Galiano Frosting.

Galiano Frosting:
⅔ cup butter
¾ pound confectioners' sugar

2 tablespoons Galiano

Cream butter. Add confectioners' sugar and Galiano, mixing well. Spread on top of Thunderbolt Kraut Chocolate Cake.

Preserve Cake

Make ahead, gets better each day

3 eggs
½ teaspoon salt
2 cups sugar
1 teaspoon vanilla
¾ cup oil
1 cup buttermilk

2 cups flour
1 teaspoon cinnamon
1 teaspoon nutmeg
1 teaspoon baking soda
1 cup pineapple preserves
¾ cup nuts

Preheat oven to 350°. Mix ingredients in order given using mixer. Fold in pineapple preserves. Bake in a well greased, not floured, bundt pan. Bake for 1½ hours. Cake forms its own chewy crust so no icing is needed.

Orange-Cranberry Torte

Serves 12
Easy to make—stays moist

2¼ cups flour
1 cup sugar
¼ teaspoon salt
1 teaspoon baking powder
1 teaspoon baking soda
1 cup chopped nuts

1 cup chopped dates
1 cup fresh cranberries
Grated rind of 2 oranges
2 eggs, beaten
1 cup buttermilk
¾ cup salad oil

Sauce:
½ cup orange juice

½ cup sugar

Preheat oven to 350°. Mix dry ingredients. Stir into fruit. Combine eggs, buttermilk and oil. Add to flour-fruit mixture. Bake in greased bundt or angel food pan for 1 hour. Let stand until lukewarm. Remove from pan and place on cake rack. Mix orange juice and sugar together and pour over cake. Collect juice that drips off and pour over and over again onto cake. Freezes well.

Key Lime Cake

Serves 8 to 10
Delightful on a hot summer day

1⅓ cups sugar
2 cups flour
⅔ teaspoon salt
1 teaspoon baking powder
1 (3 ounce) package
   lime-flavored gelatin
5 eggs

1⅓ cups oil
¾ cup orange juice
½ teaspoon vanilla
1 teaspoon lemon extract
⅓ cup Key lime juice
⅓ cup confectioners' sugar

Preheat oven to 350°. Put dry ingredients in bowl. Add eggs, oil, orange juice, vanilla and lemon extract. Beat until blended. Pour into greased 13×9 pan. Bake 25-30 minutes. Cool 15 minutes in pan. Prick cake and drizzle thoroughly with lime juice mixed with powdered sugar. Cover and refrigerate.

Pina Colada Cake

Serves 8 to 10

1 package (2 layer) white cake
  mix
1 (3½ ounce) package coconut
  cream or vanilla instant
  pudding
4 eggs

½ cup water (if using vanilla
  pudding, increase water to ¾
  cup)
⅓ cup dark rum
¼ cup oil

Preheat oven to 350°. Combine cake mix, pudding, eggs, water, rum
and oil. Beat 4 minutes at medium speed. Pour into 2 greased and
floured 9-inch layer pans. Bake for 35 minutes or until cake springs
back. Cool for 15 minutes. Remove from pan and cool on rack.

Frosting:
1 (8 ounce) can crushed
  pineapple in juice
1 (3½ ounce) package coconut
  cream or vanilla instant
  pudding

⅓ cup dark rum
1 (9 ounce) container frozen
  whipped topping, thawed
1 cup coconut

Combine pineapple, pudding and rum. Beat until well blended. Fold
in thawed whipped topping. Fill and frost cake. Sprinkle with
coconut. Refrigerate.

In 1810 the nation's first silk mill was built in Mansfield.

Fresh Plum Kuchen

Serves 12

2 pounds Italian purple plums or
  1½ pounds tart apples
1¼ cups flour
¼ cup sugar
1½ teaspoons baking powder

½ teaspoon salt
¼ cup butter
1 egg
¼ cup milk
1 teaspoon vanilla

Topping:
¼ cup sugar
1 teaspoon cinnamon

¼ cup butter, melted

Glaze:
⅓ cup currant jelly

1 tablespoon water

Preheat oven to 400°. Grease 13×9 baking pan. Wash plums; cut into thin slices. In medium bowl sift flour with sugar, baking powder and salt. With pastry blender cut in butter until it resembles coarse crumbs. In small bowl, beat egg slightly with fork; add milk and vanilla. Blend. Add to flour mixture beating vigorously with fork until smooth. Batter will be stiff. Spread over bottom of pan. Arrange plums over batter to cover completely, in 5 rows slightly overlapping. Mix topping together; spoon over fruit. Bake for 30-35 minutes. Cool slightly. In small pan melt jelly with water, stirring constantly. Serve warm. Serve with ice cream or whipped cream.

Quick Glossy Chocolate Frosting

Frosts 2 Layer Cake
Better Than a Mix—Superb Flavor

1 cup sugar
¼ cup corn starch
1 cup boiling water
2 squares unsweetened
  chocolate

½ teaspoon salt
¼ cup butter
2 teaspoons vanilla

In 2-quart saucepan thoroughly mix sugar and corn starch. Stir in boiling water, chocolate and salt. Stir until thick. Remove from heat and stir in butter and vanilla. Put on cake while frosting is warm.

Cream Pound Cake - Raspberry Sauce

Serves 8 to 10
Adaptable to many "trimmings"

4 eggs
2 cups sifted cake flour
1 teaspoon baking powder
½ teaspoon salt
1⅓ cups sugar

1 cup heavy cream, whipped
1½ teaspoons vanilla
½ teaspoon almond extract
   (optional)

Preheat oven to 350°. Beat eggs until light and fluffy. Gradually add sifted dry ingredients and beat well. Fold in whipped cream and flavorings. Bake in lightly greased tube or loaf pan for 50 minutes. Good with strawberries in Kirsch or raspberry sauce.

Raspberry Sauce:
2 boxes frozen raspberries,
   partially thawed

Break raspberries into pieces and puree in blender. Strain to remove seeds. Good topping for cake or ice cream.

Cream Cheese Frosting

½ cup butter
1 (8 ounce) package cream
   cheese

1 teaspoon pineapple juice
1 pound box confectioners'
   sugar

Cream butter and cream cheese together. Add pineapple juice and sugar. Frosts one Carrot Cake.

Apple Cheese Pie

Serves 8

½ cup butter
⅓ cup sugar
¼ teaspoon vanilla
1 cup flour
1 (8 ounce) package cream cheese
½ teaspoon vanilla

½ cup sugar
1 egg, beaten
4 cups sliced apples
½ teaspoon cinnamon
⅓ cup sugar
Chopped nuts

Preheat oven to 450°. Cream together first 4 ingredients. Spread in bottom of greased spring form pan and ½ inch up sides. Blend next 3 ingredients until smooth. Pour on top of dough. Mix remaining ingredients together except nuts. Place over cream cheese mixture. Sprinkle chopped nuts on top. Bake for 10 minutes. Lower heat to 400° and cook 25 minutes.

Blueberry-Rhubarb Pie

Serves 6 to 8
A Little Different

2 cups blueberries
2 cups rhubarb, cut in ¼-inch pieces
1½ cups sugar
3 tablespoons flour

¼ teaspoon nutmeg
⅛ teaspoon salt
¼ teaspoon cinnamon
2 tablespoons lemon juice
1 unbaked deep dish pie crust

Preheat oven to 450°. Combine all ingredients. Place in unbaked deep dish pie crust. Bake for 10 minutes. Reduce heat to 350° for 40-45 minutes.

Baked Alaska Pie

Serves 8

1 quart vanilla ice cream
9 inch baked pie crust
1 (12 ounce) jar pineapple
  preserves

½ cup chopped nuts
1 (12 ounce) jar red raspberry
  preserves

Spread ½ of ice cream in pie crust. Cover with pineapple preserves; sprinkle with nuts. Spread with remaining ice cream, cover with raspberry preserves. Freeze. Top with Elegant Meringue:

Meringue:
3 egg whites
Dash of salt

1 cup marshmallow creme

Preheat oven to 450°. Beat egg whites and salt until frothy. Add marshmallow creme, continue beating until stiff peaks form. Bake for 3-5 minutes, until lightly browned. Serve immediately.

Cran-Cherry Pie

Serves 6 to 8
Holiday Favorite

Pastry for lattice-top 9-inch pie
1 (21 ounce) can cherry pie
  filling
1 (16 ounce) can whole
  cranberry sauce
¼ cup sugar

3 tablespoons quick-cooking
  tapioca
1 teaspoon lemon juice
¼ teaspoon ground cinnamon
2 tablespoons butter or
  margarine
Milk

Preheat oven to 400°. In bowl, combine pie filling, cranberry sauce, sugar, tapioca, lemon juice and cinnamon. Let stand for 15 minutes. Line 9-inch pie plate with pastry. Fill pastry shell with fruit mixture. Dot with butter or margarine. Place lattice crust over filling, seal and flute edges. Brush lattice top with a little milk for better browning. Bake for 40-45 minutes or until crust is golden brown. Cover edges of crust with foil after 15 minutes to prevent edges from overbrowning.

Brandy Alexander Pie

Serves 8

Crust:

¼ cup butter or margarine, melted

1½ cups vanilla wafer crumbs

Filling:

3 cups miniature marshmallows or 32 large marshmallows
½ cup milk
¼ cup dark creme de cacao

¼ cup cognac or brandy
1 cup heavy cream, whipped
1 (1 ounce) semi-sweet chocolate bar

Preheat oven to 350°. Add melted butter to cookie crumbs and mix thoroughly. Press into 9-inch pie plate on bottom and sides. Bake 10 minutes. Remove from oven and cool completely. Heat marshmallows and milk in medium saucepan over low heat, stirring constantly until marshmallows are melted. Remove from heat. Add creme de cacao and cognac using a wire whisk or rotary beater. When well mixed, chill 20-30 minutes, stirring occasionally, until mixture mounds slightly when dripped from spoon. Then fold in whipped cream. Pour into pie shell. Chill for 4 hours or longer. Shortly before serving, "peel" chocolate curls off the chocolate bar with a vegetable peeler and drop onto the pie.

Blueberry Pie

Serves 6 to 8
Mother-in-law's special

1 cup sugar
3 tablespoons cornstarch
⅛ teaspoon salt
1 cup water

1 quart blueberries
1 tablespoon butter
9-inch baked pie crust
1 cup whip cream

Mix sugar, cornstarch and salt. Add water and 1 cup blueberries. Cook, stirring until thick. Add butter and rest of blueberries. Cool. Pour into cooked pie crust. Top with whipped cream.

Beverly J. Graham (Mrs. Otto Graham)
Wife of former Cleveland Browns
All-Pro Quarterback

Chocolate Coffee Toffee Pie

Serves 6 to 8

½ package pie crust or recipe
    for single crust pie
¼ cup brown sugar, firmly
    packed
¾ cup finely chopped walnuts

Filling:
¼ cup butter or
    margarine, softened
¾ cup sugar

Coffee Topping:
2 cups whipping cream
2 teaspoons instant coffee

1 square unsweetened chocolate,
    grated
1 teaspoon water
1 teaspoon vanilla

1 square unsweetened chocolate,
    melted and cooled
2 teaspoons instant coffee
2 eggs

½ cup confectioners' sugar
Chocolate curls

Preheat oven to 375°. Combine first four ingredients. Add water and vanilla. Using a fork, mix until well blended. Turn into a well-greased 9-inch pie plate. Press firmly against plate. Bake for 15 minutes. Cool on a wire rack. For filling: beat butter until creamy and gradually add sugar. Beat until light and fluffy. Blend in melted chocolate and instant coffee. Beat in 1 egg at a time until well mixed. Fill pie crust. Refrigerate overnight. For topping: combine cream, coffee and confectioners' sugar. Refrigerate 1 hour. Beat until it forms stiff peaks. Pile onto the pie and refrigerate 2 hours longer.

Never Fail Nut Pie Crust

Serves 8
Quick and Easy

1 egg white
⅛ teaspoon salt

¼ cup sugar
1½ cup finely chopped nuts

Preheat oven to 400°. Beat egg white and salt until stiff. Gradually beat in sugar. Stir in nuts. Press on well greased 8-inch pie pan. Prick well with fork. Bake for 12 minutes.

Coffee Chiffon Pie

Serves 8

1 cup graham cracker crumbs
6 tablespoons butter, melted
2 tablespoons sugar
½ cup cold water
2 teaspoons instant coffee
  powder
1 envelope unflavored gelatin
3 egg yolks
⅓ cup sugar

⅛ teaspoon salt
⅓ cup coffee liqueur
1 tablespoon vanilla
1 cup whipping cream, whipped
3 egg whites, beaten
¼ cup sugar
Shaved semisweet chocolate,
  garnish

Preheat oven to 375°. Combine crumbs, butter and sugar and mix well. Press into bottom and sides of 9 inch pie plate. Bake 8 minutes. Set aside to cool. Combine water and coffee powder in medium saucepan and stir until dissolved. Add gelatin and let stand 5 minutes. Add egg yolks, sugar and salt, whisking until well blended. Cook over low heat, stirring constantly, until gelatin is dissolved and mixture thickens (do not boil). Remove from heat. Stir in liqueur and vanilla. Pour into large bowl. Chill until thickened to consistency of unbeaten egg white, 2-3 hours. While beating egg white gradually add ¼ cup sugar, beating constantly until whites are stiff and glossy. Gently fold egg whites into gelatin mixture, then gently fold in whipped cream. Spoon into prepared pie shell. Refrigerate at least 6 hours before serving. Garnish with shaved semisweet chocolate.

Fruit Salad Pie

An easy favorite!

1 large can fruit cocktail salad,
  drained
1 pint sour cream
1 to 2 teaspoons sugar

½ teaspoon cinnamon and
  sugar, mixed
½ teaspoon nutmeg, if desired
1 unbaked graham cracker
  crumb pie crust

Preheat oven to 350°. Mix fruit, sour cream and sugar. Pour into pie crust. Sprinkle with cinnamon-sugar mixture and nutmeg. Bake for 20 minutes. Cool and refrigerate.

French Silk Pie

Serves 6 to 8

1 (9 inch) baked pie shell
1 cup sugar
1 cup butter
2 eggs
2 tablespoons instant coffee

1 cup coarsely chopped nuts
2 ounces melted unsweetened
  chocolate, slightly cooled
2 tablespoons rum or brandy

Cream butter and sugar. Add eggs, one at a time, beating at least 3 minutes between each addition. Add coffee, nuts, chocolate and rum. Turn into shell and chill.

Peach and Walnut Pie

Serves 8
Mellowed with Peach Brandy

1 (9 inch) unbaked pie shell,
  chilled
1 egg white, lightly beaten
4 eggs
1 cup dark corn syrup
⅔ cup packed brown sugar
2 tablespoons melted butter

2 tablespoons peach brandy
⅛ teaspoon salt
1¼ cups chopped walnuts
2 fresh peaches
2 tablespoons sugar
1 tablespoon fresh lemon juice
Whipped cream or ice cream

Preheat oven to 400°. Brush inside of pie shell with egg white. Combine eggs, corn syrup, brown sugar, butter, brandy and salt in large bowl and beat well. Stir in walnuts. Pour mixture into prepared shell. Bake 10 minutes. Reduce temperatures to 325° and bake an additional 35-40 minutes, or until set. Cool. Peel and slice peaches and gently mix with sugar and lemon juice; refrigerate. Just before serving, arrange peach slices on pie and top with dollops of whipped cream or small scoops of ice cream.

Daiquiri Pie

Serves 8

Chocolate Crumb Crust:

1½ cups chocolate wafer crumbs

⅓ cup butter, melted

Preheat oven to 375°. Mix together and press into 9 inch pie plate. Bake for 8 minutes.

Filling:

1 (4⅛ ounce) package lemon pie filling
1 (3 ounce) package lime-flavored gelatin
⅓ cup sugar

2½ cups cold water
2 eggs, slightly beaten
½ cup light rum
2 cups whipped topping, thawed

Mix pudding, gelatin and sugar in saucepan. Stir in ½ cup water and eggs. Blend well. Add remaining water. Stir over medium heat until mixture comes to a full boil. Remove from heat. Stir in rum. Chill about 1½ hours until cold. Blend topping into chilled mixture. Spoon into crust. Chill until firm, about 2 hours. Garnish with additional whipped topping and chocolate curls.

Peanut Butter Ice Cream Pie

Just the thing for a peanut butter junkie—and what athlete isn't?

1⅔ cups graham crackers, finely rolled
¼ cup butter or margarine, softened
¼ cup granulated sugar

1 quart vanilla ice cream, softened
½ cup chunky peanut butter
½ cup heavy cream, whipped
½ cup chopped peanuts

Preheat oven to 375°. Blend first three ingredients and press firmly against bottom and sides of a 9-inch pie plate. Bake for 8 minutes. Cool, then chill. Place ice cream in a mixing bowl. Fold in peanut butter. Gently fold in whipped cream until evenly blended. Put mixture into the crust. Freeze for about 6 hours. Garnish with chopped peanuts.

Jim Fixx
Author-Runner

Norman's Kahlua Pie

Serves 8 to 10
Easy dessert

Graham cracker crust pressed in
   spring form pan
1 pint whipping cream
4 egg yolks

1 cup sugar
⅓ cup Kahlua
Instant coffee

Make a graham cracker crust and bake in a 9-inch spring form pan.
Whip 1 pint whipping cream very stiff. Whip egg yolks with sugar.
Add Kahlua. Fold all together. Put in shell. Sprinkle instant coffee
on top. Freeze 4-5 hours.

Orange Chiffon Pie

Serves 8
One of Gramma's special treats

9 or 10-inch pie pan

Crust:
1 cup graham cracker crumbs
¼ cup sugar
1½ teaspoon cinnamon
¼ teaspoon nutmeg

⅛ teaspoon salt
1½ tablespoons butter, softened
2 tablespoons egg whites

Butter pie pan. Combine dry crust ingredients. Work in butter and
egg whites. Press firmly into pan.

Filling:
1 envelope unflavored gelatin
¼ cup cold water
4 eggs, separated
1 cup sugar

½ teaspoon salt
½ cup orange juice
1 tablespoon orange rind
1 tablespoon lemon juice

Soak gelatin in cold water. Combine beaten egg yolks, ½ cup sugar,
salt, orange and lemon juice in double boiler. Cook and stir until
smooth and thick. Add gelatin and stir until dissolved. Add orange
rind. Let cool. Beat egg whites with ½ cup sugar until stiff. Fold
into orange mixture. Put in pie crust and refrigerate. May be served
plain or with whipped cream.

State Representative, Pauline R. Kezer

Peach Bavarian Pie

Serves 6 to 8

½ cup sugar
1 envelope unflavored gelatin
⅛ teaspoon salt
1 (12 ounce) can peach nectar
3 tablespoons lemon juice

1 egg white
½ cup heavy cream
1 large can peach halves,
   drained
1 baked pie shell

Combine sugar, gelatin and salt in upper part of double boiler. Add pach nectar and stir. Heat and stir over hot water until gelatin dissolves. Remove from heat. Pour into small mixing bowl. Add lemon juice. Let cool at room temperature. When cooled, stir unbeaten egg white into mixture. Place in refrigerator. Chill until partially set, about 1½ hours. Whip partially set gelatin until light and fluffy with soft peaks. In another bowl, whip the cream stiff and fold into gelatin mixture. Arrange peach halves over bottom of baked pie shell. Pour cream and gelatin mixture over peach halves to fill the pie crust. Pour remaining mixture into small bowl or mold and chill the pie and remaining mixture overnight. Before serving, loosen remaining mixture from mold and place on top of pie. Decorate the top of pie with sliced peaches.

Pear Mincemeat

Makes 8 Pints

7 lbs. pears
6 cups white sugar
1 pound raisins
6 medium apples
2 lemons
1 tablespoon ground cloves

1 tablespoon nutmeg
1 tablespoon allspice
1 tablespoon cinnamon
1 tablespoon salt
½ cup vinegar

Grind pears, apples and lemons with a coarse blade. Add all other ingredients and simmer about 30 minutes. Stir often to keep from scorching. Can be frozen or packed in sterilized jars.

To make pie use 1 pint pear mince meat, adding a few dots of butter before placing top crush. Bake at 425° for 50-60 minutes.

Rhubarb Custard Pie

Serves 8

French pastry dough:
1¼ cups flour
¾ cup cold butter or margarine

1 tablespoon sugar
3 tablespoons ice water

Filling:
1¼ lbs. fresh rhubarb
1 cup plus 3 tablespoons sugar
1 egg
1 egg yolk
½ cup milk

½ cup heavy cream
¼ teaspoon ground cardamon or
  1 teaspoon vanilla extract
Confectioners' sugar, optional

Preheat oven to 400°. If the rhubarb is very fresh it is necessary only to trim it and cut the stems into 1-inch lengths. If it is a bit old it must be scraped or the tough outer skin pulled off. There should be about 5 cups of cut rhubarb. Place this in a saucepan with the sugar. Do not add liquid. Cover and cook for 8 minutes or longer until tender. Cool and chill. Combine remaining ingredients and add to the rhubarb. Pour the filling into the prepared pie plate. Place on a baking sheet and bake for 30 minutes. Reduce temperature to 350° and continue baking for about 10 minutes. To serve sprinkle with confectioners' sugar.

French Strawberry Pie

1 (9 inch) baked pie shell
1 (3 ounce) package cream
  cheese
3 tablespoons cream
1 quart strawberries

1 cup sugar
2 tablespoons cornstarch
Few drops lemon juice
1 cup whipping cream

Blend cream cheese until smooth. Spread in bottom of cooled pie shell. Wash and hull berries. Select the best half of berries for center of pie. Add sugar to remaining berries; let stand until juicy. Mash and rub through sieve. Mix this puree with cornstarch and lemon juice. Cook mixture until thick and transparent. Cool and pour ¼ over cream cheese. Place best berries upside down in pie shell. Pour remaining glaze over berries and chill. To serve, top with sweetened whipped cream.

Sour Cream Pumpkin Pie

Serves 6 to 8

1½ cups canned pumpkin
¾ cup firmly packed brown
  sugar
½ cup milk
2 egg yolks
1 envelope unflavored gelatin
1 teaspoon cinnamon
½ teaspoon ground ginger
½ teaspoon salt

¼ teaspoon ground cloves
2 egg whites, room temperature
⅓ cup sugar
½ cup sour cream
1 teaspoon grated orange peel
1 (9-inch) baked Nut Crust
Orange sections for garnish
Sour cream for garnish

Combine pumpkin, sugar, milk, egg yolks, gelatin, cinnamon, ginger, salt and cloves in medium saucepan. Place over medium heat and cook, stirring constantly, until mixture comes to just below boiling (do not boil). Let cool, then chill until cold and mixture mounds slightly when spooned. Beat egg whites in small bowl until soft peaks form. Gradually add sugar and continue beating until stiff and glossy. Fold into pumpkin mixture, then fold in sour cream and orange peel. Pile into crust. Chill several hours or overnight. Garnish with orange sections and sour cream.

Nut Crust:
½ cup finely ground almonds,
  walnuts, pecans or Brazil nuts

3 tablespoons sugar
2 tablespoons butter, softened

Preheat oven to 400°. Lightly butter 9 inch pie plate. Combine nuts, sugar and butter. Press firmly onto bottom and sides of plate. Bake 6-8 minutes. Cool before filling.

Nathan Hale, who was born in Coventry, graduated from Yale and taught school in East Haddam before joining General Washington's forces. At age 21, after making his famous declaration, "I regret that I have but one life to lose for my country," he was hanged by the British.

Seven Layer Cookies

A Scene Stealer

1 cup graham cracker crumbs
½ cup butter, melted
6 ounces chocolate chips
6 ounces butterscotch chips

1 cup crushed English walnuts
1 cup shredded coconut
1 cup sweetened condensed
  milk

Preheat oven to 300°. In a 9-inch square cake pan spread each ingredient in the order as listed. Bake for 30-40 minutes. Cool and cut into squares. These are very rich. I make them for Christmas giving.

Eileen Heckart
Actress

Italian Anisette Cookies

Makes 4 Dozen

Dough:
2 cups flour
½ cup sugar
3 teaspoons baking powder
½ teaspoon salt

⅓ cup oil
3 eggs
2 teaspoons anisette

Icing:
1 cup confectioners' sugar
1½ tablespoons hot water

2 teaspoons anisette

Preheat oven to 375°. Mix dough ingredients in order given to form a sticky dough. Flour dough with additional ¼ to ½ cup flour and work with hands until dough is smooth. Quarter and make 9-11 cookies from each quarter in any desired shape. Place cookies on ungreased sheet and bake 8-10 minutes. When cooled, dip cookies in icing.

Paradise Chocolate Bars

Makes 2 dozen
Rich, but oh, so good

1 pound light brown sugar
⅔ cup butter or margarine
3 eggs
2½ teaspoons baking powder
½ teaspoon salt

2⅔ cups flour
1 teaspoon vanilla
⅔ cup coarsely chopped nuts
1 (6 ounce) package milk
    chocolate morsels

Preheat oven to 350°. Melt butter with sugar over low heat. Cool; then slowly add eggs, one at a time, and beat well. Add sifted dry ingredients a little at a time, mixing well. Add vanilla, nuts and chocolate chips. Spread in greased and floured 13×9 pan and bake for 25-30 minutes. Cool slightly and cut into 24 bars.

Cream Cheese Bars

Makes 16 Bars

⅓ cup butter, softened
⅓ cup brown sugar
1 cup flour
½ cup chopped walnuts
¼ cup sugar

1 (8 ounce) package softened
    cream cheese
2 tablespoons milk
1 teaspoon lemon juice
½ teaspoon vanilla

Preheat oven to 350°. Cream butter and brown sugar. Add flour and walnuts. Reserve one cup for topping. Press remaining mixture in 8×8 pan. Bake for 12-15 minutes. Mix together remaining ingredients. Spread on top of baked mixture. Cover with reserved crumbs. Bake an additional 25 minutes. Cool and cut into bars.

Butter Horns

Makes 50 Horns
Takes time, but delicious!

Dough:

2 cups flour
⅓ cup sugar
1 cup butter, softened

1 egg, separated
¾ cup sour cream

Sugar mixture:
¾ cup sugar
¾ cup chopped walnuts

1 teaspoon cinnamon

Preheat oven to 350°. Sift flour with sugar and cut in butter. Add egg yolk, sour cream and mix well with hands. Shape into 4 balls. Sprinkle with flour and wrap each ball in waxed paper. Refrigerate overnight. Roll balls out on well floured board in circle shape. Brush with beaten egg white. Sprinkle with sugar mixture. Cut in wedges. Roll from long side. Leftover egg white and sugar mixture can be used for tops of horns before baking. Bake on greased cookie sheet for 20-30 minutes. Can be frozen after baking.

Oatmeal School Cookies

Makes 3 Dozen
Nutritious and delicious!

½ cup margarine
¾ cup brown sugar
1 egg, slightly beaten
1½ teaspoons vanilla
½ teaspoon salt
½ cup whole wheat flour

¾ teaspoon baking powder
1 cup wheat germ
¾ cup raisins
1½ cup "Quick" oats
½ cup chopped nuts or
  sunflower seeds

Preheat oven to 375°. Cream margarine and sugar. Add egg, vanilla and salt. Beat well. In separate bowl, stir flour, baking powder, wheat germ and oats together. Blend with other ingredients. Add 1 tablespoon (or a bit more) water to hold mixture together. Place by tablespoonful onto greased sheet. Flatten slightly. Bake 10-12 minutes.

Chinese Chews

Makes 32
Keeps best in refrigerator

½ cup butter
1 cup sugar
2 eggs, well beaten
1 cup sifted flour

½ teaspoon salt
1 teaspoon vanilla
¾ pound dates, cut up
1 cup chopped walnuts

Preheat oven to 350°. Cream butter. Add sugar and mix thoroughly. Add eggs, then flour, salt and vanilla. Fold in dates and walnuts. Bake in well-buttered 9×9 pan for 25-30 minutes. Cool. Cut in strips and sprinkle or roll in confectioners' sugar.

Chewey Carmel Bars

Makes 2 dozen
A definite favorite with the kids!

32 caramel candies
⅔ cup evaporated milk
1 cup flour
¾ cup oatmeal, uncooked
½ cup packed brown sugar
½ teaspoon baking soda

¼ teaspoon salt
¾ cup butter or
  margarine, softened
1 (6 ounce) package semi-sweet
  chocolate morsels

Preheat oven to 350°. In double boiler over low heat, melt caramels with evaporated milk. In separate mixing bowl combine all dry ingredients except chocolate chips. Cut in butter until mixture resembles crumbs. Press into the bottom of a 13×9 pan all of the mixture except for one cup. Bake for 12 minutes. Sprinkle with chocolate chips. Spread caramel mixture over chips evenly. Sprinkle with remaining crumbs. Continue baking 20 minutes. Cool and chill for 2 hours before cutting into bars. Store in refrigerator. Especially good in warm weather.

Date Nut Bars

Makes 2 Dozen
Easy to make—always a big hit

1 (8 ounce) package dates, cut
   up
¾ cup sugar
1 cup water
½ chopped walnuts
1 teaspoon vanilla

1½ cups flour
1¾ cups oatmeal
1 cup dark brown sugar
¾ cup margarine
1 teaspoon baking powder

Preheat oven to 350°. Cook dates, sugar, water and nuts in small pan until thick. Add vanilla. Remove from heat. While dates are cooking, mix rest of ingredients in large bowl with hands until crumbly. In a greased 13×9 pan, pat ½ of mixture on bottom. Spread on date mixture. Top evenly with rest of dry mixture. Bake for 30 minutes or until golden brown. Cool. Cut into bars. Store in cookie tin.

Lemon Bars

Makes 2 Dozen

2¼ cups flour
½ cup confectioners' sugar
1 cup butter
4 eggs, beaten

2 cups sugar
⅓ cup lemon juice
½ teaspoon baking powder

Preheat oven to 350°. Sift together 2 cups flour and confectioners' sugar. Cut in butter until mixture clings together. Press into greased 13×9 pan. Bake for 25-30 minutes, until lightly browned. Combine beaten eggs, sugar, lemon juice and beat well. Sift ¼ cup flour and baking powder. Stir into egg mixture. Pour over baked crust. Bake at 350° for 25-30 minutes. Sprinkle with confectioners' sugar. Cool and cut into bars. These can be frozen and taken out just before use.

Colonial Pumpkin Bars

Makes 3 Dozen

¾ cup margarine
2 cups sugar
4 eggs
1 (16 ounce) can pumpkin
2 cups flour
2 teaspoons baking powder

1 teaspoon cinnamon
½ teaspoon baking soda
½ teaspoon salt
¼ teaspoon nutmeg
1 cup chopped nuts

Preheat oven to 350°. Cream margarine and sugar. Blend in eggs and pumpkin. Add dry ingredients. Pour into greased and floured 15×10 pan. Bake for 25 minutes or until toothpick comes out clean. Cool and frost with vanilla cream cheese frosting or dust with confectioners' sugar. This recipe has a better texture if mixed by hand, but a mixer can be used if desired.

Pecan Tassies

Makes 2 dozen

Pastry:
1 (3 ounce) package cream
    cheese

½ cup butter or margarine
1 cup sifted flour

Let cream cheese and butter soften at room temperature. Blend together. Stir in flour. Chill about 1 hour. Shape into 2 dozen 1-inch balls. Place in ungreased 1¾ inch muffin pans. Press dough against bottom and sides to look like tarts.

Pecan Filling:
2 eggs
2 tablespoons butter, melted
Pinch of salt

1 cup light brown sugar
1 teaspoon vanilla extract
1 cup pecans, coarsely broken

Preheat oven to 325°. Beat together eggs, brown sugar, butter, vanilla and salt until smooth. Divide half the pecans among pastry lined pans. Add filling and top with remaining pecans. Bake for 25 minutes or until filling is set. Cool; remove from pans.

Golf Balls

Makes 5 Dozen

1 cup butter, melted
2 cups crushed graham crackers
1 cup peanut butter
1 pound confectioners' sugar
½ cup ground nuts
½ cup flaked coconut

1 (6 ounce) package chocolate chips
1 (6 ounce) package butterscotch chips
2 ounces paraffin

Mix together butter, graham crackers, peanut butter, confectioners' sugar, ground nuts and coconut. Form into balls the size of walnuts. Place in refrigerator until firm. In double boiler melt together chocolate chips, butterscotch chips and paraffin. Dip balls into melted mixture and place on wax paper.

Elegant Fudge Brownies

Makes 16-24 Brownies
Everyone's favorite

½ cup butter
2 squares bitter chocolate
1 cup sugar
2 eggs

⅔ cup sifted flour
½ teaspoon salt
½ cup chopped nuts
2 teaspoons vanilla

Preheat oven to 350°. Melt together butter and chocolate. Cool slightly. Add sugar and eggs. Mix well, 4-5 minutes. Blend in rest of ingredients. Place in greased 8×8 or 10×7 pan. Bake for 20-25 minutes. Do not over bake.

Frosting:
½ cup sugar
¼ cup cocoa
¼ cup milk or water

¼ cup butter
1 teaspoon vanilla

Combine all ingredients (except vanilla) and boil one minute. Add vanilla. Cool and spread on brownies.

Colossal Cookies

Makes 4 dozen

½ cup margarine
1½ cups sugar
1½ cups brown sugar
1 teaspoon vanilla
4 eggs, beaten
18 ounces quick oats

18 ounces crunchy peanut
 butter
2½ teaspoons baking soda
1 (6 ounce) package chocolate
 chips

Preheat oven to 350°. Beat together first five ingredients in large bowl. Stir in dry ingredients by hand. Drop by heaping tablespoonful on ungreased cookie sheet. Flatten with a glass dipped in sugar. Bake for 9-12 minutes. Cool a little before removing.

Ginger Krinkles

Makes 3 Dozen
Can't stop eating them

⅔ cup salad oil
1 cup sugar
1 egg, slightly beaten
2 cups sifted flour
1 teaspoon cinnamon

1 teaspoon ginger
1 teaspoon salt
2 teaspoons baking soda
1 teaspoon cream of tartar
4 tablespoons molasses

Preheat oven to 350°. Mix together first 3 ingredients. Add sifted flour with cinnamon, ginger, salt and baking soda. Add remaining ingredients. Roll into walnut sized balls then roll in sugar. Place on ungreased cookie sheet. Bake for 10 minutes. Do not over bake.

Kourabiedes (Greek Almond Cookies)

Makes 4 Dozen

1 cup unsalted butter
½ cup sifted confectioners'
　 sugar
1 egg yolk
2 tablespoons brandy

1 teaspoon vanilla
½ cup finely ground almonds
2½ cups flour
½ teaspoon baking powder

Preheat oven to 325°. In mixing bowl cream butter and sugar. Add egg yolk, brandy and vanilla; mix well. Stir together almonds, flour and baking powder. Blend into sugar mixture. Chill dough 30 minutes. Form dough into crescents or fingers. Place on ungreased cookie sheet. Bake for 20-25 minutes until light sand color. Roll in confectioners' sugar. Store in airtight container in which more sugar has been sifted.

Apple Brownies

Makes 2 dozen
Delicious

4 ounces margarine
1 cup sugar
2 eggs, beaten
¼ teaspoon salt
1 teaspoon cinnamon
1¼ cup flour

½ teaspoon baking powder
½ teaspoon baking soda
4-6 medium apples, pared and
　 chopped
½ cup chopped nut meats

Preheat oven to 350°. Cream margarine with sugar. Add eggs. Sift dry ingredients and add to mixture. Add apple and nuts. Bake for 28-30 minutes 13×9 greased pan. Sprinkle with confectioners' sugar and cut into squares.

Kyle's Scotch Shortbread

Makes 2 dozen
An old favorite

2 cups flour
1 cup butter, softened

½ cup sugar
1 teaspoon vanilla extract

Preheat oven to 375°. Blend all ingredients until smooth. Pat into ungreased 8-inch square pan. Bake for 35-40 minutes, or until golden brown. Cut into squares when cool.

Swedish or White Brownies

Makes 1 dozen

2 eggs
1 cup sugar
Pinch of salt
1 cup flour

1 teaspoon almond extract
½ cup butter, melted
Chopped nuts

Preheat oven to 325°. Combine all ingredients. Spread in 9 inch square pan. Sprinkle generously with chopped nuts and some granulated sugar. Press nuts into mixture. Bake 30-35 minutes.

Brownie Meringues

Makes 3 dozen

1 (6 ounce) package semisweet
  chocolate pieces, melted and
  slightly cooled
2 egg whites
Dash of salt

½ teaspoon vinegar
½ teaspoon vanilla
½ cup sugar
¾ cups broken walnuts

Preheat oven to 350°. Beat egg whites with salt, vinegar and vanilla until soft peaks form. Gradually add sugar, beating to stiff peaks. Fold in chocolate and nuts. Drop from teaspoon onto greased cookie sheet. Bake for 8-10 minutes.

Cranberry-Apple Crisp

Serves 6 to 8

1 (16 ounce) can whole
   cranberry sauce
2 cups chopped apples
1 teaspoon cinnamon
1 cup uncooked rolled oats
½ cup brown sugar

⅓ cup flour
½ teaspoon salt
½ cup chopped nuts
¼ cup vegetable oil
Whipped cream or ice cream

Preheat oven to 350°. In an 8 or 9-inch square pan combine cranberry sauce, apples and cinnamon. In bowl combine oats, brown sugar, flour, salt and nuts. Add oil and mix until crumbly. Sprinkle over the cranberry mixture. Bake for 45 minutes. Serve warm with whipped cream or ice cream.

Blueberry Buckle

Serves 12

¾ cup sugar
¼ cup butter or
   margarine, melted
1 egg
1 cup milk

2 cups sifted flour
2 teaspoons baking powder
¼ teaspoon salt
2 cups blueberries

Preheat oven to 375°. Mix first seven ingredients together. Gently stir in blueberries and place in well greased 8×8 floured pan.

Topping:
⅔ cup sugar
⅔ cup flour

2 teaspoons cinnamon
¼ cup butter, melted

Mix ingredients together and sprinkle over blueberries. Bake for 45-50 minutes. Serve warm or cold.

Nutritious Banana Squares

Makes 3 Dozen
Great change from brownies

¾ cup butter or margarine
⅔ cup sugar
⅔ cup brown sugar
1½ teaspoons vanilla
3 ripe bananas, mashed
1 egg
1 cup whole wheat flour

1 cup unbleached flour
t teaspoons baking powder
½ cup wheat germ
6 ounces carob chips or
    chocolate chips
Confectioners' sugar, optional

Preheat oven to 350°. Cream butter with sugars, add vanilla, bananas and egg. Sift flours with baking powder. Add to butter mixture. Add wheat germ and chips. Bake for 35 minutes in a greased 13×9 pan. Sprinkle with confectioners' sugar if desired. Cook completely before cutting into small squares.

Strawberry Bran Squares

Makes 16
A delightful snack

½ cup shortening
⅓ cup brown sugar
½ cup light corn syrup
1 egg
1 cup whole bran cereal

2 cups flour
¼ teaspoon baking soda
½ teaspoon salt
¾ cup strawberry jam

Preheat oven to 375°. Cream together shortening and brown sugar. Add corn syrup and egg; beat thoroughly. Stir in cereal. Sift together flour, baking soda and salt. Add to mixture and blend thoroughly. Press half of dough evenly in bottom of a greased 9 inch square pan. Spread jam over top of dough. Between two pieces of waxed paper, flatten remaining dough into a 9-inch square. Place dough over top of jam. Bake 20-25 minutes or until golden brown. Cool. Cut into 16 squares.

Cream Puffs (Chocolate Eclairs)

Makes 15 mini-puffs
Sells out immediately at every bake sale

Puff:
½ cup water   ½ cup flour
¼ cup butter   2 eggs

Filling:
2 (3¼ ounce) boxes vanilla   4 cups whole milk
  pudding   1 teaspoon vanilla

Icing:
2 tablespoons butter   Up to 1 box confectioners' sugar
3 tablespoons cocoa   1 teaspoon vanilla
5 tablespoons hot coffee

Preheat oven to 400°. Heat water and butter to boiling in heavy
saucepan. Stir in flour all at once and reduce heat. Stir for 2
minutes until mixture leaves edge of pan and forms a ball. Remove
from stove; add eggs, one at a time, while beating with electric
mixer at fast speed until smooth and velvety. Drop into 6 mounds
on greased baking sheet (or 15 little mounds if you desire
mini-puffs . Bake for 40 minutes. Cool slowly. Cut off lid; scoop out
and fill with vanilla pudding prepared according to package
directions. Replace tops. Mix butter, cocoa and coffee. Beat in
enough confectioners' sugar to make icing thick. Add vanilla. Have
chocolate icing cascade down cream puff. Refrigerate until served.

Mint Ambrosia

Serves 4
Light, cool summer dessert

1 (20 ounce) can chunk   ¾ cups whole fresh or frozen
  pineapple, drained   strawberries
2 cups whipped topping, thawed   2-3 tablespoons green creme de
1 cup coconut   menthe, to taste

Mix all ingredients together and chill 2 hours to blend flavors. Serve
in frosty parfait glasses.

Peach Angel Fluff

Serves 8 to 10

½ cup sugar
1 envelope unflavored gelatin
¼ teaspoon salt
½ cup water
3 fresh peaches

1 tablespoon lemon juice
4-5 drops almond extract
2 egg whites
1 cup whipping cream
8 lady fingers, split

Combine sugar, gelatin and salt. Add ½ cup water. Cook and stir over medium heat until gelatin dissolves. Chill mixture until partially set. Peel and dice peaches to measure 2 cups. Add lemon juice and extract. Place egg whites, gelatin and half of peaches in large mixing bowl. Beat mixture for 10 minutes until fluffy. Chill until partially set. Fold in peaches and whipped cream. Line sides of an 8 inch spring form pan with lady fingers. Put in mixture and chill 6 hours or overnight.

Fabulous Rice Pudding

Serves 8
An old timer

½ cup uncooked rice
2 cups light cream
2 cups milk
¾ cup sugar
¼ teaspoon salt
4 eggs

½ cup raisins
½ cup water
2 cups heavy cream
2 tablespoons vanilla
Dash nutmeg

Mix rice, light cream, milk, sugar and salt together in top of double boiler. Cover and cook over boiling water for 1 hour, stirring occasionally. Beat eggs in a bowl. Slowly add rice mixture into eggs, beating constantly and vigorously. Return mixture to top of double boiler and continue cooking until mixture coats spoon. Cool completely. While pudding cools, soak raisins in water. Beat heavy cream until it holds a definite shape. Gently fold cream into cold rice mixture with raisins and vanilla. Spoon into serving dish. Sprinkle with nutmeg and chill in refrigerator until pudding is firm.

Chocolate Mousse

Serves 12
The best ever

½ pound sweet chocolate
6 eggs, separated
3 tablespoons water
¼ cup Grand Marnier or
   Amaretto

2 cups heavy cream
6 tablespoons sugar
Whipped cream
Grated chocolate
Toasted almonds

Melt chocolate pieces in top of double boiler. Place yolks in saucepan and add water, over low heat beating vigorously until mixture starts to thicken. Add liqueur, beating constantly. Remove from heat and fold in melted chocolate. Beat the cream until stiff adding 2 tablespoons sugar. Fold this into chocolate mixture. Beat whites until soft peaks form. Beat in remaining sugar and continue beating until stiff. Fold this into the mousse. Spoon mousse into a serving bowl and chill. Garnish with whipped cream, chocolate and almonds.

Spanish Cream

Serves 6

1 envelope plain gelatin
¼ cup cold water
1½ cups scalded milk
3 eggs, separated
⅓ cup sugar
1 teaspoon vanilla

1 cup shredded canned
   pineapple, drained
1 cup raspberries
1 tablespoon lemon juice
½ cup macaroon crumbs

Soften gelatin in cold water 5 minutes. Add milk. Combine egg yolks and sugar; add gelatin mixture and cook over hot water for 5 minutes, stirring constantly until sugar is dissolved. Cool and chill until slightly thickened. Add vanilla and fruit, juice and crumbs. When well mixed fold in stiffly beaten egg whites. Turn into mold. Chill until firm. Unmold and serve with chocolate or caramel sauce or whipped cream.

Elegant Dessert

Serves 4

4 cups green seedless grapes   1 cup sour cream
½ cup light brown sugar   ¼ cup Kirsch

Combine all ingredients and refrigerate for several hours. A light but elegant topping for a dinner.

Chocolate Mousse Torte

Serves 10 to 12
Elegant dessert

3 egg whites   ½ cup butter, softened
½ cup sugar   3 egg yolks
1 cup sifted confectioners' sugar   3 egg whites
¼ cup sifted cocoa   3 tablespoons sugar
8 ounces semisweet chocolate

Preheat oven to 300°. Butter large cookie sheet. Line with foil. Butter and flour foil. With fingertips, mark two 13×11 rectangles on sheet.
Beat 3 egg whites in small mixing bowl until soft beaks form. Beat in ¼ cup of sugar, 1 tablespoon at a time, until stiff and glossy. Stir in remaining ¼ cup sugar. Fold in powdered sugar and cocoa.
Fill pastry bag with ⅜-inch plain tip and fill with meringue mixture. Pipe strips filling rectangles on baking sheet. Bake for 1 hour. Cool.
Melt chocolate in 1 quart saucepan over low heat, stirring occasionally until smooth, 3-5 minutes. Stir in butter. Heat until melted and smooth. Beat chocolate mixture and egg yolks in small mixing bowl on high speed, 5 minutes. Refrigerate covered for 10 minutes.
Beat 3 egg whites in small mixing bowl until soft peaks form. Beat in sugar, 1 tablespoon at a time, until stiff and glossy. Fold egg white mixture into chocolate mixture.
Place 1 reserved meringue on serving plate. Fit pastry bag with ½-inch star tip. Fill with ½ of chocolate mixture evenly over meringue. Top with second meringue. Press down gently. Pipe remaining mixture over top. Refrigerate until serving time.

Cinnamon Pumpkin Flan

Serves 9

1¼ cups plus one tablespoon
  sugar
½ teaspoon salt
1 teaspoon ground cinnamon
1 cup cooked pumpkin
5 large eggs, lightly beaten

1½ cups undiluted evaporated
  milk
⅓ cup water
1½ teaspoons vanilla
½ cup heavy cream, whipped
¼ teaspoon ground ginger

Preheat oven to 350°. Melt ½ cup of the sugar over medium-low heat until sugar forms a golden syrup. Stir constantly to prevent burning. Pour immediately into an 8×8 inch cake pan or 9-inch pie plate, turning and rolling pan from side to side to coat with caramel. Set aside. Combine ¾ cup of the remaining sugar with the salt and cinnamon. Add pumpkin and eggs. Mix well. Sitr in the milk, water and vanilla. Mix well and turn into the caramel-coated pan. Set in a pan of hot water. Bake 1¼ hours or until a knife inserted in the center comes out clean. Cool and chill. To serve, run a spatula around the sides of the pan. Turn cake out onto a serving plate. Cut into squares. Combine the whipped cream with the remaining sugar and the ginger and spread over the squares.

Cuban Flan

Serves 12 to 16
Very rich, serve thin slices

1 cup sugar
1 (14 ounce) can sweetened
  condensed milk
1 (13 ounce) can evaporated
  milk

3 extra large eggs
1 (8 ounce) package cream
  cheese
1 teaspoon vanilla

Preheat oven to 350°. Carmelize sugar in saucepan over low heat and pour into 9 inch cake pan, spreading evenly. Mix remaining ingredients in blender or food processor. Carefully pour into prepared cake pan. Set in larger pan with ½ inch of water. Bake 55-60 minutes until light brown. Cool Refrigerate 8 hours or overnight. Invert onto serving plate.

Cranberry Dessert Pudding

Serves 6
An old New England recipe with a real tang

1 cup cranberries
¼ cup sugar
¼ cup chopped nuts
1 egg, beaten

½ cup sugar
½ cup flour
6 tablespoons butter or
    margarine, melted

Preheat oven to 325°. Butter an 8-inch pie plate. Spread cranberries over plate. Sprinkle ¼ cup sugar and nuts over berries. Combine egg with ½ cup sugar. Add flour and melted butter. Beat well. Pour over cranberries. Bake for 45 minutes in middle of oven. Serve topped with vanilla ice cream.

Peach Melba Mold

Serves 6

1 (3 ounce) package
    raspberry-flavored gelatin
1 cup boiling water

2 cups peach ice cream
½ cup diced peaches

Dissolve gelatin in 1 cup boiling water. Stir in ice cream until melted. Add peaches. Chill until set. Garnish with whipped cream and additional peach slices.

Chocolate Peanut Clusters

Makes 34

1 (3 ounce) package chocolate
    pudding mix
1 cup sugar

½ cup evaporated milk
1 tablespoon butter
1 cup small, unsalted peanuts

Mix all ingredients, except peanuts in heavy saucepan. Cook and stir to boiling. Lower heat, and cook three minutes stirring constantly. Remove from heat. Stir in peanuts all at once. Beat until candy starts to thicken. Drop mixture by spoonful quickly onto waxed paper.

Raspberry Fanfare

Serves 6 to 8
Tart and refreshing

1 (3 ounce) package
  raspberry-flavored gelatin
1 (15 ounce) can unsweetened
  condensed milk

½ cup fresh lemon juice
1 tablespoon grated lemon rind
1 egg, separated
1 teaspoon sugar

Make gelatin according to package directions. Chill until slightly thick. Combine milk, lemon juice, rind and egg yolk. Stir until thick. Beat egg white until foamy. Gradually add sugar until soft peaks form. Fold into milk mixture. Alternate raspberry gelatin and lemon mixture into parfait glasses. Garnish with maraschino cherry. Chill at least 1 hour. May be prepared early in day or previous evening.

New England Trifle

Serves 20

1 package white or yellow cake
  mix
½ cup Kirsch, sherry or Grand
  Marnier
2 (10 ounce) packages frozen
  raspberries

1 (16 ounce) can sliced peaches
2 packages vanilla pudding
1 pint heavy cream, whipped
Toasted almonds

Prepare cake mix in 15×10 pan. Pour liqueur over warm cake. Cool. Cut into 1 inch squares and place in an attractive serving bowl. Add partially thawed raspberries and drained peaches. Prepare pudding and pour cooled pudding over peaches. Chill for several hours. Do not stir or mix. When ready to serve, top with whipped cream sprinkled with almonds.

Whiskey Balls

Makes ¾ Pound
May be frozen for holiday gifts

2 cups vanilla wafer crumbs
1 cup finely ground walnut
   meats
1 cup confectioners' sugar
1 tablespoon cocoa
¼ teaspoon salt
3 tablespoons dark corn syrup

6 tablespoons whiskey, *not*
   Scotch
Extra confectioners' sugar for
   dusting
Plastic wrap, cut into 3-inch
   squares

Combine all dry ingredients. Add corn syrup and whiskey; mix well.
Form into balls by rolling between palms of hands dusted with
confectioners' sugar. Roll balls in confectioners' sugar before
wrapping in small squares of plastic wrap. Place into container.
Freeze or store in refrigerator.

Creamy Nutcracker Fudge

Makes 4 dozen
Perfect for holidays

4½ cups sugar
1½ cups half and half
¼ cup butter
Dash salt
1 (12 ounce) package semisweet
   chocolate pieces

4 (1 ounce) squares
   unsweetened chocolate,
   chopped
1 (7 ounce) jar marshmallow
   cream
1 cup chopped nuts

Comfine first four ingredients in heavy 3 quart saucepan. Bring to
full rolling boil for 6 minutes, stirring frequently. Add chocolate and
marshmallows. Beat until melted. Add nuts. Pour into buttered
13×9 pan. Let stand several hours before cutting. Store in cool
place.

Baked Pineapple Natillas

Serves 8
A heavenly Mexican dessert

1 large fresh pineapple
¼ cup sugar

2-3 tablespoons rum or 1
    teaspoon rum flavoring
¼ cup butter

Lay pineapple on its side and take off a thick slice (off one side) that does not include the green top. Carefully scoop out the insides and cut into bite sized pieces. Or stand pineapple up and cut off top to remove the insides. Sweeten the pineapple with sugar. Flavor with rum. Put pineapple pieces back into pineapple shell. Dot top with butter. Cover with foil and bake at 350° for 20 minutes. Replace the top and serve warm, with cold sauce.

Natillas Sauce:
1 pint half and half
¼ teaspoon salt
¼ cup sugar
1 egg

2 egg yolks
1 teaspoon cornstarch
1 teaspoon vanilla

Scald half and half. Let cool slightly. Add salt, sugar beaten with 1 whole egg, and 2 egg yolks, cornstarch and vanilla. Cook over hot water, stirring constantly until smooth and slightly thickened. Chill.

Visitors to Connecticut are fascinated by the stone walls along the state's roadsides and fields. The chunks of rock cleared by pioneer farmers produced some 50,000 miles of stone fencing in the state.

Citron Fromage

Serves 16

2 envelopes unflavored geletin
¼ cup cold water
½ cup hot water
8 eggs

2 cups sugar
½ cup lemon juice or orange
  juice
¼ cup rum (optional)

Sprinkle gelatin over cold water. Stir just until absorbed into water. Add hot water. Stir well to dissolve thoroughly and set aside to cool. Separate eggs. Whip egg whites and set aside. Beat yolks until lemon colored, about 5 minutes. Add sugar gradually, continuing to beat. Gradually add juice and rum, beating at medium speed. Add gelatin gradually, using lowest speed on mixer, or stir in well. Fold in egg whites thoroughly. Be sure that there is no unbeaten egg white at the bottom of bowl. Refrigerate in serving bowl or sherbet glasses. "Sets up" in a very short time. May be made day before. Fromage is not supposed to jell and cannot be molded. It is ready when firm enough to tip bowl without it moving. Serve with whipped cream or fruit sauce and grated orange rind.

Hiram Bingham, the leader of the first missionary expedition to the Hawaiian Island, was married and ordained in the Goshen Congregational Church. A Hawaiian flag now flies year-round in the church.

Cold Mocha Souffle

Serves 6
Easy Company Dessert

1 envelope unflavored gelatin
¼ cup cold water
4 ounces German sweet
   chocolate
1 tablespoon freeze dried coffee
¼ cup water

6 egg yolks
¼ cup sugar
6 egg whites, stiffly beaten
2 cups prepared whipped
   topping

Brush inside of 2 quart souffle dish with oil. Soften gelatin in ¼ cup cold water. Heat and stir chocolate with coffee and ¼ cup water in saucepan over low heat. Add gelatin and stir to dissolve. Remove from heat. Combine egg yolks and sugar in top of double boiler. Place over hot water and beat with electric mixer until thick and light, about 4 minutes. Remove from heat. Blend in chocolate mixture and pour into bowl. Fold in beaten egg whites. Cool about 10 minutes. Then fold in whipped topping. Pour into souffle dish. Chill about 3 hours. Serve with additional topping if desired.

Butter Crunch Candy

Yummy

1 cup butter or margarine	1 cup finely chopped nuts
1 cup light brown sugar	10 thin Hershey bars

Melt butter in saucepan. Add sugar and bring to a boil, stirring constantly. When boiling, bring temperature to "hard crack" on a candy thermometer (300° to 310°). Butter a 15×10 pan and sprinkle with ½ cup nuts. Pour hot mixture over nuts by going back and forth with a fork very slowly. Place chocolate bars on top of crunch and spread until all is covered with chocolate. Sprinkle remaining nuts over the chocolate. When cold, break into pieces.

Shredded Wheat Cup Cakes

Serves 12
For "young, budding" cooks, especially preschoolers

1 (12 ounce) box shredded wheat, broken up	¾ cup chunky peanut butter
1 (12 ounce) package chocolate bits, melted	1 package jelly beans

Mix all ingredients together except jelly beans. Pack into greased measuring cup at ¼ level. Turn out on greased baking sheet and make indentation with a teaspoon on top for 2 or 3 jelly beans.

Fudgesickles

Makes 12
Kids love them

1 package instant chocolate fudge pudding	½ cup light cream
½ cup sugar	2 cups milk

Mix all ingredients together. Beat at high speed of electric mixer for 2 minutes. Fill plastic pop molds and freeze overnight.

Chocolate Ice Box Dessert

Serves 12
A delightful luncheon dessert

¾ cup butter
2 cups confectioners' sugar
2½ squares dark chocolate,
  melted

4 eggs
½ pound vanilla wafers, crushed
¾ cup chopped nuts

Cream butter. Add confectioners' sugar and melted chocolate. Add eggs, one at a time, beating well after each egg. Mix the vanilla wafer crumbs with the nuts. Grease a 9×9 pan. Place a layer of the wafer-nut mixture on bottom of pan, add some creamed mixture. Alternate, ending with a crumb layer. Chill overnight. Top with whipped cream. Can be make 2-3 days ahead.

Fresh Strawberry Ice Cream

Makes 2 Quarts

4 pints fresh strawberries
1¼ cups sugar
¼ cup orange liquer

5 egg yolks
1 cup whipping cream

Place chopped strawberries in bowl. Add sugar and orange liqueur. Stir gently, cover and refrigerate overnight. Drain berries, reserving syrup (there should be about 1½ cups). In saucepan, combine syrup, lightly beaten yolks and cream. Cook over medium heat, stirring constantly until mixture has thickened. Do not let sauce boil. Remove from heat; place pan in cold water to stop cooking, stirring constantly until cooled. Allow to cool to room temperature. Place in ice cream maker and churn until partially frozen. Add strawberries and continue churning until firm.

Rum Raisin Ice Cream

Makes 2 Quarts

1 cup dark seedless raisins	2 tablespoons cold water
¼ cup dark rum	2 cups whipping cream
2 cups half and half	½ cup evaporated milk
1 cup sugar	2 teaspoons rum extract
1 envelope unflavored gelatin	Pinch of salt

Plump raisins in rum, preferably overnight. In saucepan slowly bring half and half to boil over low heat, stirring occasionally. Add sugar and gelatin dissolved in cold water and stir to dissolve. Cool. Add remaining ingredients except raisins and refrigerate 2 hours or longer. Place in ice cream maker, add undrained raisins and churn until firm.

Watermelon Sherbet

Makes 6 Cups

6 cups ripe red watermelon
1 cup sugar
Juice of ½ lemon

Puree watermelon meat with sugar in a blender or food processor. Add lemon juice; stir until sugar is completely dissolved. Pour into ice cream maker and freeze as directed for sherbet or spoon into a 6 cup metal pan and freeze 1½ hours. Remove; beat mixture smooth and set in freezer 1 hour more. Remove and beat smooth and return to freezer until frozen. Garnish with mint when serving.

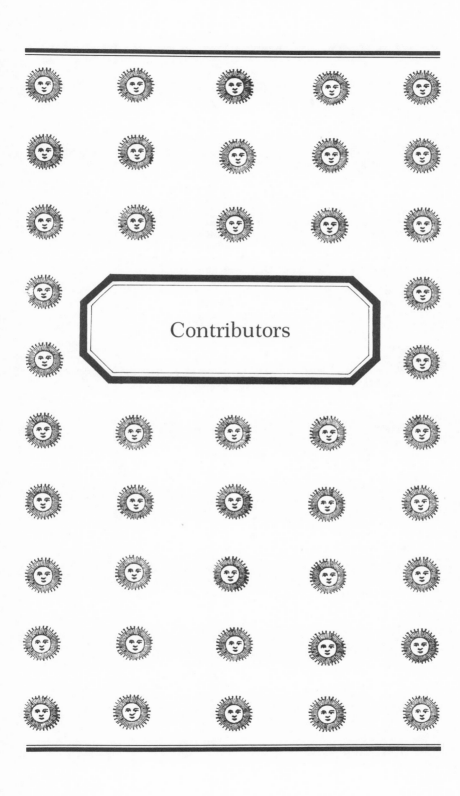

Contributors

Contibutors

Claudia Abbott
Maxwell G. Adams
Lynette J. Aey
Phyllis Alfaro
Barbara J. Allen
Phyllis Allen
Andrew Amarante
Betty C. Amon
Audrey K. Anderson
Janice Anderson
Ronni Anderson
Suzanne Andresen
Naomi S. Andrews
Ruby R. Arnold
Mary Arpaia
Rochelle Asfalg
Cornelia H. Attig
Pegge Axline
Barbara Bailey
June S. Bailey
Margaret H. Balch
Ede D. Baldridge
Mrs. Malcolm Baldrige
Mrs. John Baranski
L. Baranski
Frances Barber
Rose Marie Barone
Carol Barry
Georgia Barry
Gayle Bastianello
Mary Lou Baudean
Eileen N. Bauer
Leslie H. Belcher
Lea Bemus
Betty Benavides
Marianne Bender
Gen Bergandahl
Arlene Berkowitz
Claire M. Birdsall
Dorothy Birens
Linda Blair
Joyce B. Blackfield
Eleanor Blaskey
Maureen W. Bloss
Mary Bocash
Jane Bodgan
Mike Boguslawski
Charlotte Boland
Victor Borge

Gae Borland
Rosalie Borst
Dorothy Bortels
Angela Bowen
Dianne Bowman
June Cronen Bradley
Norman A. Brady
Christine Brail
Marion G. Brancuccio
Yvonne Brightly
Laurie Brooks
Harriet B. Brown
Janet K. Brown
Pricilla Brown
Marguerite Brungger
Rita J. Brush
Olga Bukowski
Peggy Bull
Cele Burdett
James L. Buckley
Susan Cameron
Marie Campoli
Marie Y. Camuso
Ann-Etta Cannon
Caprilands Herb Farm
Cheryl C. Carlson
Edna P. Carlson
Mrs. Herbert A. Carlson
Anita Carofino
Margaret Carrell
Pauline Carroll
Elizabeth R. Carter
Candace Casale
Dona Cassella
Ernest Cassella
Nancy Cassella
Rose Castelluccio
Mary M. Castenholz
Celia-Margaret's Specialties
Patricia Cervone
Gertrude Chandler
Ann F. Champion
Betty Chapman
Debbie Chellstorp
Joan E. Chiota
Karen Chorches
Gini Christensen
Mary Ann Cianci
Angela J. Ciempo

Alfred Cioppa, Jr.
Laura D. Clark
T. Culbertson Clark
Beverley Clarke
Virginia Coco
Nancy Colavecchio
Brenda Colgate
Peri Comollo
Sally Constant
Linda Coolidge
Mary Coppola
Jane B. Corby
Marlene G. Corkery
Kay Corl
Evelyn Cornelio
Pat Cornish
Carmel Correll
Margaret Correll
Richard Correll
Eleanor Coughlin
Myra Crasa
Lucy Bartlett Crosbie
Beth Cummings
Sona A. Current
Robert C. Current
Roberta Cutillo
Lucy Dalessio
Irene D'Ambrosio
Judy D'Ambrosio
Mary D'Amico
Mildred R. D'Apice
Phyllis Darve
Eileen Davis
Irene Davis
Polly Davis
Renate Davis
Mae Dayton
Agnes DeFilippo
Mrs. E. L. DeShong
Harriet Deutsh
Kathleen Devine
Terry Dezso
Mrs. John DiBiaggio
Mrs. A. F. DiLorenzo
Mary DiMenna
Celeste DiNello
Mary Dipalma
Elsa Dobkin
Ella K. Don
Mara Donadis
Mollie Donovan
Mary Drew
Marie F. Dugan
Peggy Dugan
Marguette Dumaine

Ellen C. M. Dunn
Tom Dunn
Elisabeth W. Dyjak
Lisa Dyslin
Bea Earle
Virginia Eckert
Mildred Ellis
Win Elliot
Bonnie C. Eriksen
Anita N. Ernst
Jane Ettershank
Patricia A. Evans
Dorothy R. Farkas
Rudy J. Favretti
Marguerite N. Fearey
Judith Ferguson
Elizabeth Ferry
Raquel L. Fialkoff
Patricia Fields
Lynne Filippone
Sue Finkenzeller
Elizabeth K. Fiore
Dorothea B. Fischer
Heidi Fischer
Bertram D. Fish
Mrs. Uria Fishbein
Mary Lou Fisher
Betsy Fithian
Mrs. Fitta
Jim Fixx
Virginia Forman
Patricia S. Forstrom
Mae Foster
Col. James Fountain
Kathleen Fox-Kukel
Hugh Franklin
Mitzi Freiman
Jo Allene Frew
Ruth M. Friend
Beverly Fuss
Mrs. Max Gagnebin
Joan Gagner
Mary Gagnon
Josephine Garufi
Joyce Gaudreault
C. B. Geer
Barbara Gess
Joan C. Gibbs
Beverly W. Gibson
Lois Gillespie
Marion Gillotti
Ethel Gilman
Noel Ginzberg
Patricia Giordano
Marge Glick

Joan Godburn
Joyce Godin
Gertrude Goldberg
Rosalind Golden
Bette Goodwin
Ethel Goodwin
Lucille Gosline
Sylvia Gottlieb
B. J. Grace
George E. Graff
Peggy Graham
Beverly J. Graham
Gov. Ella Grasso
Judy Griffin
Joan Grimm
Betty Lu Grune
Loretta M. Guise
Bridget T. Gurliaccio
Haight Vineyard
Sherman P. Haight, Jr.
Rheba Haley
Mrs. Richard Hallworth
Sue Haman
Audrey Hansen
Joanne Hansen
June Havoc
Pamela A. Hayes
Callista Healy
Eileen Heckart
Sylvia Heffley
Doris Heerlein
Rita Helming
Ruth Henderson
Mrs. Hendry
Katharine Hepburn
Cindy Herrington
Virginia Herron
Janet Hertzmark
Susan Hibbard
Mary Ellen Higgison
Phyllis Hillebrand
Joyce Hine
Loretta Hissong
Irene Hochheimer
Lorraine A. Hollman
Katherine K. Holt
Hopkins Vineyard
Judith W. Hopkins
A. E. Hotchner
Carroll Hughes
Betty Hughes
Chris Hughes
Lillian Hunter
Joan Hurwitz
Ann Ingram

Caroline J. Irace
Jean Isenberg
Fan Jacobs
Vera Jespersen
Frances A. Johnson
Marietta W. Johnson
Elizabeth Jordan
Elaine Kahaner
Ruth E. Kahn
Hattie K. Kaplan
Mary K. Karl
Teresa Karlak
Eileen Katz
Ruth B. Keeler
Rosemary Kelleher
Kay Kennedy
Pauline R. Kezer
Robert G. Kiely
Gloria Kissman
Alice Kitchen
Carol Klekotka
Estelle B. Korsonsky
Linda A. Kovacs
Linda Krasner
Rita Kraushaar
Yolanda Kruszynski
Bernice Kuzma
June Lachler
Eileen Lader
Madeleine L'Engle
Mrs. George Lamson
M. W. Landig
Stephanie Landis
Letitia E. Landry
Laurie Lane-Reticker
Gloria Langer
Helen A. Langer
Mary Langley
Ruth Lapides
Barbara Lappen
Ann Laraja
Mary R. LaRiviere
Muriel C. Larson
Mary Larke
Anne Marie Lavelle
Lucy Lavelle
Rosemary Lavelle
Ellen Lawrence
June S. LePage
Barbara Leach
Bonnie Tandy Leblang
Mrs. Robert D. Lederer
Helen J. Lee
Margaret Leiberman
Nancy Leitzes

Mary Lemoine
Lillian Lenkowski
June S. LePage
Jo Lerandowski
Karleen Lessenger
Emily Lessner
Judi Levine
Lois L. Levine
Donna O. Levy
Jennie Lewis
Ruth H. Lewis
Ann B. Lillis
Arlene M. Lipton
Jean Litke
Sylvia Little
Jane Lockrow
Geraldine Lord
Barbara Loucks
Florence Lozyniak
Beryl Lucas
Lillian Ludlaw
Irene C. MacArthur
Janice MacArthur
Wendy Madsen
Norma Magee
Adrienne Mahieu
Rosemary Malatesta
Susan Malinoski
Leela Mallon
Nina Mangiaracina
Paul Mangiaracina, D.D.S.
Ethel F. Manych
Marathon Marketing Corporation
Susan Marinelli
Alice K. Mark
Suzanne M. Markowski
Eileen Marshall
Jeanne Martin
Linda A. Martin
Olga M. Mason
Tete Masterson
Joan Mavon
Diane McAlpin
Laura McCarthy
Teresa K. McCarthy
Louise L. McGarry
Mona H. McKiernan
Eileen McMahon
Phyllis K. Medvedow
Nancy Melluzzo
Emily Membrino
Marcia Memery
Julia Merluzzi
Theodore J. Messier, Sr.
Abby Meyers

Shirley Middleton
Artemis P. Miller
Dorothy L. Miller
Mary D. Milmine
Anna Mitchell-Dunn
Susan Monaghan
Charlotte Monroe
Ruth Monzillo
Frances C. Moran
Marcea A. Morgan
Helene Morgenstern
Marion E. Morra
Alberta Morrison
Anna Morrison
Millicent Morrison
Muriel Mosler
Judy Mrosek
Nancy Munson
Arlene W. Muraszka
Anita Murphy
Loretta Murphy
Poagie Murray
Laura C. Mylchreest
Mary Napolitano
Lynn Nathan
Betty C. Nelson
New Britain General Hospital Auxiliary
Charity Nichols
Teresa Obernesser
Pamela O'Connor
Nancy O'Donnell
Gov. and Mrs. William A. O'Neill
Arline O'Rourke
Ruth L. Osterweis
Mary Ann O'Sullivan
Charles E. Otto
Martha Pallone
Doris Palumbo
Florence Pandolfi
Barbara Papacoda
Harriette Papish
Ruth Papp
Bert Parks
Ann H. Pate
Shirley Patten
Marge Peck
Don Pendzimas
Teresa Penkrot
Marilyn Peracchio
Joyce Perkins
Marilyn Perlotto
Cynthia Perno
Mrs. Perrault
Virginia Perun
Roberta Petit

G. A. Petrizzo
Marion Plant
Nettie Plumley
Bibiane Poirier
Agnes Polverari
Doris K. Pool
Barbara Porter
Eve Potts
Patricia Powell
Joanne Prague
Carmen Prelee
Dale Prescott
Denise Prindiville
Rene D. Purcell
Mrs. Giovanni Raccuglia
Linda B. Rahilly
Marie Ramsdell
Deborah Randolph
Betsy B. Ranelli
Marie Ransdell
Marion Rasmussen
Barbara Ratchford
J. LeRoy Reilly, II
JoAnne Reilly
Donna B. Reisner
Betty Reitzler
Marilyn Renfrew
Carol Renshaw
Margaret Reubelt
Marjorie F. Reynolds
Josephine Riedel
Susann Riley
Kay Roan
Gertrude Robert
Kimberly Roe
Pearl Rogers
Patricia Rosay
Myra C. Rosoff
Bernadette Ross
Ann Rossell
Vita Rotella
Helen Roth
Ellen Rovins
Donald E. Rowe
Van Rowe
Cathy Russ
Ruth Russell
Marge Rust
Beth Ruwet
Ann Saas
Lois Sabatino
Hyman Sadinsky
Ida Z. Sadinsky
Joanne Salerno
Ann Sambone

Agnes R. Sanders
Jenni P. Sanders
Terry Sanderson
Gertrude R. Sarto
Camille Savo
Jean Sawicki
Elaine Schaaf
Mildred Schadick
Betty Scherner
Marie Schlesinger
Richard F. Schneller
Elizabeth Schultz
Ann Schupack
Sharon Scorso
Gloria F. Scott
Mary   Setaro
Elsie Shanahan
Charlotte I. Shea
Ruth Shepherd
Alberta Sherman
A. Marland Shoemaker
Mari-Carole Shooks
Patricia C. Shuhi
Susie Sigmund
Frances W. Sikand
Nancy Silverstein
Mrs. Daniel Sklenar
Sandy Slaughter
Margaret Smith
Mary F. Smith
Susan S. Smith
Elinor Snider
Mim Snyder
Laura R. Soll
Lillian M. Sonstroem
Muriel Soroka
Lee Spinella
Wini Spitalnick
Linda Stankewich
Margaret Stanley
Vivian C. Stanley
Mary Stenman
Barbara Stephens
Marilyn E. Stewart
Mrs. Stinchfield
Barbara G. Stitts
Janet T. Stoddard
Janis Sullivan
Irene Sunday
Mrs. Sidney Svirsky
Virginia Swenson
Linda Szegda
Aileen M. Talbot
Jean O. Taylor
Penelope C. Taylor

Barbara Teehan
Penny Telgener
Cecile M. Terry
Al Terzi
Carolyn Terzi
Mary Thompson
Bea Thomson
JoAnn Thulin
Dorothy S. Tibbetts
Marion Tinkham
Josephine Tino
Carol Toce
Diane Tolokan
Clara Torniero
Estelle Jones Triarhos
Shirley J. Troxell
Cynthia A. Truncali
Dorothy F. Tubridy
Ben Tuerk, M.D.
Frances Ullmon
Rose J. Ushehak
Clare Usher
Bruno M. Valbona
Miriam Vannais
Frank R. Vanoni, M.D.
Bettie C. Van Valen
Pamela Vendetti
Barbara Vigars
Richard Vincent
Joyce Anne Vitelli
Diane E. Volk
Kurt E. Volk, Jr.
Kurt R. Volk,
Norma E. Volk
Dorothy O. Vosburgh
Brigitte Wade
Charlotte Wagner
Susan Wagner
Joanne Walker

Jean Walsh
LaVerne Walter
Ann Wandell
Waring Products
Diane Wasser
Sydney Watras
Connie Watson
Eunice Watstein
Leslie Weinstein
Gloria Weiss
Lynne B. Welch
Carolyn Wentworth
Rosemary R. Werner
Madeline West
Katherine Wheeler
Carl White
Charlotte White
Penelope White
Mayor & Mrs. George Whitham
Ginny Wickersham
Marlo Wiggans
Barbara Willenbrock
Olive Williams
Yvonne Williams
Susan B. Williamson
Mrs. Charles H. Wilmot
Kathryn Winter
Joy Wise
Anita L. Wolf
Alice Woodson
Joanne Woodward
Dorothy Young
Helen M. Younger
Nancy Yungk
Roselyn Zacken
Lora Zahner
Mary Jane Ziehl
Mildred G. Zucco
Helen Zychowski

Our sincere gratitude to everyone whose concern, talent, and dedication make the publishing of CONNECTICUT COOKS possible.

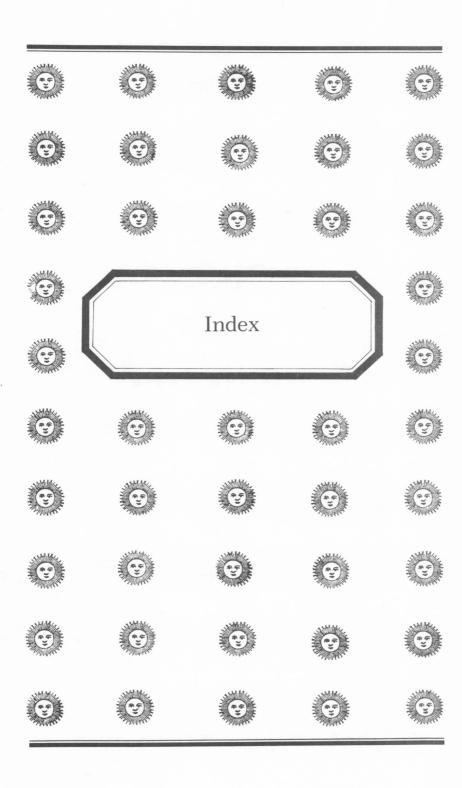

Index

Index

A

Almond
  Cake, 242
  -Lime Salad, 45
  Kourabiedes (Greek Cookies) 275
  Torte, 243
Appetizers
  Artichoke, 6
  Artichoke Pie, 3
  Black Olive Canapes, 7
  Broccoli, Marinated, 7
  Ceviche (Pickled Raw Fish) 24
  Chicken Wings, Marinated, 13
  Cheese Filled Pumpernickle, 6
  Cheese Onion Bread, 9
  Clam Rolls, 24
  Crab-Swiss Bites, 26
  Crabbies or Shrimpies, 25
  Clams, Stuffed, 25
  Derevi Sarma, (stuffed grape leaves), 8
  Dip (s)
    Artichoke, hot, 3
    Clam Bake, 4
    Guacamole Specialty, 12
    Havoc Herb, 5
    Shrimp, Hot, 5
    Shrimp, Inez Hodges, 5
    Spinach, 3
  Fritters, Foo Yung, 13
  Holiday Appetizer Pie, 4
  Kielbasa Treats, 8
  Meatballs, Brandied, 16
  Meatballs, Cocktail, 14
  Meatballs, Swedish, 9
  Mushrooms, Baked Stuffed,
    Louraine's, 14
  Mushroom Hors D'Oeuvres, 10

Mushroom Strudel, 15
Pecan Delights, Marie's Bleu, 10
Pepperoni Bread, 20
Salmon Stuffed Eggs, 27
Sausage Quiches, 19
Seed Wafers, Benne's, 7
Sesame Chicken with Honey Dip, 11
Spanish Woodcock, 22
Spinach Balls, 22
Spinach Roll-ups, 21
Spread (s)
  Caviar, Elegant, 23
  Chicken Liver Pate, 17
  Chutney-Cheese Pate, 18
  Eggplant Caviar, 11
  Homos Bi Tahini, 12
  Lentil Pate, 18
  Pate Champagne, 17
  Pineapple Cheese Ball, 20
  Potted Cheese, 21
  Salmon Ball, 26
Swordfish and Cantaloupe, Skewered,
  19
Water Chestnuts and Bacon, 27
Wieners, Glazed Spicy, 22
Zucchini Hors D'Oeuvres, 23
Apple (s)
  And Wine With Red Cabbage, 227
  Brownies, 275
  Butter Bread, 69
  Cheese Pie, 256
  Chutney, Tomato-, 210
  Crisp, Cranberry, 277
  Pie Cake, 242
  Walnut Supreme Cake, 244
  Yams, 238
Applesauce
  Cake, 243
  Pumpkin Bread, 70

Apricot Salad, 46
  Cake, 243
  Raisin Nut Bread, 70
Artichoke (s)
  Appetizer, 6
  Bottoms with Oysters and Spinach,
    218
  Casserole, Spinach, 236
  Hot dip, 3
  Pie, 3
  Quiche, Rice and, 116
Asparagus
  And Gruyere Vinaigrette, 36
  Baked With Cheese Sauce, 216
  Mushroom Casserole, 217
  Souffle, 114
Aunt Glady's Salad Dressing, 59

B

Bacon and Olive Bread, Cheddar, 72
Baked Alaska Pie, 257
Baked Beans, 220
  Connecticut, 221
Banana (s)
  Bread, 71
  Delight, 28
  Nutritious Squares, 278
Barbecued Salmon, 181
Basque Skillet Dinner, 146
Bean (s)
  Baked, 220
  Connecticut Baked, 221
  Dixie Pineapple, 219
  Green
    Chinese String, 217
    Sesame And Celery, 220
    Vinaigrette, 38
  Soup
    Black, 88
    Garbanzo and Sausage, 90
Beef
  Birds, 129
  Boeuf Bourguignonne, 136
  Boeuf Eau de Vie, 130
  Fillet of Beef with Foie Gras, 126
  German Pot Roast, 131
  Grandmother's Stew, 133
  Ground
    Bonia, 135
    Deluxe Meat Loaf, 134
    Hamburger Ring, 132
    Juarez Chili, 135
    Jumbo Shells and Meat Filling, 104
    Meatballs, Brandied, 16
    Meatballs, Cocktail, 14
    Meatballs, Swedish, 9
    Moussaka, 136
    Pastitsio, 105
    Sopa de Fideo, 137
    Stuffed Cabbage, 137
    Taco Salad, 55
    Tritini, 131

"How About Some Chinese Tonight,"
  128
In Red Wine, 127
Rollauden, 130
Salad, Marinated Roast, 56
Sauerbraten, 133
Sesame Steak, 127
Square Meal Snack, 138
Steak Pizzaiola, 128
Sweet and Sour, 134
Teriyaki Steak, 129
Tongue, Sweet and Sour, 132
Beer-Cheese Soup, 89
Beets
  In Orange And Lemon Sauce, 221
  Pickled Chinese, 206
Beggar's Marinade, 198
Bearnaise Sauce, 126
Betty's Brown Bread, 67
Beverages
  Authentic Spanish Sangria, 34
  Banana Delight, 28
  Cherry (or Fruit) Wine, 31
  Frosty, 28
  Frosty Yogurt Delight, 29
  Holiday Eggnog, 34
  Mulled Cider, 29
  Nectarine Float, 28
  Punches, *See* Punch (es)
  Spiced Ice Coffee, 30
  Spicy Instant Tea, 30
  Teetotaler's Revenge, 30
  Tomato Bouillon, 29
Bing Cherry (Sherry) Ring, 46
Blueberry (ies)
  Buckle, 277
  Cake With Lemon Sauce, 245
  Muffins, 66
  Pie, 258
  -Rhubarb Pie, 256
Boeuf
  Bourguignonne, 136
  Eau De Vie, 130
Bonia, 135
Boston Brown Bread, 72
Bourbon Marinade, 198
Braised Lamb Chops with Zucchini,
  148
Brandy Alexander Pie, 258
Bread (s)
  Apple Butter, 69
  Applesauce Pumpkin, 70
  Apricot Raisin Nut, 70
  Banana, 71
  Betty's Brown, 67
  Biscuits, Mom's, 81
  Boston Brown, 72
  Cheddar, Bacon, and Olive, 72
  Cheese Onion, 9
  Christmas Rye (Vortlimpa) 73
  Coffee Cake (s)
    Cranberry Swirl, 81
    Jewish, 79

Rhubarb, 78
Swedish Tea Ring, 82
Dill Casserole, 74
Healthy White, 77
Variations: Onion and Garlic, Pep-
peroni, Raisin and Nut, 77
Herb, 73
Honey Walnut, 75
Irish Raisin, 76
Lemon, 76
Muffins
Blueberry, 66
Cranberry, 66
In A Loaf, English, 67
Make Ahead Bran, 68
Orange Blossom, 68
Pineapple, 69
Nutritious Breakfast, 75
Nutty Orange, 74
Pepperoni, 20
Rhubarb, 78
Rolls
Dinner, 71
Onion, 64
Plain or Cinnamon, 64
Sticky Pecan, 65
Spoon, 79
Strawberry, 80
Zucchini Nut, 80
Broccoli
Casserole, Rice And, 223
Cauliflower Supreme, 218
Chowder, Mushroom, 90
Marinated, 7
Salad, Pasta Twist, 53
Souffle, 222
Soup, Chilled, 84
Brownies
Apple, 275
Elegant Fudge, 273
Swedish or White, 276
Brownie Meringues, 276
Brussels Sprouts With Yogurt, 222
Bulgur Salad (Tabbouleh) 55
Butter Horns, 269
Butterflied Leg of Lamb with Zinfandel
Sauce, 147
Buttermilk Curry Sauce, 200

C

Cabbage
Red With Apples And Wine, 227
Salad, 36
Stuffed, 137
Calcutta Shrimp Curry, 187
Candy
Butter Crunch, 290
Chocolate Peanut Clusters, 284
Creamy Nutcracker Fudge, 286
Whiskey Balls, 286
Cake (s)
Almond, 242

Almond Torte, 243
Apple Pie, 242
Apple Walnut Supreme, 244
Applesauce, 243
Blueberry With Lemon Sauce, 245
Carrot, 244
Cheesecake (s), 246
Chocoholic's Quick-fix, 246
Chocolate Swirl, 248
Individual, 247
Chocolate Crazy, 249
Chocolate Mousse Torte, 282
Chocolate Sheet Cake, 247
Coconut Cake, 248
Cream Pound-Raspberry Sauce, 255
Gingerbread, Hot Water, 245
Greek Christmas, 249
Key Lime, 252
Kuchen, Fresh Plum, 254
Mississippi Mud, 250
Orange-Cranberry Torte, 252
Pina Colada, 253
Preserve, 251
Rhubarb, 250
Shredded Wheat Cup, 290
Thunderbolt Kraut Chocolate, 251
Carrot (s)
And Cauliflower Pie, 224
Cake, 244
Gelatin, 44
Heavenly, 224
Salad, Marinated, 37
Soup, 87
Casserole (s)
Chicken Thigh, 164
Far East Celery, 227
Fish, 179
French Toast, 119
Langostino, 183
Lima-Sausage, 216
Old Fashioned Charleston Shrimp,
193
Seafood, 186
Summer Squash, 237
Sweet Potato, 231
Cauliflower
Breaded, 225
Broccoli Supreme, 218
In Sour Cream Sauce, 37
Pie, And Carrot, 224
Caviar
Eggplant, 11
Elegant, 23
Celery
Far East Casserole, 227
Italienne, 38
Sesame Beans And, 220
Ceviche (Pickled Raw Fish), 24
Champagne-Orange Punch, 32
Cheese
And Vegetable Omelet, Creamy, 114
Asparagus and Gruyere Vinaigrette, 36
Cheddar, Bacon, and Olive Bread, 72

Chutney Pate, 18
Filled
  Pumpernickle, 6
  Veal Cutlets, 142
Gorgonzola Dressing, 60
Ham Puff, Three, 123
-Mushroom Quiche, Spinach, 122
Onion Bread, 9
Potted, 21
Ring, Lemon-, 45
Souffle, Buffet Ham, 104
Soup, Beer-, 89
Swiss Baked Egg, 117
-Vegetable Medley, 223
Cherry
  (or Fruit) Wine, 31
  Pie, Cran-, 257
Chewey Carmel Bars, 270
Chicken
  and Ham Fricassee, 110
  Bihon Guisado, 157
  Breast of, Saute, 156
  Breasts, Smoked, 161
  Breasts, Walnut Stuffed, 159
  Breasts With Lemon and Brandy, 159
  Brissette, 172
  Croquettes, Baked, 156
  Elizabeth, 160
  Englaise, 162
  Gratin Italienne, 154
  In Beer and Tomatoes, Baked, 158
  Jade, 164
  Lemon, Texas Style, 165
  Liver Stroganoff, 168
  Livers in Tomato-Wine Sauce, 168
  Livers with Rice, 169
  Marinated Wings, 13
  Oven Fired, Supreme, 166
  Peruvian, 161
  Petti De Pollo Alla Bolognese, 170
  Pot Au Feu, 165
  Ratatouille, 163
  Roast, Lemon, 162
  Salad, Party, 51
  Salad, Regal, 43
  Sesame With Honey Dip, 11
  Simon and Garfunkle, 163
  Skillet Luau, 167
  Souffle, Baked, 155
  Soup, Corn, 89
  Soup, Sengalese, 94
  Stir Fry, 166
  Sweet and Sour, 158
  Thigh Casserole, 164
  Waikiki Beach, 160
  Walnut, 157
  With Herbs, 170
  With Lobster Sauce, 171
Chili, Juarez, 135
Chili Sauce, 199
Chinese
  Chews, 270
  String Beans, 217

Chocolate
  Chocoholic's Quick-Fix Cheesecake, 246
  Coffee Toffee Pie, 259
  Crazy Cake, 249
  Cream Puffs (Eclairs), 279
  Fudge, Creamy Nutcracker, 286
  Fudgesickles, 290
  Ice Box Dessert, 291
  Mousse, 281
  Mousse Torte, 282
  Paradise Bars, 268
  Peanut Clusters, 284
  Quick Glossy Frosting, 254
  Sauce, 205
  Sheet Cake, 247
  Swirl Cheesecake, 248
  Thunderbolt Kraut Cake, 251
Christmas
  Punch, 33
  Rye Bread (Vortlimpa) 73
  Souffle, 115
Cinnamon Pumpkin Flan, 283
Cinnamon Rolls, Plain or, 64
Clam (s)
  and Anchovy Sauce with Hard Cooked Eggs, 204
  Bake Dip, 4
  Chowder, 93
  Chowder, New England, 93
  Neapolitan, 195
  Rolls, 24
  Sauce and Pasta, White, 203
  Stuffed, 25
Coconut Cake, 248
Coffee
  Chiffon Pie, 260
  Ice, Spiced, 30
Colonial Pumpkin Bars, 272
Connecticut Lamb Stew, 148
Cookies, Bars, and Squares
  Apple Brownies, 275
  Brownie Meringues, 276
  Butter Horns, 269
  Chewey Carmel Bars, 270
  Chinese Chews, 270
  Colonial Pumpkin Bars, 272
  Colossal, 274
  Cream Cheese Bars, 268
  Date Nut Bars, 271
  Elegant Fudge Brownies, 273
  Ginger Krinkles, 274
  Golf Balls, 273
  Italian Anisette, 267
  Kourabiedes (Greek Almond), 275
  Kyle's Scotch Shortbread, 276
  Lemon Bars, 271
  Nutritious Banana Squares, 278
  Oatmeal School, 269
  Paradise Chocolate Bars, 268
  Pecan Tassies, 272
  Seven Layer, 267

Strawberry Bran Squares, 278
Swedish or White Brownies, 276
Corn
  Dressing for Roast Pork, 143
  Pudding, 225
  -Zucchini Bake, 228
Crab (s)
  Cakes, 188
  Crabbies or Shrimpies, 25
  Curry, 188
  Or Shrimp Delight, 184
  Sauce, 202
  Swiss-Bites, 26
Crabmeat
  Crepes, Curried Shrimp and, 108
  Quiche, 120
  Soup, 88
Cranberry
  -Apple Crisp, 277
  Catsup, 209
  Cran-Cherry Pie, 257
  Dessert Pudding, 284
  Muffins, 66
  Salad, Frozen, 47
  Swirl Coffee Cake, 81
  Torte, Orange, 252
Cream Cheese
  Bars, 268
  Frosting, 255
Cream Puffs (Chocolate Eclairs) 279
Creole, Shrimp, 192
Crepes, Curried Shrimp and Crabmeat,
  108
Crown Roast of Lamb, 151
Cuban Flan, 283
Cucumber
  Salad, Hungarian, 39
  Salad Mold, 44
  Soup, Cream of, 85
Curried Fruit, 229
Curried-Shrimp and Crabmeat Crepes,
  108
Curry Marinated Swordfish Steaks, 182

D

Daiquiri Pie, 262
Date Nut Bars, 271
Dessert (s)
  Baked Pineapple Natillas, 287
  Blueberry Buckle, 277
  Chocolate Ice Box, 291
  Chocolate Mousse, 281
  Cinnamon Pumpkin Flan, 283
  Citron Fromage, 288
  Cold Mocha Souffle, 289
  Cranberry Apple Crisp, 277
  Cream Puffs (Chocolate Eclairs), 279
  Cuban Flan, 283
  Elegant, 282
  Fabulous Rice Pudding, 280
  Mint Ambrosia, 279
  New England Trifle, 285

Peach Angel Fluff, 280
Peach Melba Mold, 284
Pudding, Cranberry, 284
Raspberry Fanfare, 285
Spanish Cream, 281
See Also Cakes, Candy, Cookies, Bars,
  and Squares, Ice Cream, Pies
Dijon Pork Chops, 143
Dill Casserole Bread, 74
Dinner Rolls, 71
Ditalini and Spinach, 98
Do-Ahead Mashed Potatoes, 230
Dressings
  Aunt Glady's Salad, 59
  Fresh Fruit Topping, 61
  Gorgonzola, 60
  Grandma Miller's Salad, 60
  Low Calorie French, 59
  Pennsylvania Dutch Salad, 60
  Poppy Seed, 61
  Sweet, 61
  Tomato French, 59
Duckling
  A L'Orange, 173
  White Peking With Orange Sauce, 172

E

Egg (s)
  And Sausage Casserole, 119
  Company, 100
  In Tomatoes, Baked, 117
  Italian Brunch, 118
  Omelets, see Omelet (s)
  Salmon Stuffed, 27
  Somerset, 118
  Souffles, see Souffle (s)
  Swiss, Baked, 117
Eggplant
  Bhurta, 229
  Caviar, 11
  Julienne, 228
  Stuffed, 219
Elegant Dessert, 282
English Muffins In A Loaf, 67

F

Family Evening Spaghetti Sauce, 203
Fettuccini with Peas and Bacon, 99
Fillet of Beef with Foie Gras, 126
Fish
  Baked Spanish Style, 184
  Barbecued Salmon, 181
  Casserole, 179
  Fillets, Stuffed, 191
  Flounder with Mushroom Caper
    Sauce, Stuffed, 180
  Salmon With Broccoli, 180
  Sea Trout, Stuffed, 187
  Sole Au Gratin, Broccoli, 185
  Sole Newburg, Stuffed, 178
  Striped Bass, Vegetable-Stuffed, 186

Swordfish, Spanish, 181
Swordfish with Mustard, Broiled, 183
Tuna Salad, German, 58
With Sweet-Sour Sauce, 179
See Also Specific Variety
Fish House Punch, 32
Florentine Rice Quiche, 120
Florentine Rice Ring, 234
Foo Yung Fritters, 13
French Silk Pie, 261
French Toast Casserole, 119
Freezer Pickles, 208
Fritata, 238
Frosting (s)
Cream Cheese, 255
Quick Glossy Chocolate, 254
Frosty Beverage, 28
Fruit
Cantaloupe Soup, Chilled, 84
Crock, 208
Curried, 229
Four Berry Sauce, 111
Leather, 213
Salad Pie, 260
Salads, *see* Salads and Specific Fruits
Strawberry Soup, Fresh, 86
Topping, Fresh, 61

G

Gae's Party Punch, 32
Gazpacho, 85
German Pot Roast, 131
Ginger Ale Salad, 47
Ginger Krinkles, 274
Glazed Ham Loaf, 144
Golf Balls, 273
Gourmet Pork Chops, 144
Grandma Miller's Salad Dressing, 60
Grandmother's Stew, 133
Grape Mold, Sherried, 48
Gratin Italienne, 154
Greek Christmas Cake, 249
Grits Souffle, 116
Guacamole Specialty, 12

H

Haight Chardonnay, Veal, 140
Ham
And Cheese Souffle, Buffet, 104
And Egg Bake, 145
Fricassee, Chicken and, 110
Loaf, Glazed, 144
Puff, Three Cheese, 123
'N Broccoli Salad, 56
Sauce, 200
Hamburger Ring, 132
Hay and Straw, 101
Healthy White Bread, 77
Heavenly Carrots, 224
Herb (s)
Bread, 73

Dip, Havoc, 5
Tomatoes, 232
Holiday Eggnog, 34
Hollandiase, Failproof, 201
Homos Bi Tahini, 12
Honey Walnut Bread, 75
Hot Water Gingerbread, 245
"How About Some Chinese Tonight,"
128

I

Ice Cream
Fudgesickles, 290
Pie, Peanut Butter, 262
Rum Raisin, 292
Strawberry, Fresh, 291
Watermelon Sherbet, 292
Individual Cheesecakes, 247
Italian
Anisette Cookies, 267
Brunch, 118
Sausage and Mushrooms, 146
Style Mushrooms, 226

J

Jane's Hot Dog Relish, 211
Jewish Coffee Cake, 79
Jumbo Shells and Meat Filling, 104

K

Key Lime Cake, 252
Kourabiedes (Greek Almond Cookies),
275
Kuchen, Fresh Plum, 254
Kyle's Scotch Shortbread, 276

L

Lake House Spinach Pasta Salad, 41
Lamb
Chops with Zucchini, Braised, 148
Crown Roast of, 151
Paprikash, 147
Stew, Connecticut, 148
Sweet-Sour Ragout of Lamb with Figs,
150
With White Beans, Leg of, 149
With Zinfandel Sauce, Butterflied Leg
of, 147
Langostino Casserole, 183
Lasagna, Gloria's Spinach, 100
Leek Soup, Cold Watercress and, 86
Lemon (s)
Bars, 271
Bread, 76
-Cheese Ring, 45
Chicken-Texas Style, 165
Citron Fromage, 288
Roast Chicken, 162
Lentil Soup, 91

Lima-Sausage Casserole, 216
Linguine with Quahog Sauce, 99
Liver (s)
    Stroganoff, Chicken 168
    With Rice, Chicken, 169
    In Tomato-Wine Sauce, Chicken, 168
Lobster
    Coquilles, 189
    with Black Beans, 189
Low Calorie French Dressing, 59
Luncheon-In-One-Dish, 123

M

Make Ahead Bran Muffins, 68
Mandarin Salad, 42
Manicotti, 102
Mandarin Salad, Sweet and Sour, 51
Marinade (s)
    Beggars, 198
    Bourbon, 198
Meat (s)
    See Beef, Ham, Lamb, Pork, Sausage,
        Veal
Marmalade
    Ground Cherry, 201
    Peach, 206
Meat Loaf, Deluxe, 134
Melba Sauce, 205
Mincemeat, 264
Mint Ambrosia, 279
Mississippi Mud Cake, 250
Mom's Bar-B-Que Sauce, 198
Mom's Biscuits, 81
Moussaka, 136
Mulled Cider, 29
Mushroom (s)
    Asparagus Casserole, 217
    -Broccoli, Chowder, 90
    Florentine, 226
    Hors D'Oeuvres, 10
    Italian Sausage and, 146
    Italian Style, 226
    Louraine's Baked Stuffed, 14
    Quiche, Spinach-Cheese-, 122
    Strudel, 15
    Stuffed Tomatoes, 233
    Stuffing, 174
Mussels, Scallops, Shrimp, with
    Spaghetti, 106

N

Nectarine Float, 28
Never Fail Piecrust, 259
New England Trifle, 285
New Orleans Oyster Loaf, 185
New Orleans Shrimp Pie, 191
Noodle Pudding, 101
Norman's Kahlua Pie, 263
Nut Bread, Apricot Raisin, 70
Nut Bread, Zucchini, 80
Nutritious Breakfast Bread, 75
Nutty Orange Bread, 74

O

Oatmeal School Cookies, 269
Olga's Hot Cakes, 111
Olive Bread, Cheddar, Bacon, 72
Omelet (s)
    Classic, 113
    Creamy Cheese and Vegetable, 114
    Smoked Oyster, 113
Onion (s)
    Rolls, 64
    Saugatuck Creamed, 230
Orange
    Bread, Nutty, 74
    Blossom Muffins, 68
    Chiffon Pie, 263
    -Cranberry Torte, 252
    Molded Salad, 48
    Pancakes, Fluffy, 115
    Sauce, 173
Osso Buco, 141
Oven Fried Chicken Supreme, 166
Oyster (s)
    Artichoke Bottoms With Spinach, 218
    Loaf, New Orleans, 185
    Omelet, Smoked, 113
    Stuffing, 175

P

Pancakes
    Fluffy Orange, 115
    German (Eierkuchen) 109
    Olga's Hot Cakes, 111
    Potato, 231
    Sourdough, 112
    Zucchini, 240
Paprikash, Lamb, 147
Pasta, 98
    Ditalini and Spinach, 98
    Fettuccini with Peas and Bacon, 99
    Gloria's Spinach Lasagna, 100
    Hay and Straw, 101
    Jumbo Shells and Meat Filling, 104
    Linguine with Quahog Sauce, 99
    Manicotti, 102
    Pastitsio, 105
    Pinwheels, Spinach, 107
    Primavera, 103
    Primavera Salad, 54
    Spaghetti with Mussels, Scallops,
        Shrimp, 106
    Twist and Broccoli Salad, 53
    White Clam Sauce and, 203
Pastitsio, 105
Pates
    A Special Note About, 16
    Champagne, 17
    Chicken Liver, 17
    Chutney Cheese, 18
    Lentil, 18
Peas Pizzicato, 39

Peach
  And Walnut Pie, 261
  Angel Fluff, 280
  Bavarian Pie, 264
  Marmalade, 206
  Melba Mold, 284
Peanut Butter Ice Cream Pie, 262
Pear
  Brandied Punch, 31
  Mincemeat, 264
Pecan (s)
  Bulgur Wheat Stuffing, 151
  Marie's Bleu Delights, 10
  Rolls, Sticky, 65
  Tassies, 272
Pennsylvania Dutch Salad Dressing, 60
Pepper (s)
  Roasted, 230
  Veal and, 140
Perfect Potato Salad, 40
Pesto Vegetable Soup, 95
Petti De Pollo Alla Bolognese, 170
Pickle (s)
  Freezer, 208
  Refrigerator, 209
  Summer Squash, 211
Pickled Chinese Beets, 206
Pickled Garden Salad, 40
Pie (s)
  Apple Cheese, 256
  Artichoke, 3
  Baked Alaska, 257
  Blueberry, 258
  Blueberry-Rhubarb, 256
  Brandy Alexander, 258
  Carrot and Cauliflower, 224
  Chocolate Coffee Toffee, 259
  Coffee Chiffon, 260
  Cran-Cherry, 257
  Daiquiri, 262
  French Silk, 261
  French Strawberry, 265
  Fruit Salad, 260
  Holiday Appetizer, 4
  New Orleans Shrimp, 191
  Norman's Kahlua, 263
  Orange Chiffon, 263
  Peach Bavarian, 264
  Peach and Walnut, 261
  Peanut Butter Ice Cream, 262
  Rhubarb Custard, 265
  Sour Cream Pumpkin, 266
Piecrust
  Never Fail Nut, 259
Pina Colada Cake, 253
Pineapple
  Beans, Dixie, 219
  Cheese Ball, 20
  Muffins, 69
  Natillas, Baked, 287
  Pot Au Feu, 165
  Spiced, 207
Plum Kuchen, Fresh, 254

Poppy Seed Dressing, 61
Pork
  Chops
    Dijon, 143
    Gourmet, 144
    Luxembourg, 145
    Real Easy, 141
  Roast
    Corn Dressing for, 143
    with Roasted Potatoes, 143
Potato (es)
  Broiled Baked Skins, 225
  Do-Ahead Mashed, 230
  Pancakes, 231
  Soup, Sweet, 91
  Sweet, Casserole, 231
  Yams, Apple, 238
Poultry
  See Chicken, Duckling, Rock Cornish
    Hens, Turkey
Praline Ice Cream Sauce, 205
Preserve (s)
  Ground Cherry Marmalade, 201
  Hot Pepper Jelly, 207
  Peach Marmalade, 206
  Spiced Pineapple, 207
  Strawberry Rhubarb Jam, 207
Preserve Cake, 251
Pudding
  Corn, 225
  Cranberry Dessert, 284
  Noodle, 101
  Rice, Fabulous, 280
Pumpkin
  Bars, Colonial, 272
  Bread, Applesauce, 70
  Flan, Cinnamon, 283
  Pie, Sour Cream, 266
Punch (es)
  Brandied Pear, 31
  Champagne-Orange, 32
  Christmas, 33
  Fish House, 32
  Gae's Party, 32
  Venezuelan Rum, 33

Q

Quiche (s)
  Crabmeat, 120
  Florentine Rice, 120
  Rice and Artichoke, 116
  Salmon, 121
  Sausage, 19
  Spinach-Cheese-Mushroom, 122

R

Raisin
  Bread, Irish, 76
  Ice Cream, Rum, 292
  Nut Bread, Apricot, 70

Sauce, 200
Sauce, Rum, 206
Raspberry
    Fanfare, 285
    Melba Sauce, 205
Ratatouille, 239
Real Easy Pork Chops, 142
Red, White, and Blue Fruit Mold, 49
Refrigerator Pickles, 209
Relish (s)
    Cranberry Catsup, 209
    Freezer Pickles, 208
    Jane's Hot Dog, 211
    Pickled Chinese Beets, 206
    Refrigerator Pickles, 209
    Rhubarb, 212
    Summer Squash Pickles, 211
    Tomato-Apple Chutney, 210
    Winchester Relish Sauce, 209
    Zucchini, 212
Rhubarb
    Bread, 78
    Cake, 250
    Coffee Cake, 78
    Custard Pie, 265
    Jam, Strawberry, 207
    Pie, Blueberry, 256
    Relish, 212
Rice
    And Artichoke Quiche, 116
    And Broccoli Casserole, 223
    And Lentil Salad, 54
    Derevi Sarma, 8
    Pilaf, 234
    Pudding, Fabulous, 280
    Quiche, Florentine, 120
    Ring, Florentine, 234
    Riscotto Alla Milanese, 235
Riscotto Alla Milanese, 235
Roast
    Pork with Roasted Potatoes, 143
Roasted Peppers, 230
Rock Cornish Hens, 169
Rum Raisin Ice Cream, 292
Rum Raisin Sauce, 206
Ruth Henderson's Sunday Lunch For
    Twelve, 109
    German Pancakes (Eierkuchen), 109
    Chicken and Ham Fricassee, 110
    Four Berry Sauce, 111

S

Salad (s)
    Bulgur (Tabbouleh) 55
    Chicken, Regal, 43
    Dressings, see Dressings
    German Tuna, 58
    Ham 'N Broccoli, 56
    Marinated Roast Beef, 56
    Molded
        Almond-Lime, 45
        Apricot, 46

Bing Cherry (Sherry) Ring, 46
Carrot Gelatin, 44
Cucumber, 44
Frozen Cranberry, 47
Ginger Ale, 47
Lemon-Cheese Ring, 45
Orange, 48
Red, White, and Blue, 49
Salmon Mousse, 57
Sea Foam, 47
Sherried Grape, 48
Shrimp Mousse, 58
Strawberry Gelatin, 50
24 Hour, 50
Pasta Primavera, 54
Pasta Twist and Broccoli, 53
Rice and Lentil, 54
Taco, 55
Tadisch's Zinovich, 57
Turkey, 52
Turkey, Hot, 53
Turkey in Melon Ring, 52
Vegetable
    Asparagus and Gruyere Vinaigrette,
        36
    Cabbage, 36
    Cauliflower in Sour Cream Sauce,
        37
    Celery Italienne, 38
    Green Bean Vinaigrette, 38
    Hungarian Cucumber, 39
    Lake House Spinach Pasta, 41
    Marinated Carrot, 37
    Peas Pizzicato, 39
    Perfect Potato, 40
    Pickled Garden Salad, 40
    Seven Layer, 39
    Spinach, 43
    Variegated, 41
    A La Greque, 42
Salmon
    and Broccoli, 180
    Ball, 26
    Barbecued, 181
    Mousse, 57
    Quiche, 121
Sauce (s)
    Basic Tomato, 202
    Bearnaise, 126
    Buttermilk Curry, 200
    Chili, 199
    Chocolate, 205
    Clam and Anchovy, with Hard Cooked
        Eggs, 204
    Crab, 202
    Family Evening Spaghetti, 203
    Four Berry, 111
    Ham, 200
    Hollandaise, Failproof, 201
    Melba, 205
    Mom's Bar-B-Que, 198
    Mushroom Caper, 180
    Orange, 173

Praline Ice Cream, 205
Raisin, 200
Raspberry, 255
Rum Raisin, 206
Sweet and Sour, 199
White Clam, and Pasta, 203
Winchester Relish, 209
Sauerbraten, 132
Saugatuck Creamed Onions, 230
Sausage
  And Mushrooms, Italian, 146
  Basque Skillet Dinner, 146
  Casserole, Egg and, 119
  Glazed Spicy Wieners, 22
  Italian Brunch, 118
  Quiches, 19
  Soup
    Garbanzo and, 90
    Zucchini, 92
Scallops
  Baked, 190
  Parisienne, 190
  Shrimp, Mussels, with Spaghetti, 106
Sea Foam Salad, 47
Seafood
  Au Gratin, 182
  Casserole, 186
  Chardonnay, 194
  Soup, Mediterranean, 94
Sengalese Soup, 94
Sesame Steak, 127
Seven Layer Cookies, 267
Seven Layer Salad, 39
Shredded Wheat Cup Cakes, 290
Shrimp
  and Crabmeat Crepes, Curried, 108
  Baked Stuffed, 192
  Bihon Guisado, 157
  Casserole, Old Fashioned Charleston,
    193
  Crabbies or Shrimpies, 25
  Creole, 192
  Curry, Calcutta, 187
  Delight, Crab or, 184
  Dip, Hot, 5
  Dip, Inez Hodges, 5
  Mousse, 58
  Mussels, Scallops, with Spaghetti, 106
  Pie, New Orleans, 191
  with Macadamia Nuts, 193
Skillet Luau, 167
Sopa de Fideo, 137
Souffle (s)
  Asparagus, 114
  Broccoli, 222
  Buffet Ham and Cheese, 104
  Chicken, Baked, 155
  Christmas, 115
  Cold Mocha, 289
  Grits, 116
Soup (s)
  Beer-Cheese, 89
  Black Bean, 88

Broccoli, Chilled, 84
Cantaloupe, Chilled, 84
Carrot, 87
Chicken Corn, 89
Clam Chowder, 93
Clam Chowder, New England, 93
Cold Watercress and Leek, 86
Crab Meat, 88
Cream of Cucumber, 85
Garbanzo and Sausage, 90
Gazpacho, 85
Lentil, 91
Mushroom-Broccoli Chowder, 90
Pesto Vegetable, 95
Seafood Mediterranean, 94
Senegalese, 94
Strawberry, Fresh, 86
Sweet Potato, 91
Viennese, With Dumplings, 92
Zucchini, 87
Zucchini Sausage, 92
Sourdough Pancakes, 112
Spaghetti with Mussels, Scallops,
  Shrimp, 106
Spanish
  Cream, 281
  Sangria, Authentic, 34
  Style Fish, Baked, 184
  Swordfish, 181
  Woodcock, 22
Spinach
  Artichoke Bottoms With Oysters And,
    218
  -Artichoke Casserole, 236
  Balls, 22
  -Cheese-Mushroom Quiche, 122
  Dip, 3
  Ditalini and, 98
  Florentine Rice Ring, 234
  Florentine Rice Quiche, 120
  Hau Pia, 236
  Lasagna, Gloria's, 100
  Mushrooms Florentine, 226
  Pasta Pinwheels, 107
  Pasta Salad, Lake House, 41
  Roll-ups, 21
  Salad, 43
Spoon Bread, 79
Square Meal Snack, 138
Squash
  Casserole, Summer, 237
  Pickles, Summer, 211
  Summer and Tomatoes, 237
Steak Pizzaiola, 128
Stir Fry Chicken, 166
Strawberry
  Bran Squares, 278
  Bread, 80
  French Pie, 265
  Gelatin Salad, 50
  Ice Cream, Fresh, 291
  Rhubarb Jam, 207
  Soup, Fresh, 86

Stuffed
  Cabbage, 137
  Eggplant, 219
  Fillets, 191
  Flounder with Mushroom Caper
    Sauce, 180
  Sea Trout, 187
  Sole Newburg, 178
  Zucchini, 240
Stuffing (s)
  Corn Dressing for Roast Pork, 143
  Mushroom, 174
  Oyster, 175
  Pecan Bulgur Wheat, 151
  Turkey, 174
Summer Squash Pickles, 211
Swedish Tea Ring, 82
Sweet and Sour
  Beef, 134
  Chicken, 158
  Mandarin Salad, 51
  Ragout of Lamb with Figs, 150
  Sauce, 199
  Sauce, Fish with, 179
  Tongue, 132
Sweet Dressing, 61
Swiss Baked Eggs, 117
Swordfish
  and Cantaloupe, Skewered, 19
  With Mustard, Broiled, 183
  Spanish, 181
  Steaks, Curry Marinated, 182

T

Taco Salad, 55
Tadisch's Zinovich Salad, 57
Tea, Spicy Instant, 30
Teetotaler's Revenge, 30
Teriyaki Steak, 129
Thunderbolt Kraut Chocolate Cake, 251
Tomato (es)
  -Apple Chutney, 210
  Baked Eggs In, 117
  Baked, Stuffed With Barley, 232
  Bouillon, 29
  Chicken Baked In Beer and, 158
  French Dressing, 59
  Herbed, 232
  Mushroom Stuffed, 233
  Rockefeller, 233
  Sauce, Basic, 202
  Summer Squash And, 237
Tritini, 131
Turkey
  Salad, 52
  Salad, Hot, 53
  Salad in Melon Ring, 52
  Stuffing, 174
  Superior, 167
24 Hour Salad, 50

V

Variegated Salad, 41
Veal
  And Peppers, 140
  Birds Marguerite (Swiss) 139
  Cutlets, Cheese Filled, 142
  Haight Chardonnay, 140
  Marsala, 141
  Osso Buco, 141
  Scaloppine Francaise, 139
  Vermouth, 138
Vegetable (s)
  Combination Dishes
    A La Greque, 42
    Asparagus-Mushroom Casserole,
      217
    Broccoli, Cauliflower Supreme, 218
    Carrot And Cauliflower Pie, 224
    Cheese-Vegetable Medley, 223
    Corn-Zucchini Bake, 228
    Florentine Rice Ring, 234
    Fritata, 238
    Lima-Sausage Casserole, 216
    Pasta Primavera, 103
    Ratatouille, 239
    Rice And Broccoli Casserole, 223
    Salads, See Salads and Specific
      Vegetables
    Sesame Beans and Celery, 220
    Spinach-Artichoke Casserole, 236
    Summer Squash and Tomatoes, 237
  Omelet, Creamy Cheese and, 114
  Soups, Pesto
  See Also Specific Variety
Viennese Soup With Dumplings, 92
Venezuelan Rum Punch, 33

W

Walnut
  Bread, Honey, 75
  Chicken, 157
  Stuffed Chicken Breasts, 159
Water Chestnuts and Bacon, 27
Watercress and Leek Soup, Cold, 86
Watermelon Sherbet, 292
Whiskey Balls, 286

Y

Yogurt
  Brussels Sprouts With, 222
  Frosty Delight, 29

Z

Zucchini
  Bake, Corn, 228
  Braised Lamb Chops with, 148
  Hors D'Oeuvres, 23
  Nut Bread, 80
  Pancakes, 240
  Relish, 212
  Sausage Soup, 92
  Soup, 87
  Stuffed, 240

Connecticut Cooks *is available at all unit offices*
of the American Cancer Society in Connecticut
or send order form to: CONNECTICUT COOKS
American Cancer Society, 14 Village Lane, P.O. Box 410
Wallingford, Connecticut 06492

Please send ____ copies of CONNECTICUT COOKS
at $8.95 per copy plus $1.25 per copy for
postage & handling: $_____
Enclosed is an additional donation of: $_____
                                  Total enclosed: $_____

SEND TO _____
STREET _____
CITY _____ STATE _____ ZIP _____
                    Please print
(   ) *Please enclose a gift card to read:*
_____
_____

Make check or money order payable to A.C.S. Cookbook

Please send ____ copies of CONNECTICUT COOKS
at $8.95 per copy plus $1.25 per copy for
postage & handling: $_____
Enclosed is an additional donation of: $_____
                                  Total enclosed: $_____

SEND TO _____
STREET _____
CITY _____ STATE _____ ZIP _____
                    Please print
(   ) *Please enclose a gift card to read:*
_____
_____

Make check or money order payable to A.C.S. Cookbook

All copies of Connecticut Cooks will be sent to same address unless otherwise specified. If you wish one or any number of books sent as gifts, furnish a list of names and addresses of recipients. If you wish to enclose your own gift card with each book, please write name of recipient on outside of the envelope, enclose with order, and we will include it with your gift.

All copies of Connecticut Cooks will be sent to same address unless otherwise specified. If you wish one or any number of books sent as gifts, furnish a list of names and addresses of recipients. If you wish to enclose your own gift card with each book, please write name of recipient on outside of the envelope, enclose with order, and we will include it with your gift.